Doubting Darwin?

CREATIONIST DESIGNS
ON EVOLUTION

Blackwell Public Philosophy

Edited by Michael Boylan, Marymount University

In a world of 24-hour news cycles and increasingly specialized knowledge, the Blackwell Public Philosophy series takes seriously the idea that there is a need and demand for engaging and thoughtful discussion of topics of broad public importance. Philosophy itself is historically grounded in the public square, bringing people together to try to understand the various issues that shape their lives and give them meaning. This "love of wisdom" – the essence of philosophy – lies at the heart of the series. Written in an accessible, jargon-free manner by internationally renowned authors, each book is an invitation to the world beyond newsflashes and soundbites and into public wisdom.

Permission to Steal: Revealing the Roots of Corporate Scandal by Lisa H. Newton
The Extinction of Desire: A Tale of Enlightenment by Michael Boylan
Doubting Darwin? Creationist Designs on Evolution by Sahotra Sarkar
Torture and the Ticking Bomb by Robert Brecher

Forthcoming:

Terrorism and Counter-Terrorism: An Applied Philosophical Approach by Seumas Miller
Spiritual But Not Religious: The Evolving Science of the Soul by Christian Erickson
In Defense of Dolphins: The New Moral Frontier by Thomas I. White
Evil On-Line: Explorations of Evil and Wickedness on the Web by Dean Cocking and Jeroen van den Hoven

SAHOTRA SARKAR

Doubting Darwin?

CREATIONIST DESIGNS
ON EVOLUTION

Blackwell
Publishing

BLACKWELL PUBLISHING
350 Main Street, Malden, MA 02148-5020, USA
9600 Garsington Road, Oxford OX4 2DQ, UK
550 Swanston Street, Carlton, Victoria 3053, Australia

First published 2007 by Blackwell Publishing Ltd

1   2007

Library of Congress Cataloging-in-Publication Data

Sarkar, Sahotra.
    Doubting Darwin? : creationist designs on evolution / Sahotra Sarkar.
      p. cm.
    Includes bibliographical references and index.
    ISBN-13: 978-1-4051-5490-1 (hbk.: alk. paper)
    ISBN-13: 978-1-4051-5491-8 (pbk.: alk. paper)
    1. Creationism.   2. Intelligent design (Teleology)   3. Evolution (Biology)   4.
Evolution—Religious aspects.   5. Religion and science.   I. Title.

    BS651.S3167 2007
    231.7′652—dc22

                                                                            2006033450

A catalogue record for this title is available from the British Library.

Set in 11/13.5pt Dante
by Graphicraft Limited, Hong Kong
Printed and bound in Singapore
by Markono Print Media Pte Ltd

For further information on
Blackwell Publishing, visit our website:
www.blackwellpublishing.com

Contents

CONTENTS

For John Stachel, comrade and friend

Figures

Preface

In the United States, its President, George W. Bush, does not get due credit for a war he is actually winning, his Administration's ongoing war on science.[1] The battle is being fought under the banners of God and Big Business. It has many fronts including global warming, stem cell research, and most importantly for the purpose of this book, biological evolution. On August 1, 2005, during a round-table interview with reporters from five Texas newspapers, Bush proposed that Intelligent Design (our contemporary version of anti-evolution creationism – see Chapter 1) should be taught in schools along with the biological theory of evolution.[2] Bush's remarks came in a context in which a School Board in Dover, Pennsylvania, had mandated the teaching of Intelligent Design (ID) in its *biology* classes[3] and the Kansas State Board of Education was well on its way to dilute the teaching of evolutionary biology in high schools.[4] A legal challenge by a group of parents against the Dover policy, and joined by the American Civil Liberties Union (ACLU), was making its way through the courts (see below).

Meanwhile, in California, in 2005, the University of California system faced a lawsuit which argued that it violated the constitutional rights of applicants from Christian schools by deeming that some of their high school coursework was inadequate preparation for college. Creationism was at stake in this complaint because the plaintiffs cited the University system's policy of rejecting high school biology courses that used creationist-inspired textbooks published by Bob Jones University Press and A Beka Book. Lawyers representing the plaintiffs included Wendell Bird, a former staff attorney for the Institute for Creation Research.[5] In 2004, the Ohio State Board of Education had passed a proposed model science curriculum which included a controversial model lesson plan, "Critical Analysis of Evolution," designed to generate skepticism about evolutionary biology. A similar measure had also been passed in 2002.[6] On only a slightly lighter note, in June 2005, the Park and Recreation Board of Tulsa, Oklahoma voted to have a display depicting the Biblical account of creation at the Tulsa Zoo. In July, though, they rescinded this entertaining decision.[7]

The assault on the teaching of sound science in schools in the United States has reached a level not seen for over two decades.[8] Largely this is due to well-funded religious fundamentalist think tanks such as the so-called Discovery Institute's Center for Science and Culture (originally, the Center for *the Renewal of*[9] Science and Culture) in Seattle which have been successfully peddling creationist propaganda to media outlets throughout the United States and making inroads in a few other countries, especially Australia, Britain, and Turkey.[10]

Outside the United States, the situation in Britain is perhaps the most pathetic. In 2002, the Prime Minister, Tony Blair, told Parliament that he was happy that creationism was taught along with evolution in controversial state schools run by the private Emmanuel Schools Foundation.[11] And, in 2005, under question in the House of Lords, Junior Education Minister, Geoffrey Filkin, explicitly refused to preclude the teaching of creationism in state schools.[12] The rest of the world is not entirely without bizarre incidents. In 2004, Rio de Janeiro State in Brazil authorized the teaching of creationism in state schools while, over a few days, Serbia banned and then reinstated the teaching of evolution in biology classes.[13] In July 2005, in a *New York Times* opinion piece, Archbishop Cardinal Christof Schonborn of Vienna called neo-Darwinian evolution incompatible with the Catholic Church and in conflict with nature itself.[14] The Archbishop seemed to support Intelligent Design and contradict the Vatican's acceptance of the theory of evolution. This did not sit well with the Vatican. Its astronomer, Rev. George Coyne, the Jesuit director of the Vatican Observatory, went out of his way to declare explicitly that Intelligent Design was not science.[15]

On some occasions, scientists, conscientious educators, and their supporters have managed to fend off religious challenges to science education. A 2003 battle over textbooks in Texas had loomed large in the picture in the United States because the Texas State Board of Education, with a solid Republican majority, was the largest textbook buyer in the country. Biologists were drawn into participating in the political debate by many organizations, most notably, the Texas Freedom Network. Creationists' efforts to change textbooks to include skeptical and derogatory remarks about evolution failed comprehensively in Texas even though, in 2002, conservatives in the same Board had managed to ban a textbook on environmental science that they found offensive to their corporate instincts. (Should too much be read into this about the maturity of Texas' political culture, in January 2006, the Texas Governor, Rick Perry, voiced support for teaching Intelligent Design in schools.[16])

There have been several other recent successes at resisting the creationists. In 2005 the Alaska State Board of Education strengthened the teaching of evolution in its curriculum.[17] In Utah, the State Board reaffirmed the teaching of evolution in 2005 even though some legislators continued to threaten legislation mandating the teaching of Intelligent Design.[18] Since 2002, Cobb County in Georgia had required the placement of a disclaimer about evolution in school biology textbooks. The disclaimer warned students: "This textbook contains material on evolution. Evolution is a theory, not a fact, regarding the origin of living things. This material should be approached with an open mind, studied carefully and critically considered." In 2005 a federal court ruled against the stickers in a lawsuit brought by local parents and supported by the ACLU though, in May 2006, an appeals court vacated the ruling and sent it back to the lower court.[19] In February 2006, Ohio's State Board of Education reversed its earlier attempts to sneak Intelligent Design into the school curriculum under the guise of requiring a critical discussion of evolution.[20] And in December, 2005, a federal court in Pennsylvania ruled comprehensively against the Dover School Board, accepting the plaintiff's arguments that Intelligent Design is a religious doctrine. Meanwhile, the creationist School Board had been voted out in November and no appeals were expected.[21] Judge John E. Jones, a Republican appointed by George W. Bush, who ruled in this case, held $2 million to be a reasonable amount for plaintiffs' costs. The School Board settled the case for $1 million.[22] The amount awarded should deter future efforts to impair the teaching of sound science in schools throughout the United States.

But, by and large, so far, these are isolated examples of sanity. Alabama has had a disclaimer on its biology textbooks since 1995.[23] There are few states in the United States that have not seen some challenge to the teaching of evolution during the past decade.[24] When the Thomas B. Fordham Institute evaluated state science standards in the United States in 2000, twenty-four states received what they deemed a "sound" (that is, good) or at least a passing grade for the teaching of evolution; in 2005, when it repeated that exercise, that number had decreased to twenty.[25] On both occasions only seven other states received passing scores. Poor science standards were not limited to the teaching of evolution. When all of science is considered, in 2005, only nineteen states received a "sound" grade, a number unchanged since 2000.

The attacks on the teaching of evolution in public schools in the United States and attempts to replace it with creationism are motivated by a religious fundamentalist agenda that would like to see a return of sectarian religion into public life. (Some Intelligent Design creationists, for instance, Philip Johnson, freely admit this goal.[26]) However, what makes this attack dangerous, and not merely to be dismissed like the old-fashioned creationism of the 1970s and 1980s, is that Intelligent Design (ID) creationism is a somewhat more sophisticated doctrine and often presented by its proponents disguised as science, replete with apparently impressive mathematical formalism and arguments.

In the United States the courts have presumably removed the possibility of teaching Biblical creation as science in public schools for the foreseeable future. But ID claims to be science, and thus not subject to these precedents. This book is about the claim of ID to be good science (if it is science at all), something with sufficient achievement and sufficient promise to be introduced in our schools. It also attempts to describe some biology, its history, and its philosophy through its examination of ID.

Beyond scientific critique, this book also includes an examination of the philosophical arguments over ID. Though this book is written by a professional biologist and philosopher of science, it is intended for a more general audience, including a religious audience interested in understanding the intellectual debate about ID. The idea of this book arose during the discussion following a short talk I gave to theologians at the annual meeting of the American Academy of Religion (San Antonio, 2004) in response to a presentation by William Dembski. Many theologians in the audience were embarrassed by ID and critically and deeply interested in what biology actually said, and why biologists, even those who were critical of the neo-Darwinian orthodoxy in evolutionary biology, had no sympathy for ID. This book is intended as much for them, to delineate the intellectual terrain of the dispute between biology and ID, as it is to provide more arguments for non-religious critics of ID. But this book does not delve into theology. The occasionally polemical tone of this book is directed at ID creationists, not theologians or scholars of religion. There is also no claim in this book about whether religion (let alone any particular religious faith) is rational or irrational, or whether it is appropriate to practice or teach it at homes or temples. The concern that has motivated this book is about what happens in *science* classes.

The emphasis throughout this book will be on general arguments and positions, rather than on each individual variant of ID creationism. It is a book about ideas and arguments, not individuals and idiosyncrasies. It is also not about the politics of the ID movement or of the "scientific" creationism that preceded it. There are several excellent recent books mapping that important terrain.[27] This book does not, for instance, have anything to say about the so-called Wedge strategy, allegedly an originally surreptitious strategy formulated by ID creationists to promote their religious worldview in every aspect of our collective cultural life.[28] Besides this Preface, with one exception in Chapter 7, political remarks are confined to the last chapter and, even there, restricted to general principles, ignoring the particular political battles raging today. This is not to deny the importance of the political context of science but, rather, to leave it for a different book in which it can receive the full attention that it deserves. Nevertheless, this book does have an implicit political agenda: to remind the reader that ID is no credible alternative to evolutionary biology when we decide what to embrace and teach *as science* in our schools.

Acknowledgments

For discussions, sometimes over the course of years, as well as comments and criticisms of parts of this manuscript, thanks are due to Dan Bolnick, Jeff Dean, Raphael Falk, Justin Garson, the late Stephen Jay Gould, Benjamin Jantzen, Cory Juhl, James Justus, Manfred Laubichler, Richard Lewontin, Arturo de Lozanne, Antonio Madrid, the late John Maynard Smith, Stephen Menn, Alexander Moffett, Ian Musgrave, Anya Plutynski, Michael Ruse, Tom Schneider, Jeffrey Shallit, Mike Singer, Elliott Sober, John Taylor, John Wilkins, William Wimsatt, and David Wolpert. If I have inadvertently missed someone, I apologize in advance.

Material on which this book is based was presented to audiences at the Conference on Fundamentalism's Threat to Democracy (Texas Freedom Network, Dallas, Fall 2003), the American Academy of Religion (San Antonio, Fall 2004), the University of Chicago (Big Problems Lectures, Spring 2005), the University of California at Santa Cruz (Department of Philosophy, Spring 2006), and the University of Texas (Humanities Institute Free Thinking Lunch, Fall 2005; Dean's Scholar Seminar, College of Natural Sciences, Spring 2006; and during a debate organized by the Undergraduate Philosophy Association, Spring 2006). Thanks are due to the many respondents from the audiences who provided useful feedback.

Three anonymous reviewers for Blackwell provided very useful comments. Throughout, Anna Zaigraeva helped maintain my often-flagging enthusiasm for the project by feeding me with timely instances of creationist crimes and misdemeanors. Finally, this book only saw the light of the day because of Jeff Dean's initial suggestion and continued enthusiasm for the project.

1

Introduction

Good old-fashioned Creationism was the doctrine that the Book of Genesis is a scientific text that provides a historical record of the origin of the Earth's biota. It claimed that the world is about 10,000 years old and that the fossil record has to be reinterpreted to accommodate this chronology. Good old-fashioned Creationism was bold and fun: if the reinterpretation of the fossil record requires a change in the laws of physics, Creationism said, so be it. Creationism accepted that the Flood happened as the Bible records it. Sloths would have had to migrate from West Asia to the neotropics in the allotted time, wombats to Australia. These sloths would have to move very, very fast, something that they are physiologically not prone to do. Old-fashioned Creationism could live with all of that. Biogeography places formidable challenges to Creationism – but those who are unconstrained by the laws of physics would presumably find it child's play to alter the facts of mere biogeography. Creationism can even live with the fact, first described by Andreas Vesalius in 1543, that, very strangely, men have the same number of ribs as women.[1]

But Creationism underwent a long-overdue Reformation in the 1990s in an attempt to make it more compatible with the findings of modern science. Unreformed Creationism lives on, in places such as the Creation Evidence Museum in Glen Rose, Texas. The museum sells books with titles such as *Crash Goes Darwin . . . and His Origin of Species*, *Dinosaurs by Design*, and *Noah's Ark: A Feasibility Study*;[2] fascinating books, but largely irrelevant as the Reformation has swept across all those institutions which urge the rejection of contemporary science and a return to an essentially fundamentalist religious view of the world. These institutions – for instance, the so-called Discovery Institute in Seattle – want to reform biological curricula in high schools in the United States and elsewhere to bring God back into science classrooms. But they do not want unreformed Creationism – at least that is the official story. They want Reformed Creationism.[3]

According to Reformed Creationism, we need no longer believe that the world is only about 10,000 years old, or that all extant animals are descended from those that jumped off Noah's Ark on Mount Ararat some 8,000 years ago. Darwin and evolution are no longer always equated with evil and blasphemy.[4] Instead, Reformed Creationism accepts parts of evolutionary biology, including some role for natural selection. It accepts that blind variation and natural selection – "Darwin's law of higgledy-piggledy" as the physicist John Herschel dismissively called it[5] – can explain phenomena such as the evolution of drug resistance in bacteria or pesticide resistance in insects. Most versions of Reformed Creationism even accept that natural selection may have modified traits such as the size and shape of bird beaks. For instance, they sometimes accept that natural selection molded the beaks of Darwin's finches in the Galápagos Islands where the size of available seeds selected for the form of beaks.[6] These versions of Reformed Creationism generally accept common descent: that all extant organisms are descended from a single ancestor in the recesses of deep time,[7] presumably the first cell.

Nevertheless, Reformed Creationism urges us to reject the view that evolutionary theory, coupled with our increasing knowledge of the physics and chemistry of living organisms, will eventually explain the emergence of all biological phenomena. Moreover, to get a full theory, it claims, we will have to embrace supernatural (or at least extra-natural) mechanisms. In particular, we will have to invoke the operation of a designing intelligence guiding the process of organic change. Reformed Creationism is called Intelligent Design (ID). Its intellectual stalwarts are Philip Johnson, William A. Dembski, and Michael J. Behe and much of this book will concern their arguments, though several lesser players will also enter the stage.[8]

The Central Argument

ID creationists' most fundamental biological claim is that complex adaptations could not have been produced by natural selection or any other natural process. Their emergence requires the intervention of an extra-natural designer. Bacterial flagella and the blood clotting cascade in mammals are their favorite examples though there are several others (see Chapter 6). This claim of impossibility is supposed to be bolstered by some alleged mathematical results from computer science and information theory – we will examine all these issues in this book.

One central argument underpins all of ID creationism. Briefly, that argument runs as follows: *first*, evolutionary theory is supposed to allow only: (i) the inheritance of traits; (ii) the occurrence of blind variation; and (iii) natural selection. (Chapter 2 will contain a detailed examination of these assumptions.) *Second*, according to this argument, evolutionary theory cannot at present explain many natural phenomena, in particular, the evolutionary emergence of biological complexity. *Third*, this failure is so blatant that it shows that evolutionary theory does not even have the conceptual resources to explain the emergence of complexity. (This "no conceptual resources" claim is critical to the success of the argument because, without it, evolutionary biologists have an obvious response: wait and see – as our science progresses, we will resolve the present difficulties.) *Fourth*, proponents of ID go on to claim, there is good reason to believe that the required resources must include intelligent mechanisms.

The aim of this book is to examine this argument – for ease of future reference, we will call it the "Central Argument" of Intelligent Design. Though the rejection of the Central Argument is the main conclusion defended in this book, what evolutionary biology actually says – and does not say – receives just as much critical attention as the Central Argument. This is also a book about biology, its philosophy, and its history – a feature of this book which makes it different from several very competent critiques of ID that have appeared recently.[9] However, Ken Miller's 1999 book, *Finding Darwin's God*, discusses a lot of the biology excellently.[10] Miller's book focuses on the ID creationists' major claims from the late 1990s. This book concentrates on the period since 2000 and, in that sense, complements Miller's treatment though there is some overlap (mainly in Chapter 6). Finally, this book is also a qualified defense of *naturalism*, the claim that the methods of science and their extensions are all we have to guide us through the enterprise of obtaining knowledge of the world. Here it parts company with Miller and his theological preoccupation of reclaiming God from the creationists – see Chapters 8 and 9. Naturalism, as we shall see later in the book (particularly in Chapter 9), is the real target of ID creationists and we will see how it fares under their criticisms.

Let us return to the "no conceptual resources" claim which, as we noted earlier, is critical to ID's Central Argument. There are two ways in which this claim can be fleshed out: (i) there is an abstract characterization of what is permitted by a theory, and a theorem or some such result that shows that some specific observed phenomenon is not permitted by the theory. This provides, essentially, a *reductio ad absurdum* argument against the theory; or, (ii) there is a body of phenomena that has proved recalcitrant to explanation over a sustained period of time, and these phenomena are better explained by some other fundamentally different theory even if that theory calls into question what was then the dominant scientific metaphysics. (Metaphysics, here, is taken to mean the most general assumptions about the world which all scientific theories must satisfy even when they disagree with each other.) ID creationists have tried both the options mentioned above. We will call the former the "inconsistency" option and the latter the "incompleteness" option.

Note that, if we accept the Central Argument, we must first give up one of the most successful scientific theories of our time – the theory of evolution by natural mechanisms. (Recall the evolutionary geneticist Theodosius Dobzhansky's famous, though perhaps rhetorically overstated, dictum: "Nothing in biology makes sense except in the light of evolution."[11]) We must next give up the dominant and even more successful metaphysics that has grounded science since at least the Copernican era: naturalism. Naturalism is often taken to claim that all that exists in the universe is processes and entities knowable to us through scientific methods, that is, through logic and our senses, with no recourse to entities and processes entirely inaccessible to these methods. When formulated in this way, naturalism makes both metaphysical and epistemological claims, about what may exist and how we may come to know about them. Ultimately, naturalism is the real target of ID because it forbids the reintroduction of divinity into the empirical world. The attack on evolutionary theory is a necessary stage in this campaign because evolutionary theory claims that, not only the entire biological world, but even our most fundamental human features – our minds, our morals – should be accounted for without appeal to extra-natural intervention.

However, a defense of evolution in the present context of what constitutes *science* does not require the metaphysical component of naturalism. All it requires is a very weak form of epistemological naturalism, usually called methodological naturalism, which limits science to those facts that are accessible to naturalistic methods as defined above.

Methodological naturalism allows the possibility of a religious realm to be explored using religious practices. It merely asks that this realm be kept distinct from science. Though Chapter 9 of this book will defend a stronger form of naturalism than methodological naturalism, the weak doctrine is all that we need to defend evolutionary biology against ID creationism.

A demand that we give up a particular scientific theory is not radical: the history of science is littered with examples of highly successful scientific theories being replaced by successors that are even better. The caloric theory of heat gave way to the kinetic theory in the nineteenth century.[12] Heat turns out not to be a fluid called "caloric"; rather, it is the agitation of matter in motion as the kinetic theory demands. Darwin's blending theory of inheritance was similarly replaced by Mendel's particulate theory.[13] Offspring traits are not intermediates between parental traits produced by a mingling of hereditary material. Rather, parents pass on discrete factors or "genes" (more accurately, *alleles* or versions of genes) which help specify offspring traits. Offspring traits may well be identical to those of one of the parents or even one of the grandparents. The growth of science requires the replacement of old theories and their replacement by better new ones.

The Evidence for Evolution

We can reasonably be asked to give up a theory if it fails to save the phenomena. A central claim of ID is that, indeed, there are many phenomena that evolutionary theory cannot explain. We will examine those claims in detail in later chapters of the book. Meanwhile, it will suffice here to sample some of the phenomena that evolutionary theory does explain and which, therefore, provide our evidence for evolution. This is not to suggest that evolutionary theory is complete or that there are no legitimate debates about evolution. We will discuss a host of problems in Chapter 4. But, here, we present the case *for* evolutionary theory.

Evolution means modification by common descent through a variety of natural mechanisms. Most, though not all, evolutionary biologists believe that the most important of these mechanisms is natural selection, the production of more offspring by some types over others. Assuming that some of the traits of the parental types are inherited by the offspring, these traits will spread because of the higher number of such offspring – there is nothing mysterious about natural selection. Modifications arise because of changes in the genes through which parental characteristics are transmitted to the next generation. Some modifications are minor. For instance, a mutation in a single gene in humans can make the bearer produce a different form of hemoglobin than the usual one and become susceptible to sickle cell disease (a painful form of anemia). However, this mutation also makes bearers, provided they also carry a copy of the normal gene, resistant to many types of malaria. Thus, in an environment in which these forms of malaria are prevalent, the modification would be selected for.

Not all modifications are minor and, according to evolutionary theory, the accumulation of many minor modifications may lead to major changes. Thus, humans and the great apes all descended from a common ancestor from which humans have diverged quite radically through successive small modifications. Similarly, birds are generally believed to have evolved out of theropod dinosaurs through small modifications though some recent findings suggest a more complicated story.[14] All mammals similarly evolved from a group of reptiles that lived over 200 million years ago.[15] We will encounter many other examples later in the book.

Though this level of detail is atypical for an Introduction to a book, the rest of this section will document some of the specific evidence for evolution. The aim is to drive home the variety and depth of the evidence that makes the theory so compelling for biologists. ID creationists must seriously confront all this evidence if they are intellectually honest. As the noted evolutionary biologist Ernst Mayr points out, our confidence for evolution comes from the consilience of four major types of evidence: (i) the fossil record; (ii) morphological similarities between organisms; (iii) biogeography; and (iv), of late, the molecular constitution of organisms.[16] What follows is not intended as a systematic survey of all of the evidence for evolution: even a cursory such survey would fill a book much longer than this. Moreover, because contemporary ID creationists generally do not deny either the fact of evolution or the operation of the standard mechanisms of evolutionary change, denying only that these mechanisms suffice to explain *all* of organic change, such a survey is not strictly necessary. Nevertheless, having the concrete evidence of the achievements of evolutionary theory fresh in our minds will help us navigate the issues discussed in this book:

(i)   *The Fossil Record.* Darwin and the early proponents of evolution all started from the fossil record, and so shall we. Fossils of extinct organisms are found in geological strata that can be accurately dated using a variety of techniques including radioactive dating with carbon (C-14), potassium (K-40), uranium (U-238), and other isotopes. Fossils found in recent strata are closely related to – and sometimes indistinguishable from – extant organisms. But this similarity diminishes steadily, layer by layer, as we examine fossils from more distant strata. There are gaps in the fossil record but, as time has gone on, these gaps or missing links have become less numerous. Sometimes spectacular discoveries have filled these missing links. For instance, in 1861, a fossil of a bird found in the upper Jurassic era (145 million years ago [Mya]), Archaeopteryx, was discovered in southern Germany. It had teeth, a long tail, and other characteristics of the reptilian ancestor posited for birds by evolutionary biologists. But it also had a large brain, large eyes, feathers, and wings. The latter set of features showed it to be a transitional form between modern birds and the common more reptilian ancestor of both modern reptiles and birds. It was almost certainly capable of flight. Since 1940, at least 12 other "missing" links between birds and their reptilian ancestors have been discovered.[17]

In some cases the fossil record is remarkably complete with most expected transitional forms having already been found.[18] These cases include the lineage leading from therapsid reptiles to mammals and that leading from Eohippus (the ancestral horse) to Equus (the modern horse). Moreover, with virtually no exception, fossils have been found only in the time period evolutionary theory predicts that they should be found. There are no anomalous fossils, for instance, fossils of the same species found in inconsistent geological strata. If we found a fossil rabbit in strata from the Jurassic era (206–144 Mya), as the great evolutionary biologist, J. B. S. Haldane, once remarked, we would consider abandoning the theory of evolution. The fossil record supports evolution – descent with modification – though, by itself, it cannot give direct evidence of the mechanisms of that change, whether it is entirely due to natural selection. To get a handle on why evolution occurred, we must turn to morphological variation among the organisms that exist today.

(ii) *Morphology.* As evidence for evolution, morphological similarity performs even better than the fossil record in providing support for evolution and even helps to resolve the problem of identifying mechanisms of evolution. Morphological similarity is ubiquitous, not only between ancestor and descendant as determined from the fossil record, but also between related organisms today. Even before Darwin, starting especially with the work of the Swedish botanist Carl Linnaeus in the eighteenth century, morphological similarity was used by systematicists to organize all known species in a taxonomic hierarchy allegedly created by God. Evolution, that is, descent with modification from a common ancestor,[20] gave a straightforward earthly explanation of this hierarchy. Descent with modification is why the wings of birds resemble the anterior extremities of mammals – the two structures are *homologous* because their similarity is explained by the fact that they share a common ancestor. Homologies – similarities due to common ancestry – are critical to our arguments because even ID creationists admit that close homologies (that is, overwhelming similarities) between related species point to gradual changes from the common ancestor. We will often argue from homology throughout this book.

In cases such as that of wings we can infer – though not prove conclusively, as skeptics love to point out – the role of natural selection in modifying the form. We can tell a consistent story of such modification through the extensive fossil record. Vestigial organs – for instance, the human appendix – are similarly explained as homologs of functional similar organs in related organisms. Moreover, once we go beyond fossils and also focus on organisms living today, we can elucidate the mechanisms of evolutionary change and, ideally, even test quantitative models of natural selection. Comparative morphology begins to fill in the gap left by the fossil record about the possible mechanisms of descent with modification.

(iii) *Biogeography*. Biogeography provides equally compelling evidence for evolution. For many observed biogeographical patterns there is no explanation other than evolution with branching descent. There is only one species of mockingbird in continental South America (*Mimus gilvus*).[19] However, during the voyage of the *Beagle* Darwin found three different mockingbird species, now called *Nesomimus trifasciatus*, *N. parvulus*, and *N. melanotis*, in three different islands of the Galápagos group. Evolution explains how each of these diverged from a common ancestor they shared with *M. gilvus*. In the case of Darwin's finches, also from the Galápagos islands, quantitative work has detailed how changes in beak morphology in different islands are brought about by natural selection.[20] Evolution explains biogeography at every spatial scale, as Darwin's co-discoverer of the theory of natural selection, Alfred Russel Wallace, showed in detail in the 1870s.[21]

Evolution explains why the faunas of Europe and North America on different sides of the north Atlantic ocean are similar while the faunas of Africa and South America on different sides of the south Atlantic ocean are not. It even explains puzzling discontinuous geographical distributions of related species. For instance, true camels (*Camelus dromedarius* and *C. bactrianus*) are found only in Asia and Africa. Their closest relatives are the llamas (*Lama glama*, *L. glama pacos* or alpaca, and *L. guanicoe* or guanaco) and vicuñas (*Vicugna vicugna*) of South America. But, if evolution is the continuous process that we believe it to be, there should be camels of some sort or other in North America. There are none at present, but the fossil record includes a large fauna of Tertiary era North American camels, now long extinct. Camels are believed to have originated in North America and migrated to South America, Eurasia, and Africa. The fauna of Europe and North America are similar because a land bridge connected the two in the early Tertiary era, 40 Mya. In contrast, continental drift separated Africa and South America 80 Mya and their fauna have diverged ever since. Biogeography, morphology, and the fossil record mutually reinforce each other in the service of evolutionary theory.

(iv) *Molecular evidence.* Finally, the past fifty years have churned out a vast body of molecular evidence all pointing towards evolution. The more related that two organisms are according to evolutionary theory, the more similar should be the molecules constituting them. The agreement between theory and evidence has often been spectacular. Molecules evolve in the same way as other structural elements of organisms: descent with modification is ubiquitous. However, different types of molecules evolve at different rates: fibrinopeptides, molecules involved in the clotting of blood, evolve very rapidly; histones, small chromosomal proteins, are exceedingly conservative, that is, resistant to evolutionary change. Molecular analysis has also cleared up many evolutionary puzzles. Fungi were long regarded as being plants or at least close to plants. Yet, their cell walls consist of chitin, also found in the hard parts of insects, but never in plants. Molecular analysis revealed that the basic chemistry of fungi is close to that of animals. Today, fungi are classified in a separate kingdom distinct from both plants and animals. Once we turn to the DNA in our genetic material, we see evolutionary theory quantitatively confirmed in many cases. For instance, if natural selection is a major force of evolution, we would expect DNA sequences coding for functional protein molecules to be much more constrained, and evolving much more slowly, than non-coding non-functional DNA sequences. That is exactly what we find. Molecular evidence also dispels the view – once also held by the majority of evolutionary biologists – that all modern animal phyla appeared more or less fully formed and almost suddenly, in the pre-Cambrian era, about 550 Mya – there will be more on this in Chapters 4 and 7. Molecular homologies are ubiquitous and we will turn to them in Chapter 6. These homologies are now extensively used to reconstruct evolutionary history.

Rejecting Theories

Convincing scientists – or even the educated public – to give up a theory as powerful as the theory of evolution will not be easy. But, recall that the ID creationists would not be satisfied with merely that; they also want a transformation of our metaphysics. They want us to give up naturalism. On occasion, we do give up metaphysical assumptions. Though naturalism itself has not been called into question within science since its rise to dominance in the seventeenth century, there are several examples of deeply held – and empirically successful – theories being replaced by successors deemed metaphysically impossible in earlier times.

Consider the following four examples, keeping in mind the question whether contemporary ID is on par with any of them. We range over the sciences also to highlight the fact that ID's assault on naturalism is an assault on all of science, and not only evolutionary biology:

(i) *Newton's mechanics.* Let us begin with the part of physics we teach first in high school, and which we continue to use in most of our everyday life: classical mechanics. In 1687 Isaac Newton published *Principia Mathematica* in which he propounded the three laws of motion that still bear his name. He also propounded a new theory of gravitation – the "Law of Universal Gravitation." Newton's theory unified celestial and terrestrial mechanics: it showed that the laws governing the fall of bodies on earth (for instance, Galileo's law of the pendulum) explained the laws which governed the motion of planets, that is, Kepler's three laws. Newton's theory correctly predicted the return of Halley's comet in 1758. There was never much doubt about its predictive power and success.

The trouble was that Newton's theory assumed action-at-a-distance, that distant bodies influence each other instantaneously through gravitation. The dominant scientific metaphysics of the day, the mechanical philosophy of Boyle, Descartes, and Huygens, did not permit action-at-a-distance: all interactions were supposed to be mediated by local contact between impenetrable particles of matter. From the point of view of the mechanical philosophy, action-at-a-distance was "occult," as Leibniz put it, or even "absurd," as Huygens opined.[22] But the mechanical philosophy had no convincing account, let alone a quantitative explanation, of planetary motion. Descartes, for instance, had a purely qualitative theory of vortices that was never successfully quantified. Attempts to find a quantitative mechanical explanation of planetary phenomena continued well into the eighteenth century, at times co-opting the efforts of such eminent mathematicians as Leonhard Euler.

But all this effort was expended to no avail. By the end of the eighteenth century it was clear that the mechanical philosophy probably did not have the conceptual resources to account for all physical phenomena: gravitation had remained recalcitrant for over a century, and Newton's simple law saved the phenomena though it required a change of metaphysics. Action-at-a-distance had come to stay and the mechanical philosophy was on its way out by the nineteenth century. In a last-ditch effort, some figures such as Hermann von Helmholtz tried to resuscitate the mechanical philosophy by changing its assumptions to allow action-at-a-distance so long as it was governed by "central" forces (roughly, forces directed along lines joining the centers of material bodies). But these efforts were of no avail. The phenomena had forced a change of metaphysics.

(ii) *General relativity.* Newton's eminence in the eighteenth century is aptly captured by Alexander Pope's intended epitaph for him:

> "Nature and Nature's Laws lay hid in night
> God said: let Newton be and all was light."

Central to Newton's reputation was his law of gravitation discussed earlier. By 1798 Henry Cavendish had measured the gravitational constant found in Newton's law, obtaining a value the accuracy of which has not been very significantly improved to this day. The early nineteenth century only saw Newton's theory of gravitation extend its success. Using

Newton's law, in the 1840s, John Couch Adams and Jean Joseph Le Verrier showed that well-known anomalies in the motion of Uranus, that is, deviations from what was predicted by Newton's law, could be explained by positing the existence of an eighth planet and retaining Newton's law. Le Verrier's prediction was immediately confirmed in Berlin by Johann Gottfried Galle in 1846. Adams was English, Le Verrier French, and a bitter priority dispute broke out with each backed by his own national scientific establishment. At stake was the name of the new planet which eventually came to be called "Neptune."

The discovery of Neptune was the high point of the history of Newton's theory of gravitation because another much more recalcitrant anomaly soon emerged. In 1859 Le Verrier pointed out that there was a discrepancy between the observed motion and the predicted motion of the perihelion of Mercury (the point at which it is closest to the Sun) as predicted by Newton's law.[23] Le Verrier found the discrepancy to be 38″ per century; by 1882 it was known to be 43″. Over the years many solutions were proposed: Venus was 10% more massive than believed; there was another planet or a ring of matter within Mercury's orbit; Mercury had a moon; the Sun was more oblate than observed; and so on. It was also proposed that Newton's theory required modification, and this was the only proposal not soon ruled out by experiment or observation. At the beginning of the twentieth century the perihelion problem remained unresolved.

The solution came from Einstein around 1915.[24] But it required more than any ordinary modification of Newton's law of gravitation. Einstein's new theory of gravitation, also known as general relativity, reinterpreted gravitation as the curvature of space-time. It cast aside the view, then doubted by no one, that space and matter were independent of each other. Along with that metaphysical principle went the claim that the Euclidean (or flat) geometry of space is a necessary truth. We live in a curved space-time, one in which that curvature is continually changing as pieces of matter move around. General relativity did more than only explain the perihelion shift of Mercury. It predicted that light would bend around matter. A 1919 British expedition led by Arthur Eddington to the western Pacific to record the passage of light during an eclipse found just what was predicted. Subsequent experiments have only added to our confidence in the theory in spite of the metaphysical readjustments it has demanded. It is fitting to conclude with an addendum, by John Colling Squires, a British journalist, to the couplet by Pope with which we started:

"It did not last: the Devil howling 'Ho!
Let Einstein be!' restored the status quo."

(iii) *Quantum mechanics.* Let us turn to what is regarded as the most radical conceptual change in physics in the twentieth century: quantum mechanics. One important innovation of early nineteenth-century physics was the wave theory of light, a departure from Newton's view that light consisted of particles. Shortly afterwards, in the 1830s and 1840s, Michael Faraday and others showed that electricity and magnetism were related phenomena. Between the 1850s and 1870s James Clerk Maxwell developed Faraday's intuitive ideas about "fields" of electrical and magnetic forces to formulate a unified mathematical theory of electromagnetism. One consequence of this theory was that light consisted of electromagnetic waves. Like all other waves, light waves were believed to be continuous. Light is both emitted and absorbed by matter creating what are called emission and absorption spectra: the precise distributions of the wavelengths at which light is either emitted or absorbed. These spectra are characteristic of the material being studied. By the 1890s several laws governing these spectra were empirically well established.

However, between 1900 and 1905 Max Planck and, especially, Einstein showed that these laws could be made consistent with the rest of physics only if we deny the unlimited validity of Maxwell's theory of light and accept that light comes in discrete chunks or "quanta." It took a quarter-century, until the late 1920s, to make any sense of quantum theory. It was a joint effort, with contributions from many physicists including Niels Bohr, Werner Heisenberg, Max Born, Erwin Schrödinger, and Paul Dirac. The result, quantum mechanics, is arguably the greatest achievement of physics to date. Quantum mechanics provides the foundation for chemistry, explaining the rules of valency. At the practical level, it provides the basis for electronics. It is indispensable for the understanding of particle physics. As the physicist Eugene Wigner liked to point out, with quantum mechanics, for the first time, we can explain the stability of matter, why matter does not decay spontaneously. Indeed, within the biological context, Schrödinger believed, erroneously as it turned out, that quantum mechanics would be necessary to explain the stability of genes (alleles) across hundreds of generations.[25]

But the acceptance of quantum mechanics came at an unprecedented metaphysical cost. We have been forced to abandon determinism: the doctrine that, given the present state of the world, the laws of nature are such that, at any future instant of time, there is only one possible state of affairs.[26] Traditionally, that assumption lay at the foundations of the scientific enterprise, the attempt to understand the universe in terms of exceptionless general laws. Quantum mechanics denies that. Moreover, it decrees that some individual systems may also not be in a determinate (or definite) state at all times, contrary to anything permitted in classical physics (and, indeed, the rest of science). Yet the empirical success of quantum mechanics forced a re-evaluation of such foundational claims. Einstein, for one, was never satisfied with the new metaphysics that quantum mechanics requires, and contemporary philosophers of science (and some physicists) continue to debate its interpretation. There are even those who retain the hope that future developments will allow us to regain the metaphysical certainties of old without eschewing the empirical success of the new physics. We will return to quantum mechanics in Chapter 10.

(iv)   *Natural selection.* The fourth example is the one central to the concerns of this book: Darwin's and Wallace's theory of evolution by natural selection which will be treated in detail in Chapters 2 and 3. The success of the theory of natural selection removed design and teleology from nature, replacing them with explanations in which causes always precede effects, and nothing but physical law guides the course of all systems, including biological ones. As Francisco Ayala puts it: "It was Darwin's greatest accomplishment to show that the directive organization of living beings can be explained as a result of natural process, natural selection, without any need to resort to a Creator or other external agent."[27] ID creationists want to resuscitate design and teleology – *ipso facto*, they have to reject evolutionary theory or at least seriously delimit its domain.

Each of these examples is a successful path-breaking episode in the history of science. In each case a revision of metaphysics was forced by the astounding empirical success of a new bold theory which challenged established metaphysical principles. If ID creationists want their claims of revolutionary success to be taken seriously, what they must show is that the choice between ID and conventional evolutionary theory is similar to the choices faced in these examples. Otherwise we would have no reason to forsake well-established metaphysical principles. Moreover, in none of the first three examples, radical as they are, is naturalism itself at stake. To make us question naturalism itself, ID creationists must do even better than the proponents of the new theories in all these cases.

They must do at least as well as Darwin and Wallace and their followers when they reinterpreted the history of life in the nineteenth century without recourse to a designer.

In fact, they must do better. With respect to naturalism, the case of the theory of natural selection is curious. Before the acceptance of that theory, the adaptation of organisms was beyond what natural law could explain:[28] they were yet to be brought within the realm of science in the same way many aspects of our mental and cultural lives today are beyond what contemporary science can explain. (This is not to say that some scientists, for instance, human sociobiologists and Evolutionary Psychologists, do not claim to provide such explanations. It is to deny that these claims are credible – there will be more on this point in Chapters 2 and 4.) What the theory of natural selection did was to draw adaptation into the realm of science. Now ID wants to reclaim complex adaptations from the scientists. But they are faced with the situation that naturalism works not only for the study of adaptations, but for all of the rest of science.[29] So, ID creationists are faced with an even more difficult task than the one that confronted Darwin and Wallace. The founders of evolutionary theory were only establishing consistency between a recalcitrant domain (the study of adaptations) and the rest of science. ID creationists want to reject all of it. We should be impressed by the audacity of the project though, as this book will show, some humility would have served the ID creationists better.

Let us set aside evolutionary theory for the time being – after this chapter, the rest of this book, except Chapter 8, will only concern it. The other three examples provide reliable methodological principles for us to adopt.[30] There are at least six lessons to be learned:

(i)   we should abandon theories only when there is compelling unimpeachable evidence against them, unimpeachable in the sense of not being merely a question of controversial interpretation of the evidence.[31] There was no doubt about whether the successful predictions made by Newton's law of gravitation posed a problem for the mechanical philosophy. There was also no doubt about the relevance of the anomalous motion of the perihelion of Mercury to Newton's law of gravitation: even proponents of the law regarded the anomaly as a problem;

(ii)   before abandoning a theory altogether, it is reasonable to attempt to modify it minimally or change our other less important assumptions to see if we can accommodate the recalcitrant data. This point is exemplified by the relatively minor modifications of Newton's law attempted in the nineteenth century, as well as the modifications of assumptions about the mass of Venus, the shape of the Sun, and so on, all to save Newton's law of gravitation;

(iii)   in the face of problems with a theory, before abandoning the metaphysical principles underlying the theory, it is again reasonable to try to find alternatives to the theory that remain consistent with those principles. Trying to find mechanical explanations of planetary phenomena was entirely appropriate. Trying to modify Newton's law minimally to save the basic framework of his theory was also appropriate. Metaphysical principles which lie at the foundation of a science are not for everyday exchange, as Thomas Kuhn and Imre Lakatos pointed out long ago;[32]

(iv)   we should abandon an old metaphysical principle and adopt a theory based on new ones only when there is clear and compelling evidence for the latter – every example above illustrates this point;

(v)   mere metaphysical difficulty with a theory is not sufficient for its rejection: there must be a compelling empirically successful alternative. Contrary to Philip Johnson, "purely negative arguments," criticizing alleged explanatory failures of evolutionary theory, is not good enough.[33] Thus Newton's law triumphed over the mechanical philosophy, relativity eventually replaced Newton's mechanics, etc., only because of unimpeachable positive evidence supporting the successful alternatives. Moreover, so long as a theory is empirically successful, in the absence of such an alternative, we will tolerate any deviant metaphysics it embraces. Empirical success trumps metaphysical scruples. Action-at-a-distance was palatable so long as Newton's law faced no anomaly. Quantum mechanics continues to be endorsed in spite of all its discomfiting metaphysical commitments; and

(vi)   all these examples and the preceding points show that confidence in metaphysical principles is based, ultimately, on empirical facts, in exactly the same way that confidence in a particular theory is. Yet, this is what proponents of ID try to deny.[34]

Two final comments about these four examples are relevant to our context: (a) we continue to tolerate empirically successful theories, while we hope to do better eventually, even if they invoke inconsistent scientific or metaphysical principles. It is well known that the deterministic world of general relativity is in conflict with the indeterminism of quantum mechanics, and both theories claim to have all physical systems within their domains. Theories that would resolve this conflict remain speculative at present. Nevertheless, we continue to hold both theories because, in practice, they are used in sufficiently different domains so that the potential conflict can be ignored: quantum mechanics is used for atoms and smaller entities, general relativity for planets, stars, galaxies, and larger entities. Good theories are rare: we use them wherever we have them and we do not give them up easily; (b) our examples come from both physics and biology. This is important because part of the rhetoric of ID is to argue that there are relevant differences between physics and biology which show that the reliability of mature biological theories is not anything like that of mature physical theories. To show that changes of metaphysics and changes of theory in physics follows the same pattern as in biology undercuts that claim.

The first three lessons listed above are relevant to the "no conceptual resources" claim of the Central Argument but only when that claim is based on the incompleteness option (that is, there remain recalcitrant phenomena unexplained). The inconsistency option – rejecting a theory because what it permits, at a very general level, is inconsistent with observed phenomena – has rarely been deployed in the history of empirical science though there is one ambiguous example among the cases we have already introduced.[35] Einstein's dissatisfaction with quantum mechanics led him to formulate an alternative deterministic framework in the 1930s.[36] These ideas were developed by John S. Bell in the 1960s to derive a mathematical inequality which violated quantum mechanical predictions.[37] A large number of experimental tests since have uniformly come out in favor of quantum mechanics. This example may be regarded simply as a case in which two theories make definite predictions and one of them does so correctly. However, it is probably more useful to regard it as a case where the inconsistency option is being deployed against a theory. The Einstein–Bell argument is based on very general and compelling assumptions of what any deterministic theory should look like, rather than being an explicit theory, and the theoretical predictions of quantum mechanics are inconsistent with what is permitted by this deterministic framework.[38]

In spite of the rarity of its deployment in the history of science, much of this book will concern the inconsistency option because of its systematic use by ID creationists. To that extent we will charitably allow negative argumentation: it will not make any difference to the conclusions we reach. Typically ID creationists provide what they take to be an abstract characterization of evolutionary theory, then examine what they claim to be the range of possibilities that are permitted by it, and then produce an alleged empirical counter-example from the biological world. Rare though it may be in the history of science, this is a legitimate strategy so long as the characterization, the derivation of the range of possible outcomes, and counter-example, is each correct. (Moreover, *reductio ad absurdum* proofs, which provide a useful analogy, are commonplace in mathematics.) But the very fact that ID creationists use an option so rarely used in the history of science already suggests that ID creationists do not wish to play by the everyday rules of scientific practice. But, perhaps, this is inevitable since their claims are so radical – after all, in demanding a rejection of naturalism, they want a change of metaphysics more fundamental than all but the last of our examples.

Plan of the Book

We will conclude this Introduction by sketching the course of the book. Chapter 2 of this book deals with Darwin, Wallace, and the first formulation of the theory of natural selection. It delves into some details of those aspects of the development of evolutionary theory that remain salient to discussions of ID today. It includes a discussion of Wallace's heresy, his endorsement of the existence of a spiritual world interacting with ours, which has been surprisingly ignored by ID creationists. Chapter 3, which is also mainly historical, turns to the question why the theory of natural selection required a change of worldview or metaphysics at least as profound as that required by Newton's theory of gravitation, relativity theory, or quantum mechanics. This chapter also disposes of the most traditional objection to natural selection, Paley's argument from design, and its attempted recent resurrection by Dembski. This refutation is not particularly difficult or insightful but, nevertheless, is included here for the sake of completeness. For all the wild enthusiasm of ID supporters, Dembski's resurrection is ultimately no better than Paley's original argument.

Chapter 4 gives a historical account of the emergence of contemporary evolutionary theory and of its central claims today. The history is used to provide a survey of contemporary evolutionary theory. The chapter also includes a discussion of several issues that remain in legitimate debate within evolutionary theory. It also introduces distinctions that will be enforced throughout the rest of this book: those between contemporary evolutionary theory, the more restricted theory of natural selection, and Darwinism in the sense of what Darwin historically said. ID creationists routinely conflate these categories for rhetorical purposes, for instance, to use some limitation of Darwinism to argue against contemporary evolutionary theory. The illegitimacy of such a move will be a recurrent theme in this book.

Chapter 5 turns to the so-called No Free Lunch (NFL) theorems from computation theory that are supposed to show that natural selection is no better than random search in attempting to find a well-designed solution to evolutionary problems. This chapter points out that evolution is largely not an optimization process and very rarely falls within the orbit of such theorems. Even where it does, the ID creationists' interpretation of the NFL theorems is illegitimate. Chapter 6 turns to what Behe calls "irreducibly complex systems" that are supposed to be "in principle" unevolvable because their functioning requires the coordinated action of unsubstitutable parts. This chapter shows through the detailed examination of a variety of examples – both Behe's and others – that the claim of "in principle" unevolvability is false. Moreover, though there are many instances of complexity that continue to challenge evolutionary explanations, there is a growing set of cases in which this challenge has already been met.

Chapter 7 turns to the question whether modern information theory poses a challenge to the theory of evolution. It points out that the standard quantitative models of information allow accumulation of information through evolution by natural selection. It notes that Dembski's account of "information" is idiosyncratic. Consequently, information theory cannot be legitimately be used to challenge – or defend – evolutionary theory. This chapter also analyzes – and disposes of – Dembski's claims about the challenge posed by "complex specified information" to evolutionary theory. Claims such as Dembski's law of the conservation of information are largely figments of an apparently over-excited imagination.

Chapter 8 turns to an issue somewhat beyond the mainly biological concerns of this book: the "fine-tuning" argument which is supposed to show that certain cosmic coincidences lie beyond the scope of naturalistic explanation. It shows that this argument is no better than Dembski's failed argument from design. Chapter 9 turns to the question of whether ID – including the fine-tuning argument – poses a credible challenge to naturalism. Distinguishing between methodological and metaphysical naturalism, it argues that no such challenge has been launched against the former, noting that this modest conclusion is all that is required to fully defend evolutionary theory. In contrast, the legitimacy of meta-physical naturalism (even if that doctrine is correct) is irrelevant to that question. Nevertheless, to the extent that practice of science brings with it metaphysical commitments, it defends metaphysical naturalism. But this defense is limited – the practice of science does not require religious belief or disbelief properly understood, when religion and science are seen to perform different, perhaps complementary, individual and social functions. Chapter 10 draws some conclusions, pointing out that scient-ists do take credible challenges to evolutionary theory seriously, exam-ines the ways in which ID fails to be *science*, and considers whether it belongs in high school curricula.

An alert reader will have noticed that though this chapter has re-capitulated ID's Central Argument against evolutionary theory and, in the process, has given a cursory description of what evolutionary theory claims (at least, as described by ID creationists), we have not been pre-sented with a summary of ID theory: though books entitled *Intelligent Design* have appeared, ID creationists are remarkably evasive about what their theory is besides vague claims such as intelligence guides organic evolution or that ID has something to do with the transfer of informa-tion.[39] ID creationists have largely concentrated on attacks on evolution-ary theory – hence the focus of this book.

Finally, though this chapter began with a mention of the socio-political agenda of the ID movement – to return God to the classrooms, and though the Preface laid out the political context in which we work as philosophers and scientists, this book is not about the politics of the ID movement. We only return to the socio-political arena in Chapter 10 and, even there, do so only very briefly. As the outline above delineates, the aim of this book is to provide a general analysis of the arguments and evidence presented by ID creationists and to do so accurately but acces-sibly because some ID creationists tend to mislead ordinary readers by clothing disreputable claims in vestments of impenetrable symbolism.[40]

2

The Legacy of Darwin
and Wallace

In June 1858, Charles Darwin received a thin package mailed from the distant island of Ternate in the Malay Archipelago (now in Indonesia).[1] Darwin's correspondent was Alfred Russel Wallace, a relatively unknown young naturalist with whom Darwin had only a cursory acquaintance. Unlike Darwin, Wallace came from an impoverished background, had no formal education beyond elementary schooling, and was traveling in the Malay Archipelago to collect specimens for a living while studying the natural history of the region.[2] Earlier, in 1855, Darwin had been impressed by another paper from Wallace which argued that every species had come into existence in spatial and temporal contiguity with some closely allied species.[3] For Wallace, this observation of the contiguity of allied species set the stage for an investigation of the mechanism by which one species may have directly arisen from another, a question which had fascinated him for decades. The package that Darwin received in 1858 contained a handwritten 3,764-word paper summarizing the results of that investigation. It was called "On the Tendency of Varieties to Depart Indefinitely from the Original Type."[4]

The rest of the story is well known. Wallace's manuscript was an expository masterpiece presenting the theory of evolution by natural selection with such clarity that it remains of pedagogic value even today. During the preceding two decades Darwin had been patiently collecting data for a major work on evolution. Wallace's manuscript seemed to have preempted him completely, so much so that Darwin considered abandoning his own project. Darwin was emotionally devastated. At this point, two of his closest friends, the geologist Charles Lyell and the botanist Joseph Dalton Hooker, both leading luminaries of English science, intervened to protect Darwin's interests. They decided that Wallace's paper was to be presented to the prestigious Linnaean Society and published in its *Proceedings*, but only along with something by Darwin, thus protecting the latter's claim to priority. The trouble was that Darwin had nothing presentable. So Lyell and Hooker, with Darwin's collaboration, salvaged extracts from an unpublished essay written in 1844 and from a letter written to the Harvard botanist Asa Gray. These were all presented to the Linnaean Society on July 1, 1858 and published in August; Darwin's contributions were placed ahead of Wallace's on both occasions to suggest that Wallace had no claim to priority. On the other side of the globe, Wallace remained unaware of these developments and had no say on how his manuscript was handled. Meanwhile Darwin rushed to prepare a 540-page Abstract of a larger work he had envisioned. In 1859 it was published as *On the Origin of Species by Means of Natural Selection* – thus was born the theory of evolution by natural selection or, more succinctly, the theory of natural selection.

The Theory of Natural Selection

The structure of the Darwin–Wallace theory, that is, the theory of natural selection, is straightforward.[5] Its three assumptions have already been outlined in the exposition of ID's Central Argument in Chapter 1:

(i) traits are inherited from generation to generation though the rules of inheritance were then unknown. Over the years Darwin developed an incorrect theory of pangenesis and blending inheritance, already mentioned in Chapter 1. That theory assumed that there were "gemmules" generated by all bodily organs which entered the blood and eventually arrived at the germinal cells to be transmitted to the next generation. The eventual demise of this implausible theory was mourned by no one; luckily for the future of biology and for the subsequent reputation of that book, it was not part of the *Origin*. But the correct rules of inheritance were being established in the 1860s by Darwin's contemporary, Gregor Mendel, though his work would not be noticed until around 1900 – there will be more on this story in Chapter 4;

(ii) the spontaneous occurrence of "blind" variation. By "blind" Darwin meant both that the causes of such variation were unknown and that variation itself was not an adaptive process leading to an increasing fit between organism and environment. In the first edition of the *Origin*, Darwin rejected the importance of the inheritance of acquired characters, a position he eventually felt forced to soften, as we shall see later in this chapter; and

(iii) of course, differentia reproduction, generally of individuals within a population, due either to greater fertility of some individuals or to a better fit between an individual and its environment. The better fit typically led to better survival rates and, from that, to more offspring. Fitness increase is the inevitable result of natural selection. Fitness, as used here, is a relative concept: what is at stake in this model of evolution by natural selection is how individuals fare with respect to other individuals within a population. According to Darwin, the theory of natural selection was supposed to explain many facets of organic evolution, including the origin of species, but it was never supposed by itself to explain evolution in its entirety, a point to which we will return below.

That the *Origin* created an intellectual revolution is an understatement: it permanently changed the way we view nature, including ourselves. By the late 1860s, or at most the 1870s, most biologists had come to accept both the fact of evolution and that natural selection was its major mechanism, though doubts about the latter would emerge by the end of the nineteenth century. The details of this history have been reconstructed many times with only slightly varying interpretations. Four aspects of that history are relevant to our context:

(a) Darwin had a profound awareness of the problem of explaining complex functional structures only on the basis of blind variation and natural selection. This awareness, as we shall see later in this chapter, shows much more sophistication than the arguments of our contemporary ID creationists and Darwin's detailed response remains relevant today;

(b) Darwin himself had a pluralistic vision of evolution. For reasons, some good but mostly poor (at least from a twenty-first-century perspective), he accepted the view that besides natural selection there were other mechanisms of evolutionary change;

(c) while doubts about the possibility of transformation of species largely – though not entirely – disappeared in the wake of the *Origin*, a large variety of mechanisms other than natural selection came to be proposed, especially in the 1890s, including some that relied on extra-natural mechanisms. Though none of these eventually survived careful scrutiny in the light of empirical data, by 1900, the theory of natural selection was a theory in retreat; and

(d) Darwin explicitly tried to interpret the evolution of human cognitive and emotional faculties in terms of natural selection, setting the stage for what has become contemporary human sociobiology and Evolutionary Psychology.[6] Along with the dismissal of design and teleology from nature, this attempt to interpret the "higher" human faculties as having evolved from animal "instincts" was perhaps the greatest challenge that Darwin posed to the worldviews preceding him.

Each of these four aspects of the early history of evolutionary biology will merit some further discussion before we turn to the question of design and teleology in the next chapter. They capture those parts of Darwin's legacy, and Wallace's, that continue to be relevant to the ID movement today. (Late twentieth-century writers on evolution have deified Darwin to the detriment of an appreciation of Wallace's achievements. The account given here will try to avoid this unfortunate elision while recognizing both Darwin's genius and Wallace's occasional foibles.)

"Absurd in the Highest Possible Degree"

Part of Darwin's scientific acumen lay in knowing exactly what his favored mechanism of evolutionary change, natural selection, can easily achieve and what it cannot. Darwin was far more aware of the problems faced by the theory of natural selection than his contemporaneous critics or, for that matter, the ID creationists today – his preemptive replies to potential criticisms arguably played a major role in the relatively easy early acceptance of the theory within the biological community in the decades immediately following the publication of the *Origin*. Chapter 6 of the *Origin* is entitled "Difficulties on Theory" and Chapters 7 and 8 ("Instinct" and "Hybridism") are all concerned with elaborating apparent problems with the theory of natural selection and their possible resolution.

In fact, what is most surprising is that ID creationists have focused on only one of the potential problems that the *Origin* addresses. Darwin was equally troubled with several other putative flaws:

Firstly, why, if species have descended from other species by insensibly fine gradations, do we not everywhere see innumerable transitional forms? Why is not all nature in confusion instead of the species being, as we see them, well defined?

Second, is it possible that an animal having, for instance, the structure and habits of a bat, could have been formed by the modification of some animal with wholly different habits? Can we believe that natural selection could produce . . . organs of such wonderful structure, as the eye, of which we hardly as yet fully understand the inimitable perfection?

Thirdly, can instincts be acquired and modified through natural selection? . . .

Fourthly, how can we account for species, when crossed, being sterile and producing sterile offspring, whereas, when varieties are crossed, their fertility is unimpaired?[7]

ID creationism has been somewhat myopic and remiss in focusing only on the problem of complex organs of extreme perfection. Old-fashioned Creationists were better in this respect in the sense that they were more catholic in their criticisms of evolutionary theory – at least, they harped *ad nauseum* on the problem of missing transitional forms. (There are occasional exceptions among ID creationists – Johnson, in some of his writings, and David Berlinski, for example, do question what the fossil record shows.[8])

We will restrict attention to ID creationism and, therefore, to the problem of complex adaptations. In Chapter 6 of the *Origin*, Darwin begins his discussion of "organs of extreme perfection and complication" with a free acknowledgment:

To suppose that the eye, with all its inimitable contrivances for adjusting the focus to different distances, for admitting different amounts of light, and for the correction of spherical and chromatic aberration, could have been formed by natural selection, seems, I freely confess, *absurd in the highest possible degree.*[9]

No ID creationist, certainly not Behe (as we shall see in Chapter 6), has posed the problem more forcefully. However, the evolution of the eye – whether it be the compound eye of insects and crustaceans or the single-chambered "simple" eye of vertebrates – is no longer regarded as a salient puzzle for evolutionary explanation; eyes have evolved far too often and easily (that is, through small steps in many different lineages).[10]

Consequently, contemporary ID creationists do not dwell on the eye. Instead, they attempt to resuscitate Darwin's problem with molecular mechanisms as if evolutionary theorists were unaware of the problem of explaining complex features until the advent of ID creationism – we will return to this issue in Chapter 6.

But Darwin went on to indicate, at least for one scenario, how his question may be answered:

> Yet reason tells me, that if numerous gradations from a perfect and complex eye to one very imperfect and simple, each grade being useful to its possessor, can be shown to exist; if further, the eye does vary ever so slightly, and the variations be inherited, which is certainly the case; and if any variation or modification in the organ be ever useful to an animal under changing conditions of life, then the difficulty of believing that a perfect and complex eye could be formed by natural selection, though insuperable by our imagination, can hardly be considered real.[11]

The argument is compelling though not one to which no response is possible: to strengthen the argument we must go beyond Darwin. Suppose that all gradations of some structure exist in different species, each being functional for that species in its environment. Now, and here we go beyond Darwin, suppose that these species are related enough to share a fairly close common ancestor, preferably one shared with no other species. (Technically, the group of species then forms a *clade*.) Then it is entirely reasonable to assume that all the graded variation arose through divergence from a common ancestor. For this argument, it is irrelevant whether there is a plausible evolutionary pathway – through natural selection or any other mechanism of evolutionary change – from the simplest extant form to the most complex extant form: they could have diverged in different directions from the common ancestor (see Figure 2.1).[12] All that is now required is a plausible pathway to each extant form from a common ancestor. Consequently, it is irrelevant whether we now see every grade between the two extant forms.

In fact, it is even irrelevant if any simple form still persists though, in the case of the eye, rudimentary organs with a few light-sensitive cells happen to be found in nature. These are the intricacies of evolutionary reasoning that ID creationism must deal with. Note that, by insisting that we see both a simple and a complex form, as well as all intermediate grades of complexity, Darwin makes the problem appear more difficult

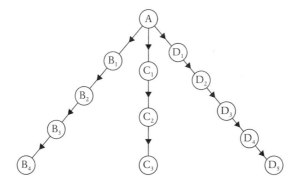

Figure 2.1 Accessibility through evolution. Suppose that some trait is "primitive" in a contemporary species, C_3, but takes a more complex form in two other such species, B_4, and D_5. If these forms of the trait are evolutionarily related, then there must be a common ancestral species, A, and sequences of species, $B_i (i = 1, 2, 3, 4)$, $C_i (i = 1, 2, 3)$, and $D_i (i = 1, 2, 3, 4, 5)$, that evolve into each other through sufficiently small steps. It is not even required that there are such paths between C_3 and B_4, or C_3 and D_5.

for evolutionary theory than it is. In the *Origin*, potential critics of evolutionary theory got more than what was justly their due – Darwin's intellectual charity remains legendary.

Darwin's Unfortunate Retreat

Much of ID creationism's – in particular, Dembski's – putatively technical objections to evolutionary theory are based on interpreting that theory as identical to the theory of natural selection and viewing the latter as a simple hill-climbing process. The details of these arguments – how they misinterpret the evolutionary process – will be a concern of Chapter 5. But, to get a fair picture of what Darwin himself believed, we should note his eventual ambivalence, if not skepticism, about the ability of natural selection alone to effect the observed evolutionary changes. In the sixth and final edition of the *Origin*, in 1872, Darwin observed:

As my conclusions have lately been much misrepresented, and it has been stated that I attribute the modification of species exclusively to natural selection, I may be permitted to remark that in the first edition of this work, and subsequently, I placed in a most conspicuous position – namely at the close of the Introduction – the following words: "I am convinced that natural selection has been the main, but not the exclusive means of modification." This has been of no avail. Great is the power of steady misinterpretation.[13]

This much-quoted excerpt is often taken to imply that Darwin was a pluralist about mechanisms of evolutionary change in the sense that the conceptual framework of modern evolutionary theory admits a variety of evolutionary forces and constraints.[14]

But, for once, such a view gives Darwin more credit than is his due. In 1867, Fleeming Jenkin, a Scottish engineer and associate of the physicist William Thomson (who later became Lord Kelvin), published a scathing review of the *Origin* in the *North British Review*.[15] Jenkin's criticisms centered on the observation – accepted by Darwin – that evolution by natural selection was an extraordinarily slow process. Not only is selection slow because it acts on minute "insensible" differences between individuals, the time required is made much greater by the fact that Jenkin and Darwin believed that traits blended during transmission from parents to offspring in sexually reproducing organisms. Thus, any novel variant that arose in a population would be swamped (or blended away) by sexual reproduction with the commoner members of the population. For a novel variant to be passed on to the next generation with no loss of variation, and therefore, to be fodder for immediate natural selection, two novel variants would have to be simultaneously present and mate with each other. Any blind variant that has higher fitness is rare. The simultaneous appearance of two such variants in a population must be a very rare event. For natural selection to account for the observed differences of the Earth's biota would require billions of years.

But, on the basis of a physical calculation by Kelvin, Jenkin argued that the Earth was simply not that old. Kelvin had assumed that the energy transmitted by the Sun, which could be estimated from the amount received on Earth, was entirely due to gravitational energy stored in the Sun. Given the mass of the Sun, it was then possible to estimate the total available energy of the Sun and its loss per year. From this, he estimated that the Sun and, consequently, the Earth, was not more than a few hundred million years old, certainly not old enough for natural selection to have wrought the observed organic changes required by the theory of evolution. Over the next half-century Kelvin and his students reduced the estimate to mere tens of millions of years.[16]

Kelvin's objection to Darwin, that there has not been enough time for evolution to take place through natural selection, has been a recurrent theme in the history of evolutionary biology. As we shall see in Chapter 4, when the same objection was deployed by religious critics in the 1920s, it motivated the biologist J. B. S. Haldane to develop a mathematical theory of evolution that would silence these critics. This objection lurked behind much of the skepticism once expressed by mathematicians and physicists about the theory of natural selection in the 1960s.[17] It continues to form the basis for Behe's rejection of evolution, which we shall examine in detail in Chapter 6.

Returning to Kelvin, he had wisely observed that his estimates of the age of the Earth were entirely invalid if there were other sources of energy than gravitation in the Sun. What saved the day for the theory of evolution (and for Kelvin's ultimate reputation as a physicist) was the discovery of radioactivity and subsequent realization that nuclear, not gravitational, interactions were responsible for the Sun's energy. The crucial point is this: evolution did not come to be accepted by the scientific community because of fashion or blind faith, as "dissenting" ID creationists such as Berlinski and Johnson try to insinuate.[18] Rather, evolutionary theory had to fight for its place in science, subject to public criticism, scrutiny, and, especially, peer review, like any other science.

In the late 1860s Darwin obviously would not have known of radioactivity which was only discovered in the 1890s. It is unclear whether Darwin specifically learned of the problems posed by physics from Jenkin's review or was aware of most of them from a variety of other earlier sources.[19] But he took them seriously. By the fifth edition of the *Origin* in 1869, Darwin had begun to downplay blind variation and embrace the inheritance of characteristics acquired through environmentally induced changes, especially through the Lamarckian mechanism of use and disuse. Evolution became a speedier process: similar variants were produced in similar environments, and variants were not swamped through mating because acquired characteristics were routinely inherited. These were the mechanisms that Darwin had in mind in his 1872 remarks, and they were rejected by the next generation on sound empirical grounds.

The important point to note is that Darwin was not always correct and today's evolutionary biologists (and historians of biology) explicitly recognize that. ID creationists misrepresent the practice of evolutionary biology when they present it as *Darwinism*, as if it were a doctrine based on a prophet like their own theologies of revelation. Science does not operate that way. Great scientists sometimes only merely glimpse what later generations regard as correct; sometimes they make mistakes, and science is always subject to revision. Evolutionary biology is no different in that respect. In physics, our respect for Newton is not diminished because his theory of gravitation was replaced by Einstein's theory of general relativity. Similarly, our respect for Darwin and his achievement is not diminished by recognizing that his theory of evolution has to be modified in the light of modern knowledge. Darwin is not on trial, contrary to Philip Johnson, nor is Darwinism.[20] What is at stake is the theory of evolution. Science does not have revealed texts to be interpreted, nor does science, done well, tolerate dogma. It proceeds by continuous readjustment of assumptions in the face of recalcitrant data. The rest of this chapter will document the many challenges faced by the theory of evolution in the last two decades of the nineteenth century, including some of the foibles of its founders. These only helped the emergence of the truly robust theory of evolution which we have had since the 1930s, as will be discussed in Chapter 4.

Wallace and Weismann

In spite of the reservations noted in the last section, Darwin's attitude towards the mechanisms of evolutionary change was genuinely pluralistic in the sense that he was never committed to natural selection alone. Recall that the passage quoted above includes within it a quote from the first edition of the *Origin* indicating that natural selection was not the sole evolutionary force, and this was written long before Darwin recanted his reliance on purely blind variation. Moreover, Darwin was not committed to the idea that every trait in every organism was the result of its own selection or even that it was due to its correlation with some other character that was directly selected. The expression of emotions in humans, for instance, according to Darwin, usually had no selective value. The contrast here is with Wallace and also with August Weismann, the most important evolutionary theorist in the generation after Darwin. Both endorsed what has come to be called "pan-selectionism," the view that natural selection was the sole force of evolution, though, in Weismann's case, his commitment to selection was not quite as strong as what his contemporaries took it to be.[21]

In Wallace's case, pan-selectionism led to what most biologists have since regarded as heresy, the invocation of a spiritual essence guiding human evolution.[22] Wallace accepted that Darwin and others had established continuity between the mental and moral faculties of "lower" animals and those of *Homo sapiens*. As we will see later in this chapter, Darwin went on to give an evolutionary, selectionist, story for the evolutionary emergence of these faculties. But, Wallace correctly argued, establishing continuity does not by itself establish etiology. According to Wallace, in contrast to the physical characteristics of *H. sapiens*, Darwin had not established that human mental and moral faculties had evolved by natural selection. Wallace observed – as many others have since – that, for instance, mathematical ability does not confer any advantage in the "survival of the fittest":

> The Greeks did not successfully resist the Persian invaders by any aid from their few mathematicians, but by military training, patriotism, and self-sacrifice.[23] The barbarous conquerors of the East, Timurlane and Genghis Khan,[24] did not owe their success to any superiority of intellect or of mathematical faculty in themselves or in their followers . . . We conclude, then, that the present gigantic development of the mathematical faculty is wholly unexplained by the theory of natural selection, and must be due to some other distinct cause.[25]

For Wallace, the musical and artistic faculties were similar to the mathematical – they, too, could not have evolved by natural selection.

Moreover, Wallace claimed, no more than one percent of the human population showed genuine mathematical, artistic or musical or, for that matter, "metaphysical" ability or displayed the faculty of wit and humor – consequently, selection could not account for their presence. However, these observations did not lead Wallace to question his pan-selectionism and wonder whether forces and constraints other than natural selection may have a role in their evolution. Wallace's pan-selectionism seemed to require that organic evolution admit no biological mechanism other than natural selection. Therefore, Wallace argued:

> The special faculties we have been discussing clearly point to the existence in man of something which he has not derived from his animal progenitors – something we may best refer to as being of a spiritual essence or nature, capable of progressive development under favourable conditions.[26]

The development of these faculties was not the only time that such extra-natural factors impinged upon evolution: according to Wallace, the origin of life itself and the emergence of consciousness in animals were similarly inexplicable by natural selection and, therefore, material mechanisms of evolution. He concluded:

> These three distinct stages of progress from the inorganic world of matter and motion up to man, point clearly to an unseen universe – to a world of spirit, to which the world of matter is clearly subordinate.[27]

It merely remained to show, in more detail, that these transitions between stages were governed by "causes of a higher order than those of the material universe" and, like the typical contemporary ID creationist, Wallace claimed to have arrived at this position through "strictly scientific evidence in its appeal to facts."[28] It is somewhat strange that ID creationists have not adopted Wallace as their patron saint. After all, here we have one of the two founders of the theory of evolution by natural selection endorsing the existence of a transcendent world inhabited by spirits. Pan-selectionism comes at a cost.

Weismann was equally convinced that such mental faculties or "talents" could not be the product of natural selection.[29] But, unlike Wallace, he concluded that they were by-products of the human mind which, as a whole, was selected. Wallace was not impressed, arguing that Weismann's "view hardly accounts for the existence of the highly peculiar human faculties in question."[30] For Wallace, even a slight retreat from pan-selectionism – the acceptance of the possibility that not every trait is adaptive – was unacceptable. Weismann was never quite as dogmatic.

Weismann's main contribution to the development of evolutionary theory was a blanket rejection, through both argument and experiment, of the ubiquitous inheritance of acquired characters which Darwin and many others had come to accept since the 1860s, in contrast to the position taken in the first 1859 edition of the *Origin*. Weismann also distinguished sharply between the germinal cells (or germ-line) and the other *somatic* cells (or *soma*) in animals. He argued that the early sequestration of the former from the latter led to their protection from environmental influences. Unlike what was permitted in Darwin's theory of pangenesis, Weismann's germ-line could suffer no environmentally induced changes that could potentially be transmitted to future generations. Since the germ-line produced the next generation, from this point of view, the germ-line was immortal. This conceptual framework lies at the foundation of what has become the framework for the modern theory of evolution. However, for Weismann's contemporaries, what largely became a matter of concern was his perceived insistence that natural selection was the only major force of evolution. This was a view that came increasingly under attack during the decades around 1900.

The Decline of Darwinism

If the 1870s and early 1880s may be regarded as a triumphant period for the theory of natural selection, the 1890s must be regarded as a period of retreat.[31] Biologists did not question evolution, that is, the transformation of species, as they had done before 1858. Rather, they questioned whether natural selection was a major force of evolution. Some even claimed that natural selection was not even a force of any substance. A wide range of non-selectionist evolutionary theories appeared; the most important of them can be loosely organized under the rubric of neo-Lamarckism and orthogenesis. Speaking broadly, there were two motivations for the rejection of the theory of natural selection:

(i) general skepticism about how far natural selection alone can modify a species, in particular whether it can result in speciation. Experimental evidence did not settle the issue in favor of the selectionists. Darwin did not have a single experimental test of natural selection in the *Origin*; all he had were plausible "just-so" stories about how a trait could evolve by natural selection. Even today field tests of natural selection (that is, tests beyond the laboratory using "artificial" selection) are difficult to perform.[32] In the 1890s, W. F. R. Weldon established some quantitative cases of natural selection in the wild, but these were perceived to be trivial changes, for instance, in the size of the Naples crab, *Carcinus moenas*;[33] and

(ii) a general dissatisfaction with the purposelessness of evolution through blind variation and natural selection. Critics perceived such evolution as nihilistic, especially if *Homo sapiens* is no more than yet another animal produced in this manner.

Both motivations are shared by contemporary ID creationists; they, too, deny the power of natural selection to render significant organic change and hope to replace the blindness of that change with what they call intelligence.

Given the lack of much experimental data, Weismann's insistence on the ubiquity and power of natural selection and his tirades against neo-Lamarckism also did not help the popularity of natural selection. Neo-Lamarckism emphasized the importance of use-inheritance (the hereditary transmission of characters acquired through use for the benefit of organisms). Its enthusiasts included Herbert Spencer, coiner of the phrase "survival of the fittest," who came to prefer neo-Lamarckism to natural selection, and the writers Samuel Butler and George Bernard Shaw, besides many biologists in Europe and the United States including Edward Drinker Cope, George Henslow, Alpheus Hyatt, and Alpheus Packard.[34]

The faintly more plausible doctrine of orthogenesis (which was also known by other names such as Henry Fairfield Osborne's "aristogenesis" in the United States and Leo S. Berg's "nomogenesis" in Russia) posited an internal drive in organisms leading to linear rather than divergent, but not necessarily adaptive evolution. Besides Berg and Osborne, its enthusiasts included Theodor Eimer in Germany. Strangely, the enthusiasts for orthogenesis did not pay much attention to why such a drive would exist, especially in cases where it is maladaptive. Orthogenesis remained sufficiently popular for J. B. S. Haldane to have to spend considerable space refuting it in *The Causes of Evolution* in 1932.[35]

Both neo-Lamarckism and orthogenesis addressed the two motivations that had led to skepticism about natural selection: both provided a mechanism of evolutionary change more powerful than mere natural selection, and both allowed organic change to have a purpose though, in the case of maladaptive orthogenetic change, this purpose remained somewhat mysterious. Ultimately, neither doctrine survived empirical scrutiny during the early decades of the twentieth century, though rare instances of the apparent inheritance of acquired characters continue to be found.[36] The main reason they have been discussed here is to emphasize that the theory of evolution and the mechanism of natural selection were not dogmatically embraced by biologists, as ID creationists sometimes claim. Rather, they survived the careful scrutiny of evidence, competed with conflicting accounts, and came to be accepted only because they performed better. But the theory that became the modern theory of evolution is much transformed from the original theory of Darwin and Wallace – we will take up that story in Chapter 4.

Mind and Culture

From the beginnings of his speculations on the transformation of species, Darwin was interested in the evolution of human mentality. His most detailed account of the subject appeared in *The Descent of Man* in 1871. Here, as in the case of physical evolution, Darwin relied on the continuity from animals to humans:

> We have seen . . . that man bears in his bodily structure clear traces of his descent from some lower form; but it may be urged that, man differs so greatly in his mental power from all other animals, there must be some error in this conclusion [of the gradual evolution of mentality] . . . If no organic being excepting man had possessed any mental power, or if his powers had been of a wholly different nature than those of lower animals, then we should never have been able to convince ourselves that our high faculties had been gradually developed. But it can be shown that there is no fundamental difference of this kind.[37]

The differences were ones of degree, with intermediate gradations filled, as expected from the theory of natural selection.

For Darwin, both human reason and emotional expression had their origin in animal instincts as displayed by our ancestors: "With mankind some expression, such as the bristling of the hair under the influence of extreme terror . . . can hardly be understood, except on the belief that man once existed in a much lower animal-like condition."[38] Darwin's confidence in the instinctual origin of human cognitive faculties remained constant even though many aspects of Darwin's views about the evolution of mentality underwent significant change over the years. A belief that animal instinct and human reason and emotion were related did not distinguish Darwin much from his contemporaries: even the natural theologians who did not accept evolution were willing to find aspects of reason and emotion in "lower" animals.[39] However, going beyond his contemporaries, Darwin assumed that even moral qualities – parental nurture, group cooperation, community defense, etc. – would persist over many generations and become part of the repertoire of inherited instincts of a species.

But, now, Darwin faced a critical difficulty: such social instincts conferred benefits to the recipients, not to the agents, of actions. How could natural selection, acting to increase individual fitness, maintain, let alone augment, such instincts? The problem was not limited to human cooperation. As Darwin realized as early as the 1840s, social insects such as ants and wasps, with sterile worker castes laboring on with no prospect of reproductive success, exhibited this paradox even more distinctly. Darwin's solution lay in group selection: individuals would have their moral instincts calibrated not by individual selection but by natural selection acting to preserve more of those groups with individuals displaying such group-oriented instincts. But how did such behavior arise in the first place? Darwin suggested two mechanisms, both involving transmission across generations through use-inheritance: what has come to be called reciprocal altruism (altruistic behavior on the expectation of future reciprocation) and social approbation or blame. These mechanisms may have solved the moral problem but other intellectual traits such as intelligence, linguistic ability, etc., remained recalcitrant and required an elaborate story beyond mundane group selection.

Darwin's solution of the problem of the evolution of intellectual traits also relied on ubiquitous use-inheritance and an insistence on the continuity between other animals and *Homo sapiens*. Darwin insisted on such continuity even for traits showing apparently unbridgeable discontinuity, in particular, linguistic ability of which there is no clear analog in non-human animals. Darwin's solution was to proclaim the co-evolution of language and brain, starting with a primitive proto-linguistic form of communication, and mediated by the use-inheritance of altered brain structures. In the *Descent*, an evolving language would exercise and enlarge the brain, and such inherited larger, more complex, brains would produce more complex languages. Darwin effectively conceded Wallace's argument, described earlier, that complex mental abilities did not confer immediate individual fitness benefits, but the argument from co-evolution muted the thrust of that objection.

Barely more plausibly, against Wallace, Darwin also urged the possibility of sexual selection leading to the evolution of intellectual traits, at least in human males. Male mental acuity was a result of competing for access to females. This is supposed to be similar to how selection gave the peacock its fantastic tail. But why do human females also display mental acuity? It is unclear that Darwin had any answer. But, then, Darwin also had no doubt that female intellectual abilities – and those of non-white "races" – were inferior to those of white males.

Thus, for Darwin, all moral and mental qualities are part of the human *biological*, rather than cultural, inheritance.[40] To some extent, this was an inevitable consequence of his acceptance of the Lamarckian mechanism of use-inheritance. If environmentally induced traits including, necessarily, all cultural traits were somehow transferred to the hereditary material for transmission to future generations, cultural inheritance independent of biological inheritance could be only a fleeting phenomenon. Biology would take over anything culture began. But Darwin's commitment to a biological account of mind and morals ran deeper: not having such a biological account opened the possibility of divinity reentering nature, denying the triumph of naturalism in all the sciences, including the human sciences.

Are Darwin's speculations about the origin of human mental faculties correct? Some probably are while others are almost certainly not, for instance, when they rely on use-inheritance. In any case, in spite of all the continuing popular excitement over the dubious disciplines of human sociobiology and Evolutionary Psychology, we are still far from sure (see Chapter 4). More importantly, are these stories essential, or even central, to the theory of evolution? Certainly not, as Weismann's dissent, mentioned earlier, amply demonstrates.

Contemporary Implications

This chapter began with an account of the first formulation of the theory of natural selection by Darwin and Wallace but continued with a description of the vagaries of evolutionary thought during the generation after the publication of the *Origin*. For all the enthusiasm with which the theory of natural selection was initially embraced by biologists, it came to be severely criticized – and therefore subject to skeptical scrutiny – very early in its history. As we shall see in Chapter 4, a robust, generally accepted, theory of evolution based on natural selection only emerged in the 1930s, and the importance of natural selection has again been questioned and subject to rigorous tests since the late 1960s. Contrary to ID creationists,[41] evolutionary theory does not owe its acceptance to dogmatic belief or some other irrational factor.

We also saw that attempts to use natural selection to explain the origin of many of our mental and cultural features were controversial when Darwin first embarked on that project. They remain equally controversial today but they are not central to accepting the theory of biological evolution by natural selection and other natural mechanisms. We will return to this important theme several times in this book. The point deserving emphasis is that accepting the theory of evolution, as we must if we have any respect for science, does not require commitment to the idea that all aspects of human mentality and culture can be reduced to biology, let alone be explained by the effects of natural selection. Evolution is more than pan-selectionism.

3

The Argument from Design

Evolution, as Darwin and Wallace understood it – and as we understand it today – consists of three major processes: (i) adaptation; (ii) speciation or, more generally, divergence at every level of the taxonomic hierarchy (from sub-species and species to kingdom and domain); and (iii) extinction. Neither Wallace nor the *Origin* says much about extinction: it is even unclear whether Darwin and Wallace thought extinction was largely a matter of weeding out the unfit, or whether it was a matter of luck. Even today a general theory of extinction remains out of sight.[1] Surprisingly, in spite of its title, the *Origin* says little about speciation.[2] The *Origin* is ambivalent on such central questions as the role of geographical isolation in speciation[3] though Wallace is less ambivalent, generally denying the necessity of isolation. We do much better about speciation today,[4] and we have gone a long way towards explaining diversity at higher levels of taxonomic organization though the problem is far from fully solved. However, in the case of adaptation Darwin and Wallace provided a novel explanation that has stood the test of time and that, in an important sense, has permanently removed divinity from nature, ensuring that the organic world should never again be regarded as the special handiwork of a divine "Creator."

Adaptation and Design

That adaptation is ubiquitous in the living world was recognized long before the *Origin*. Take the case of neotropical sloths, often regarded as among the most ungainly of creatures. Sloths were first systematically studied by the somewhat eccentric English naturalist and traveler, Charles

Waterton, who lived in British Guiana (now Guyana) from 1804 to 1812, returning there in 1816, 1820, and 1824.[5] Waterton's fascination with sloths led him even to keep one in his room for several months. His initial description of a sloth, in his entertaining 1825 travelogue, *Wanderings in South America*, emphasizes its apparent maladaptiveness:

> On comparing him to other animals, you would say that you could perceive deficiency, deficiency and super-abundance in his composition. He has no cutting teeth, and though four stomachs, he still wants the long intestines of ruminating animals. He has only one inferior aperture, as in birds. He has no soles to his feet, nor has he the power of moving his toes separately. His hair is flat, and puts you in mind of grass withered by the wintry blast. His legs are too short; they appear deformed by the manner in which they are joined to the body, . . . and his claws are disproportionately long. Were you to mark down upon a graduated scale, the different claims to superiority amongst the four-footed animals, this poor, ill-formed creature's claim would be the last upon the lowest degree.[6]

But, Waterton wisely observes later: "This singular animal is destined by nature to be produced, to live and to die in the trees; and to do justice to him, naturalists must examine him in his upper element."[7] Once the arboreal perspective is adopted, the sloth's apparent malformations get recognized as adaptations for a life largely spent hanging from branches. Waterton proceeded to give one of the first reasonably accurate descriptions of the natural history of sloths and justly took the Comte de Buffon to task for assuming that the sloth must live its life in misery because of the poverty of its design. Modern research has fully vindicated Waterton's assessment.[8]

Before Darwin and Wallace, in the Western intellectual tradition, the adaptedness of living organisms to their environment was often taken to be evidence for the existence of God. This argument, usually called the argument from design, is of ancient vintage, going back at least to Plato,[9] but was perhaps most famously elaborated by the natural theologian William Paley in 1802:

> In crossing a heath suppose I pitched my foot against a *stone*, and were asked how the stone came to be there, I might possibly answer, that for any thing I knew to the contrary it had lain there for ever; nor would it, perhaps, be very easy to show the absurdity of this answer. But supposing I had found a *watch* upon the ground, and it should be inquired how the

watch happened to be in that place, I should hardly think of the answer which I had before given, that for any thing I knew the watch might have always been there. Yet why should not this answer serve for the watch as well as for the stone; why is it not as admissible in the second case as in the first? For this reason, and for no other, namely, that when we come to inspect the watch, we perceive – and we could not discover in the stone – that its several parts are framed and put together for a purpose, e.g. that they are so formed and adjusted as to produce motion so regulated as to point out the hour of the day; that if the different parts had been shaped different from what they are, or placed after any other manner or in any other order than that in which they are placed, either no motion at all would have been carried on in the machine, or none which would have answered the use that is now served by it.[10]

Now, just as a watch implies a watch-maker, as Michael Ruse puts it, "the adaptations of the living world imply an adaptation maker, a deity."[11] Paley's most compelling example was the eye, which he compared to the telescope. He discussed the eye's functionality in elaborate detail: for instance, light rays passing from water into the eye had to be refracted by a more convex surface than those passing from air into the eye in order to have the same bending effect. "Accordingly," Paley observed, "we find that the eye of a fish, in that part of it called the crystalline lens, is much rounder than the eye of terrestrial animals."[12]

Though the argument from design is usually regarded as a single argument, it actually consists of two distinct arguments joined together. The first is an argument for there being something special in genuine artifacts such as watches, as well as in living organisms. That special something, as Paley makes it clear, is functionality in the sense of some sort of goal-directedness. We will call this the argument for functionality.[13] The second argument purports to show that functionality implies the existence of a conscious – in most versions, intelligent – designer: we will call this the argument to a designer.

Long before Darwin and Wallace, and even before Paley, the argument for functionality had been challenged, in the context of a discussion whether the world as a whole, rather than only organisms, could be used as evidence of the handiwork of a deity. In his 1779 *Dialogues Concerning Natural Religion*, the philosopher, David Hume, interjected his own view through one of the participants, Philo, who questioned whether the world was more like a machine rather than an animal or vegetable. If the latter were true, then the world would not require a conscious designer.

Hume also had other arguments against design which are not relevant to our purposes here. Some of these are typically not regarded as cogent objections to the design argument: for instance, Hume wondered whether the world could have been created by a relatively unsophisticated mechanic by rote repetition of learned techniques, just like the work of the mechanics who create even the best-designed ships. For Paley, the design argument was supposed to establish the *existence* of a designer, not identify what its features are. But this retort will not help Paley's argument in the end: as we shall see below, we cannot identify design without some idea of what these features are.

Function, Design, and Selection

For Hume, the analogy between the world and an animal or a vegetable might have provided a convincing argument against the existence of a designer but, for anyone with a deep appreciation of the biological world, it is beside the point. Living organisms display functionality, as every biological theory at least since Aristotle has recognized. We routinely explain aspects of the biological world by referring to functions: we have eyes in order to see, ears in order to hear, hearts in order to circulate blood, ovaries and testes in order to reproduce, and so on – in each case the organs have well-defined functions. Without talk of functions, doing biology is well-nigh impossible.

We typically explain the existence of entities performing functions by referring to those functions: each such entity exists *because* of its function. But, explaining the existence of any entity on the basis of its function is philosophically precarious.[14] A basic rule about causes, accepted since the scientific revolution of the seventeenth century, is that a cause precedes its effect. But when we refer to the function of an organ – or any other entity – we refer to something it will do in the future, after the organ already exists, when it begins to perform its function. Moreover, for organisms, the future is often uncertain, and some organs may not achieve their function – for instance, in spite of having adequate ovaries or testes, a nun or a monk may fail to reproduce. What, in such a situation, is the function of the ovaries and testes?

The "traditional answer," as Ruse argues, "is that this all goes to show that we humans are not the only beings with intentions. Adaptations are God's handiwork, fashioned to help organisms . . . to function down here on earth . . . [T]he genitalia that went unexercised . . . were nevertheless fashioned by God with future purposes or circumstances in mind."[15] This is a claim of the existence of teleology or purposiveness in nature, impregnated into the natural world by the will of God. In Western science, before Darwin and Wallace, this view of the origin of adaptations was largely found satisfactory though there was occasional dissent going back at least as far as Epicurus and Democritus among the ancient Greeks.

What the theory of natural selection provided was a way to naturalize functional explanations of the origin of adaptations, *naturalize* in the sense that it showed how adaptations can exist without violating the cause-precedes-effect rule and without recourse to any extra-natural mechanisms. In the process it killed the argument to a designer and, because of that, the argument from design. Let us return to the nun's ovaries and to that ancient animal ancestor of the nun which had the first differentiated ovary tissue that could be inherited by its female offspring. According to the theory of natural selection, that ancestor would have either higher fertility or higher viability than those conspecifics which lacked the ovary tissue. The latter possibility, higher viability, is less plausible in this example and we will ignore it in favor of the former, that is, higher fertility. Because of higher fertility of the animals with ovarian tissue, over generations, this trait would spread and eventually come to dominate the population. The function of the ovary is to enhance fertility by producing offspring. The nun's ovary today has the same function – in spite of the nun's odd sexual behavior – but, in saying so, we do not have to refer to the nun's future offspring and we do not have to refer to any god and its intentions. Thus any teleology in nature is thus naturalized, tamed – selection takes over from a god's intentions.[16] But there is a cost: the explanation must refer to history in a way that typical mechanistic or causal physical explanations do not – there will be more on this below.

Such functional explanations of the origin of organismic traits are ubiquitous in biology. Arthropods (which include insects) usually have a hardened cuticle with waxy waterproofing. They do so because these functioned to protect the body from desiccation when the first arthropods invaded the land after their evolutionary origin in the oceans.[17] Many mammals sweat, but humans sweat most profusely and efficiently. Sweating functions for heat tolerance. Human sweat is produced by eccrine glands and has low salt and almost no fat content compared to other mammals in which sweat is produced by apocrine glands. The low mineral content of human sweat and the general hairlessness of the human body ensure rapid evaporation of the sweat. The result is a very efficient way of cooling the body.[18] (Among mammals, probably only camels are more heat tolerant than humans.) All these functions exist *now* because of natural selection: we need not assume that they exist in a future that may not even happen let alone in the mind of a designer in the distant past.

The nun's ovary is thus not like Paley's stone. It may be like his watch insofar as it has a function but it is not like his watch with respect to its origin. Evolution by natural selection accepts the argument for functionality. But it rejects the argument to a designer. Looking at the watch or the eye Paley had assumed that two hypotheses about its origin exhausted the range of possible hypotheses: (i) it was the work of a conscious designer; or (ii) it was the work of blind chance aided by no other mechanism. If these are the only two possible hypotheses we may still prefer the second because we have never had independent experience of a designer of eyes. But, at least, we would have to concede that the first is not unreasonable.

The trouble is that these two alternatives are not the only ones. Chance may be aided by a potentially infinite number of natural processes. Crystals form patterns by physical law but there is no question of function here. Stalactites grow downwards because of gravitation; stalagmites grow upwards to meet them. There seems to be some goal-directedness here but this type of goal-directedness in physical systems can easily be explained away: there are versions of successful physical theory that admit no teleology. In the nineteenth century most physicists came to believe that versions of physical theory that do appeal to principles that seem to be teleological – for instance, the principle of least action – can ultimately be reduced to a physical theory with no goal-directedness. For Paley's argument to work at all, the functionality of the structure is critical. But this is exactly where natural selection strikes a deadly blow: it is a natural process that, by its internal logic, provides an account of functionality with no appeal to teleology.

Once we have even three hypotheses: (i) conscious design; (ii) blind chance; and (iii) blind chance coupled with natural selection, at most what Paley's argument shows is that (ii) is less likely than (i) or (iii). (Note, moreover, there is nothing that says that we are restricted to three hypotheses, that no more are possible. We reserve the right to introduce more hypotheses in the future if the present set proves inadequate.) Now, when we compare (i) and (iii), that is, the hypothesis

Let h_1 be the hypothesis of design, h_3 be the hypothesis of natural selection, and o the observed adaptation. Let $p(h_1)$ and $p(h_3)$ be the two prior probabilities and $p(h_1|o)$ and $p(h_3|o)$ be the two posterior probabilities. Let $p(o)$ be the probability of the observation, and $p(o|h_1)$ and $p(o|h_3)$ be the probabilities of the two hypotheses. Bayes' theorem (an uncontroversial result in probability theory) says that $p(h_1|o) = \dfrac{p(o|h_1)p(h_1)}{p(o)}$ and $p(h_3|o) = \dfrac{p(o|h_3)p(h_3)}{p(o)}$. Therefore, for $p(h_1|o)$ to be greater than $p(h_3|o)$, $p(o|h_1)p(h_1)$ must be greater than $p(o|h_3)p(h_3)$. If $p(h_1)$ is equal to $p(h_3)$, then what is required is that the probability $p(o|h_1)$ is greater than the probability $p(o|h_3)$. (If $p(h_1)$ is less than $p(h_3)$, then what must be required is that $p(o|h_1)$ be sufficiently greater than $p(o|h_3)$ to compensate for the difference between $p(o|h_1)$ and $p(o|h_3)$.) But $p(o|h_1)$ is what we do not know how to compute because we have no independent access to the putative designer's intentions and abilities.

Figure 3.1   The argument from design: a Bayesian analysis

of a designer and the hypothesis of natural selection, what do Paley's observations show?

Let us consider the general situation before we begin our analysis of any specific adaptation. The argument that will be given below assumes that we are attributing some probability of being true to the two hypotheses we are considering. As we get more knowledge of the world, we update these probabilities in the light of the new data. This is what philosophers call a Bayesian perspective and Figure 3.1 gives the formal argument in full detail. This is not the only way to think about scientific inference but it seems to be the approach Paley usually had in mind. Analyzing the same example, the philosopher, Elliott Sober, used an approach in which he compares the probability of seeing the evidence according to each of the two hypotheses; he reaches the same conclusion as the one reached here.[19] The conclusion does not depend on the details of the framework for describing scientific inference.

Returning to the argument, the important point is that we have some evidence about what natural selection is and what it may produce. However, we have no evidence about the existence or abilities of potential designers of adaptations. (We cannot point to the adaptations themselves: we need *independent* evidence about what these designers can and cannot do[20] – otherwise our reasoning becomes circular.) Because natural selection has explained other adaptations in the past and we have no independent evidence of the existence of a designer, we should attribute a higher initial or prior probability – that is, prior to the analysis of the new adaptation – to the hypothesis of natural selection than the hypothesis of a designer. But let us be charitable to our opponents and give both the same prior probability. Then we must show that the probability of the hypothesis of a designer, given our observed adaptation, is greater than that for the hypothesis of natural selection, given the same observation. However, it is an elementary result of probability theory that this can be so only if the probability of observing this adaptation, given the hypothesis of design, is higher than the probability of observing the same adaptation, given the hypothesis of natural selection.

But this is precisely what we cannot establish. The theological purpose of the design argument is to establish the existence of a designer sufficiently powerful and different from us to be identified with some god. Even if we tame most of our theological aspirations, at the very least, we must show that the putative designer must be a designer of natural adaptations, and not only clocks. But, as Sober and others have correctly pointed out, we do not have independent access to what the goals and abilities of such a designer are and, once again, we need independent access to these features before we can begin assessing the relevant probabilities.[21] We do not know if the adaptation could or should have been better – or, perhaps, worse, given the ultimate goals of the designer. We have no way to use our observation of an adaptation to estimate probabilities about what such a designer may or may not accomplish. We may or may not want to believe in the existence of such a designer but the observation of adaptations is irrelevant to the question. As Darwin asked: "Have we any right to assume that the Creator works by intellectual powers like those of man?"[22] (In passing, we should also notice that Paley's assumption that the stone was not put in the place where he found it by the divine designer for some cosmic purpose is also unwarranted. We do not even know that – Paley's argument may be even worse than how it is usually presented, even by its critics.)

Meanwhile, in the case of the hypothesis of natural selection, we can at least qualitatively assign probabilities to observed adaptations, given the hypothesis. We can construct alternative selectionist scenarios, and evaluate these probabilities for each of them. We may then even decide that none of our scenarios is plausible – that some other scenario is required or even that selection is not the explanation of the existence of a trait in spite of its present apparent adaptation. We often decide that the adaptations we see are less than perfect. With Paley in mind, and returning to the eye, Darwin observed: "The correction for the aberration of light is said, on high authority, not to be perfect even in the most perfect organ, the human eye."[23] The relative importance and power of natural selection, compared to other mechanisms of evolutionary change, remain controversial issues within evolutionary theory – we will return to this question in Chapter 4. Meanwhile, confronted with an apparent adaptation, the hypothesis of natural selection remains the only game in town. Given an adaptation, the only rational course of action is to assume its evolution by natural selection and then attempt to identify the appropriate selectionist scenario.

Note, also, an important disanalogy between Paley's watch and any natural adaptation. In the case of the watch, in contrast to the adaptation, we are supposed to evaluate the probability of the hypothesis of a human designer, not some potential deity with whom we are not conversant.[24] The evaluation of such probabilities presents no insurmountable problem: it would be eccentric if we did not infer the existence of a human designer for the observation of a watch. Now, in the case of the watch, we know what the function is. The eminent evolutionary biologist, John Maynard Smith, liked to tell the story of how he had the job of inspecting a warehouse of German war materials during World War II. He had no difficulty in inferring the existence of an intelligent designer for the machines even though he had no idea what their functions were. But, once again, Maynard Smith knew that any putative designer must have been human. Moreover, the functions of many parts of these machines were clear to him – given that he could assume that these parts were assembled by humans. It is not, therefore, implausible to infer the existence of an intelligent designer. Archaeologists confronted with unfamiliar artifacts have similar experiences. For instance, they were able to decipher what the function of the initially mysterious Antikythera Device was because they could assume it was created by humans with human abilities, needs, desires, and interests.[25] An argument to a human designer is often sound; cosmic designers are the ones that are beyond our abilities.

There are many other objections to the argument to a conscious designer. Hume, for instance, also pointed out that it is at best an argument by analogy, from a human designer to a divine designer of adaptations. But we have no way of deciding the aptness of the analogy. Such additional objections only bolster the argument from probabilities given above. Meanwhile, what is the upshot of all of this? Unlike Hume, biologists will concede the argument for functionality for adaptations. But any argument from functionality to a conscious designer is not only unsound, but because we cannot assign the relevant probabilities, simply incoherent. Meanwhile natural selection acting on blind variation gives us a handle on the origin of organic adaptations. *This* is the most important legacy of Darwin and Wallace. Perhaps the only rational theological claim that can be made about the design argument is the one that was once made by John Henry Newman, the leader of the Oxford Movement in the Anglican Church in the nineteenth century: "I believe in design because I believe in God; not in a God because I see design."[26]

Blind Variation

The theological and metaphysical force of the theory of evolution by natural selection comes from the blindness of variation. Even the neo-Lamarckian mechanism of use inheritance allowed some directionality in evolution and, therefore, the possibility of recovering some teleology in nature. Evolution could occur towards some future goal or set of goals. But evolution based on blind variation leaves open no such option: it is evolution away from a point, that is, from the first organism, endlessly diverging, and never to a point, a final goal that will eventually be reached. There is no plan, no purpose. Humans appear in the universe entirely by accident and natural selection. We, humans, allegedly the pinnacles of divine creation, have no purpose. As Douglas Futuyma puts it: "Some shrink from the conclusion that the human species was not designed, has no purpose, and is the product of mere material mechanisms – but this seems to be the message of evolution."[27]

Some of Darwin's followers reveled in what they took to be the complete removal of teleology from nature. As his self-styled "bulldog," Thomas Henry Huxley, put it: "That which struck the present writer most forcibly in his first perusal of the 'Origin of Species' was the conviction that Teleology, as commonly understood, had received its death-blow at Mr. Darwin's hands."[28] However, Huxley identified teleology with an acceptance of the argument from design: "For the teleological argument runs thus: an organ or organism (A) is precisely fitted to perform a function or purpose (B); therefore, it was specially constructed to perform that function."[29] Instead, Huxley went on to argue:

For the notion that every organism has been created as it is and launched straight at a purpose, Mr. Darwin substitutes the conception of something which may fairly be termed as trial and error. Organisms vary incessantly; of these variations the few meet with surrounding conditions which suit them and thrive; the many are unsuited and become extinguished.[30]

Huxley downplayed function; trained as an anatomist, his emphasis was always on the recognition of morphological homologies due to shared descent, whether or not these were functional.

In sharp contrast, and more plausibly, Asa Gray argued: "Darwin's great service to Natural Science [was] in bringing back to it Teleology; so that, instead of Morphology *versus* Teleology, we shall have Morphology wedded to Teleology."[31] Retaining teleology served Gray well insofar as it helped his cause of making evolution compatible with Christianity. But his true insight was in seeing – as both Darwin and Wallace also had seen – that whatever teleology that still remained in nature was now naturalized. Unlike Darwin, though, Gray did not appreciate the point that the "new teleology" (a term that Gray introduced) allowed only a very mitigated, contingent, and local concept of purpose: ultimately it relied on blind variation.

If evolution's reliance on blindness challenged the pre-Darwinian metaphysical conception of human selves and their purposes, its reliance on natural selection was equally foundationally important, though in a very different way. Natural selection potentially made functional biology a mechanistic science, in principle no different from physics and chemistry, the sciences of inanimate matter. There is, however, one important difference: as noted earlier, functional explanations routinely bring history into play. Physical explanations also sometimes refer to history, for instance, in explaining the origin of our galaxy or our solar system, but not as often as biological explanations. Moreover, except in cases such as that of geological explanation of individual rock formations, historical explanations in the physical sciences do not focus upon differences between individuals. Biological explanations must, not only because variation is ubiquitous and diversity itself is interesting and calls for further explanation, but because these are the differences on which natural selection must act. (Without variation there is no prospect for change by natural selection.) History plays a dual role here: variations are a result of evolutionary history in the sense that blind chance causes these variations, but variations are also lost or enhanced because of the past history of selective forces acting on an evolutionary lineage over time.

Parts of organisms have functions not because of some future for which they are prepared but because of the history of blind variation and natural selection in the past. All causes precede effects. There is never any final cause. The transition from Aristotelian to modern science in the seventeenth century had removed teleology from inanimate matter; Darwin and Wallace's theory of natural selection now removed any irreducible teleology even from living matter. For Huxley, Marx, and Engels, Darwin had also cleared the way for a thoroughgoing materialism; for Engels, in particular, scientific materialism would provide the basis of what was to be a new "scientific" metaphysics that was supposed to replace all older systems of thought.

Dembski's Resurrection

Ever since Darwin and Wallace, the customary philosophical and scientific attitude has been that, if there is design in living organisms, the designer is natural selection. Design is no more than a metaphor. By the end of the twentieth century, metaphorical design seemed to be gaining ground in biology in at least one sense. After having been routinely questioned during the preceding century, the view that natural selection is the most important force of evolution was gaining acceptance – there will be more on this in the next chapter. Except in theological circles, well removed from the natural sciences, the argument from design seemed dead, though some thought it was killed by Hume rather than Darwin and Wallace. However, one of the first major skirmishes in ID creationism's campaign against evolutionary theory consisted of the publication of *The Design Inference* in 1998, an attempt by Dembski to resuscitate the argument from design. We will end this chapter with a close look at that argument. Though it is presented with a lot of unusually – and unnecessary – formal apparatus,[32] the basic idea is quite simple and the argument falls apart almost before it gets started.

Design, for Dembski, is a "logical rather than causal" category though every instance of design that he considers in the book emanates from conscious human agency.[33] Dembski argues that an inference to a design hypothesis for the explanation of an event E is correct provided it survives passage through a procedure which he called an "explanatory filter."[34] Unlike the traditional argument from design, instead of just hypotheses of chance and design, we are also supposed to consider a hypothesis of regularity (that is, occurrence because of a law of nature).

These three hypotheses are supposed to be mutually exclusive and exhaust all possibilities – Dembski does not permit us to consider any other possibility. Dembski's explanatory filter is a multi-stage decision procedure in which we first consider regularity and do not reject it if the event to be explained, E, has a high probability. (High probability is supposed to indicate the operation of a regularity.) If it does not, we next ask if chance confers a low probability on E. If it does not, we assume that E is due to chance. If it does, we go on to ask whether E is "specified," intuitively, whether if fits a pattern.[35] If it does not, once again we attribute E to chance. If it does, the filter requires that we attribute E to design.

The filter is illustrated in Figure 3.2 and consists of the following protocol:

(i)   assume that three explanations, Regularity (R), Chance (C), and Design (D), are mutually exclusive and jointly exhaustive as possible explanations of E;

(ii)   assume that we have a method for determining if E is "specified" or not;

(iii)   assume that R is preferred over C and C over D by some criterion.[36] Thus we should consider R first, C and D only after we reject R, C next, and D only if we reject C;

(iv)   because of this ranking, we should try to eliminate R, C, and D in that order;

(v)   if E has a high probability, we should accept R; otherwise, we should reject R and begin considering C and D;[37]

(vi)   if C does not confer a low probability on E or E is not "specified," we should accept C; otherwise, we should reject C and consider D;

(vii)   since we have rejected both R and C, we should accept D as the explanation of E. In other words, we never reject D.

Thus, design is supposed to be inferred if we cannot explain something by regularity or chance. As Dembski puts it: "To attribute an event to design is to say that it cannot reasonably be referred to either regularity or chance."[38] Notice, immediately, that: (a) we are never even supposed to consider the probability that D attributes to E. In other words, we are never even told what design means – what a design hypothesis says; (b) perhaps even more strangely, Dembski's filter starts with an evaluation of the probability of E, not what probability R attributes to E; and (c) the filter by itself does not tell us how low the threshold probability of E must be before we must reject R, or what probability C must assign to E

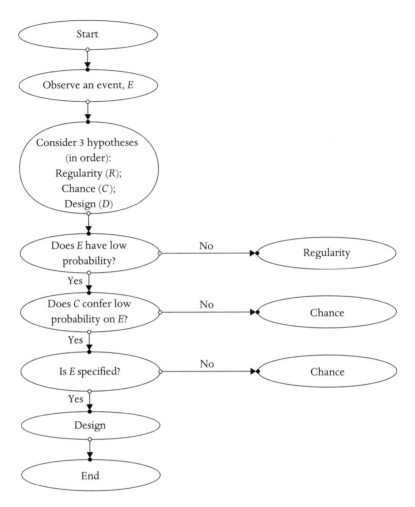

Figure 3.2 Dembski's explanatory filter. This flowchart is based on Dembski's (1998) *The Design Inference*. Notice how this procedure never allows design to be rejected even though Dembski never indicates what design is supposed to be. A simpler scheme, omitting the calculation of the probability of *E* on the basis of *C* is to be found in Dembski's (2002) *No Free Lunch*.

before we must reject *C*. However, independent of the filter, Dembski posits that the latter probability, for the total number of times *E* occurs in the history of the universe, must be less than $\frac{1}{2}$.

The entire process begins with trying to reject *R* and Dembski's instructions for doing so are incoherent. We are supposed not to give up any particular regularity hypothesis – for instance, a particular putative law of nature – but all regularity hypotheses in one swoop. Here we are supposed to evaluate the probability of E itself, not according to any specific hypothesis. All this can possibly mean is that we ask whether E is a rare or a common event in the universe. Now consider the physical theory of weak interactions, the only hypothesis we need to consider for many situations such as the radioactive decay of matter. Let E be the event that a particular neutrino be detected in a particular instrument of known characteristics. Now, let us select our materials and instruments carefully so that our hypothesis predicts the probability of E very accurately, but with a very low probability – this is easy since we have a good theory of weak interactions and neutrinos interact very weakly with other types of matter and are, therefore, notoriously hard to detect. Dembski's filter will have us reject R as an explanation of E because the probability is low, no matter how accurately our hypothesis predicted R. But, as the example shows, just because an event has low probability does not mean that it could not have been produced by a regularity. There are many other such examples.

But there is a much deeper problem here. When we attribute a probability to an event E (even when it is a probability that some hypothesis assigns to E), that probability depends on how we describe E (or, in technical terms, what the relevant reference class is). Consider the following event reported by the BBC on October 28, 1998:[39] in the Democratic Republic of Congo, all 11 members of a soccer team were killed by a bolt of lightning that did no harm to the other team. Now suppose we describe this event exactly as such, requiring that lightning must strike during a soccer match *and* that it must kill all 11 members of one team *and* that it must leave the other team unharmed. Such an event would be rather infrequent. In Dembski's explanatory filter, we would almost certainly reject R. But suppose we describe this event as lightning striking a soccer field and injuring players in southern Africa. It turns out, according to the BBC, that during the previous weekend a bolt of lightning struck the ground and injured several players during a match in Johannesburg, South Africa. Now, the event does not seem to have so low a probability after all. There may well be some regularity here, and that regularity tells us that it may be dangerous to play soccer in southern Africa in spring.

But suppose we do not know about the Johannesburg match. In Dembski's explanatory filter, after rejecting R, we turn to a consideration of C and D. For C to be rejected, two conditions must be satisfied: (i) C must confer a sufficiently low probability (less than $\frac{1}{2}$) to E; and (ii) E must be "specified." Recall that C must confer this low probability for all events of the type of E in the history of the universe. Now, let us return to the Congolese soccer match and use our first description of it. Let p be the probability that our chance hypothesis confers on an individual even E. Let an event of this type occur n times in the history of soccer and that, because we have already rejected regularity, these are independent events.[40] Then the probability that must be less than $\frac{1}{2}$ is $1 - (1 - p)^n$. Let us say that C attributes to E a probability, p, of 0.1 (or 1 in 10). Then n must be about 8 or C will not be rejected. If p is 0.01 (or 1 in 100), n must be about 750. These are much larger probabilities than what any plausible chance hypothesis would ever assign to what happened at the Congolese soccer match. Now, as p gets lower, n gets rapidly larger. So, unless we believe that events of this type have occurred thousands of times in the brief history of soccer, we are well on the way to rejecting C.[41]

All that remains to be shown is that C is specified in Dembski's sense. Assuming that our description of what happened during the match gives all the relevant detail, it is trivially true that the event follows a pattern and that we have an adequate tractable description of what it is: we have already described it in very few words. So, the inexorable conclusion is that the event must be explained by the hypothesis of design.[42] In one sense, at least, this inference is reassuring because it is consilient with another related hypothesis: reportedly, many residents of Bena Tshadi village in the province of Eastern Kasai, the home of the team that lost all its members, attributed our event E to witchcraft.[43]

Mark Perakh gives another example.[44] While living in the erstwhile Soviet Union, Perakh had not seen his cousin Kot since 1939 because of World War II. In 1949, when he lived in Odessa, Ukraine, he went to Moscow for a few days and ran into Kot. Kot, who now lived in the city of Balkash, several thousand miles away in Kazakhstan, was accidentally in Moscow for a few hours. The example also sails through Dembski's filter – once again we are supposed to endorse design. Twenty years later, in 1969, on the same street in Moscow, during another short visit to Moscow, this time for a few hours, Perakh encountered a friend, Karl, whom he had also not seen for exactly ten years. Moreover Karl, too, lived in Balkash and was in Moscow for a few days. Note that both of Perakh's associates had names beginning with "K." In both cases one of the two individuals destined to meet was visiting Moscow for a few hours while the other was visiting for a few days. In both cases, the one visiting Moscow for a few days first recognized the other. Now consider the joint event as a single event – it sails through Dembski's filter even more easily.

Purely scientific examples are also not hard to find. During the fall of 1967, an astronomy graduate student, S. Jocelyn Bell, began observing a strange radio signal with a very uniform period of $1\,^1/_3$ seconds emanating from a specific region of the sky.[45] Terrestrial sources were easily ruled out. Less easily, it was determined that the source was outside our solar system but inside our galaxy in the Vulpecala constellation. The research group named it "LGM" for "Little Green Men," but only in jest. Dembski's filter would have led to something similar, but not in jest, perhaps naming it "LGG" for "Little Green God." Signals of such regularity from extra-terrestrial sources in 1967 were of very low probability, given what sources radio telescopes could easily detect. It is also clearly specified, so much so that extraterrestrial intelligence could not be trivially ruled out. The signals came from a pulsar, now known to be a rotating neutron star. Bell's super-visor, Anthony Hewish, received a Nobel Prize in physics in 1974 for the discovery. The story may reveal something negative about the organiza-tional and gender relationships within science. But what it reveals more clearly, and more negatively, is the irrelevance of Dembski's filter.

What all of these examples show is that Dembski's explanatory filter is useless as an inferential procedure, and this point is independent of whether the filter is supposed to be used to bolster any theological agenda. Now recall that, for Dembski, design is a logical rather than causal category. By itself, this leaves open the possibility that we could detect design in organic forms but that the causal story to be told is the stand-ard one based on natural selection. What excludes this possibility is an interesting bit of logical trickery. It is obviously highly unlikely that almost any complex adaptation would arise by chance but much less unlikely that it would arise by ubiquitous natural selection acting on sequences of chance variation – indeed, this, essentially, was how Darwin and Wallace disposed of Paley. The logical trickery consists of Dembski setting up his filter in such a way that we sequentially consider regularity alone, chance alone, and then end up with design.[46] We do not get to consider regularity along with chance, that is, natural selection along with blind variation. If we could have done so, and especially if we were allowed, as we should be allowed, to look at every combination of every selectionist and every variational hypothesis, then there is no reason to believe that we could eliminate a single adaptation even if we followed the basic flow of Dembski's filter.

The point just made is quite obviously true when we look at adaptive traits that evolve many times, and hence there are many events of type E for which we must compute the probability on the assumption of natural selection and blind variation. Examples include the eye that had so troubled Paley. By now, molecular evidence is conclusive in suggesting that there have been multiple independent origins of complex eyes.[47] Of the thirty or more animal phyla about a third include species with well-formed identifiable eyes and another third include species with light-sensitive patches of cells.[48] Among animals with proper eyes there is a near-continuous gradation of variation between the simplest and the most complex. Recent theoretical work shows that even a very pessimistic estimate of eye evolution requires only 300–400,000 generations to evolve a lens eye from a patch of pigmented light-sensitive epithelial cells.[49] Now, recall that the organisms in which the first eyes evolved are likely to have had very short generation times, usually less than a year. On the average it would not even take half a million years to evolve an eye. Eyes are easy to evolve. A hypothesis of blind variation and natural selection would confer a fairly high probability of the evolution of the eye.

For some events, for instance, the origin of the first cell, we are not on equally firm ground and we should be free to say so. We do not even know whether there were many different types of cells generated from non-living matter, and that only a few types survived the first phase of evolution and were then integrated by symbiosis. If so, the probability assigned to these events by natural selection and blind variation would not be particularly low. On the other hand, if there only arose at most a very few types of cell, the probability would be lower. At present we do not know, but our uncertainty about models of the origin of life does not constitute uncertainty about the mechanisms of the evolution of life on Earth no matter where the first living thing came from. The origin of life is not a test case for evolutionary theory.[50] Life may possibly have come from outer space as some biologists have speculated.[51] Even if life originated elsewhere, evolutionary biologists still face the burden of explaining how it evolved on Earth. If all that ID creationists can do is to point out that we have not solved the problem of the origin of life, they would only be parroting what Darwin said in the *Origin* while ignoring that we know a lot more today, with the problem appearing in much clearer resolution now than even a generation ago. But, even in this case, there are enough alternative hypotheses about the origin of life that there is no reason to believe that Dembski's filter can dispose of all explanations based on regularity *and* chance.

Ultimately, in *The Design Inference*, all of Dembski's work is really done by his "Law of Small Probability" and an appeal to an intuitive recognition of pattern: "Specified events of low probability do not occur by chance."[52] This is no conceptual advance from Paley, and a lot less elegant. It also shows a lot less intellectual integrity, as becomes apparent when we recall that Paley, unlike Dembski, was writing before the theory of natural selection provided an alternative to design as an explanation of functionality. Finally, since there is no mention of a designer in *The Design Inference* (recall that design was a logical category, not a causal mechanism), even if we accepted the argument for design, we still have no argument for a designer.[53] What makes it worse is that, because design, according to Dembski, is simply the "set-theoretic complement of the disjunction of regularity-or-chance,"[54] it consists, by definition, of anything not explained by the hypotheses of regularity alone or chance alone.[55] This includes events explained by human agency and those explained by our combination or blind regularity *and* chance, including those explained by the theory of natural selection. But suppose that human agency is also explainable by some combination of regularity and chance, and that regularity *or* chance[56] allows the use of both. Then is there any reason to suspect that the complement is non-empty? Dembski provides none. If ID creationists want biologists to take their objections seriously, they will have to do better.

4

Mere Evolution

Natural selection – Darwin and Wallace's seminal discovery – lies at the foundation of the modern theory of evolution which we accept today. But it is not the only principle at that foundation; indeed, as we shall see below, discoveries at the molecular level sometimes challenge any excessive confidence in the preponderant role of natural selection in evolution. The developments that led to the modern theory of evolution, which will be reviewed in this chapter, had two major sources. Darwin and Wallace's theory of natural selection is one of them. The other is the work of a Moravian monk, Gregor Mendel, who remained unknown in his lifetime. The developments discussed in this chapter underscore the extent to which modern evolutionary theory is more than the "Darwinism" glibly criticized by Dembski and other ID creationists.[1]

Mendel's Legacy

We begin with Mendel, who was born in 1822 in Heinzendorf, Moravia (now, Hyncice in the Czech Republic), the son of a peasant farmer. He entered the Augustinian order in 1843 at the St. Thomas Monastery in Brünn (now, Brno) and was ordained in 1847. He was assigned to teaching duties in 1849 but failed the state teacher certification examination. One of the examiners advised that the largely self-taught Mendel be sent to university for a proper education in the natural sciences. During 1851–3 Mendel attended the University of Vienna, studying the natural sciences and mathematics. Returning to Brünn, from 1856 Mendel began experimenting with plant hybridization in the monastery garden with thirty-four different varieties of the common garden pea (of the genus

Pisum). Presumably inspired by his education in Vienna, and unlike his predecessors in the field of hybridization, Mendel's goal was to give a quantitative account of the inheritance of traits during hybridization. The results were presented to the Brünn Society for the Study of Natural Science in February and March 1865 and published in its *Proceedings* in 1866.[2]

Mendel interpreted his quantitative results on the observed patterns of inheritance in the peas as showing that characters or traits (such as height, flower color, seed shape, seed color, etc.) were each controlled by two factors, now called *alleles* (which are different forms of a gene), one inherited from each parent during sexual reproduction. Mendel's analysis produced three rules governing the behavior of these alleles:

(i)   dominance – one allele could be dominant over another, that is, an individual that had both alleles (say, A and a) would display the trait observed when only the dominant allele was present (in two copies, say A and A). (The former type of individual is called a heterozygote, the latter a homozygote.) Thus, because the color green of pea seeds is dominant over the color yellow, an individual plant with one allele for green color and one allele for yellow will produce only green seeds;

(ii)   segregation – any gamete (or germ cell, namely, the ovum or the sperm) was equally likely to receive an allele from the male as from the female parent of the reproducing individual; and

(iii)   independent assortment – different sets of alleles, now called alleles at different *loci*, are inherited independently of each other. (For example, an allele for seed color would be inherited independent of an allele for the height of a plant.)

Mendel's paper generated no immediate attention. A reprint sent to Darwin remained unread. Mendel died in 1884 with no reason to believe that the next century would regard his work as among the most important innovations biology had seen to date, for some even more important than the formulation of the theory of natural selection. Around 1900, Mendel's work was recovered almost simultaneously by three botanists, Hugo de Vries, Carl Correns, and Erich von Tschermak-Seysenegg, though there is considerable controversy as to whether any of them obtained the same results and produced the correct interpretation before reading Mendel's paper.[3] All three did give Mendel due credit as a predecessor. Meanwhile, the English zoologist, William Bateson, who coined the term "genetics" in 1905 to describe the study of heredity based on Mendel's rules, soon emerged as Mendel's greatest champion in the scientific world.

Bateson did not believe that evolution took place through natural selection acting on quantitative variation, or minor variations in degree, rather than in kind. Rather, he was firmly convinced of the importance of discontinuous variation for evolution. In Britain, the idea of discontinuity was strongly resisted by the so-called biometricians, such as Karl Pearson and W. F. R. Weldon, who claimed to have assumed Darwin's mantle, and were attempting to construct a statistical theory of evolution. Pearson and Weldon, in turn, doubted that Mendel's rules were obeyed in any but very exceptional cases. They also dismissed the possibility that distinguishing between factors and characters, and following what happened to factors, would lead to a better account of evolutionary change than an account based on changes in the characters themselves. Instead, they formulated a set of rules such as the "Law of Ancestral Heredity" which governed the inheritance of characters from generation to generation. This law claimed that all ancestral generations contributed to the degree to which an individual displayed a trait though this contribution decreased geometrically with receding generations. Coupled to this intellectual disagreement was a strong personal animosity between Bateson and Weldon.

It is therefore not particularly surprising that the recovery of Mendel's work sparked an acrimonious dispute between the biometricians and Mendelians in Britain at the turn of the twentieth century. Bateson, in particular, insisted on the importance of discontinuous changes – for instance, between Mendelian alleles – for evolution. This view was backed by de Vries' "mutation theory" of evolution, once again underscoring the point made in Chapter 2 that natural selection as a major mechanism of evolution was a theory in retreat by 1900. The immediate dispute came to an end with Weldon's death in 1906 but the conceptual divide remained.

The Modern Framework for Evolutionary Theory

That divide was eventually bridged between 1918 and 1930 by two sets of developments: (i) in 1918 R. A. Fisher showed that the rules formulated by the biometricians, including the Law of Ancestral Heredity, could be approximately explained on the basis of Mendelian inheritance; and (ii), more importantly, starting with the work of H. T. J. Norton, H. S. Jennings, and R. B. Robbins in the 1910s, and continuing particularly with the work of J. B. S. Haldane, R. A. Fisher, and Sewall Wright in the 1920s, a theory of natural selection based on Mendelian models of inheritance was constructed. What we consider to be the modern framework for evolutionary theory emerged from these developments, taking its mature form in the early 1930s – that framework owes as much to Mendel as to Darwin (and Wallace).[4]

Crucial to the construction of this framework was the elaboration of Mendel's distinction between character (or trait) and factor into a distinction between *genotype* and *phenotype*, first clarified by Wilhelm Johannsen in 1909.[5] The genotype was an abstract description of the inherited specificities of an individual consisting of Mendel's factors, what we customarily call genes or, more accurately, alleles. This description needed to be abstract at the turn of the twentieth century because, even though it was becoming clear that the alleles were carried by chromosomes from generation to generation, it was far from clear what the genetic material was. Chromosomes were known to consist of proteins and DNA. Until the 1940s, the genetic material was believed to consist of proteins because DNA, constructed from only four building blocks (or nucleotide *bases* – adenine [A], cysteine [C], guanine [G], and thymine [T]), was not supposed to be complex enough to specify the hundreds of known alleles. Experimental results from the 1940s finally established that DNA was the genetic material.[6] With the construction of the DNA double helix model by Watson and Crick in 1953,[7] it became clear that individual alleles were specified by linear sequences (or arrangement) of A, C, T, and G. These sequences specified amino-acid residue sequences which formed proteins. The relation between DNA sequence and proteins is usually viewed as one of *coding*, with genes encoding proteins. One unexpected discovery of the 1960s was that this code is degenerate: different DNA sequences may code the same protein.

In contrast to the abstract genotype of classical genetics, the phenotype consisted of the physical traits of organisms, their structures and behaviors, what Mendel had also called characters. The proteins specified by the genes constitute the phenotype at the most basic level. To get complex structures and behaviors requires many intermediate levels of biological specification. Now, because only the genotype gets transmitted during reproduction, it was natural to assume that the genotype – in some way or the other – specified the phenotype and was, in this sense, more fundamental than the latter. Moreover, for many traits, the specification of the phenotype by the genotype was sufficiently precise that all the details of development, how the phenotype arose from the history of interactions between the genes and the environment, could be ignored for the purpose of studying the rules of inheritance with modification, that is, evolution. As Thomas Hunt Morgan, the premier geneticist of the first decades of the twentieth century, put it:

> Between the characters, that furnish the data for the [Mendelian inheritance] theory and the postulated genes, to which the characters are referred, lies the whole field of embryonic development. The theory of the gene . . . states nothing with respect to the way in which the genes are connected with the end-product or character. The absence of information relating to this interval does not mean that the process of embryonic development is not of interest for genetics . . . but the fact remains that the sorting out of the characters in successive generations can be explained at present without reference to the way in which the gene affects the developmental process.[8]

Morgan's *heuristic*, treating development as a black box, allowed organismic evolution to be tracked by following what happened to the genotypes from one generation to the next. All that needed to be assumed was that natural selection can be modeled through changes in genotypic frequencies.

Following Morgan's heuristic, genotypes, rather than phenotypes, were assigned differential fitnesses capturing differences in the viabilities and fertilities of individual organisms themselves. The *fitness* of a genotype is the expected number of offspring it produces in the next generation relative to other genotypes in the population. (The *mean fitness* of a population is its expected change in size in the next generation relative to its present size.) All of evolution was to be explained from a genetic basis. As Morgan's student, H. J. Muller, put it: "in all probability all specific, generic, and phyletic differences, of every order, between the highest and lowest organisms, the most diverse metaphyta and metazoa, are ultimately referable to changes in . . . genes."[9] For the time being, cases in which the relationship between the genotype and phenotype was more complex, and dependent on environmental cues, were deliberately largely ignored.

Starting in 1924, J. B. S. Haldane published a series of papers containing a detailed treatment of a genetical theory of natural selection, analyzing a wide variety of genetic models.[10] These models differed with respect to the dominance relationships between alleles, assumptions about whether one or several loci controlled a phenotypic trait, the size of the population, patterns of mating, and, most importantly, modes of natural selection (whether it was weak or intense, or constant, cyclic, or fluctuating), and so on. A surprising general, and welcome, conclusion was that even small fitness differences can lead to rapid evolution. Darwin's old worry (see Chapter 2), whether there was sufficient time for evolution by natural selection acting on blind variation, was finally and decisively laid to rest. Even in the early 1920s, religious critics of evolution had continued to harp on the problem of whether there was sufficient time for natural selection to have brought about the observed patterns of evolutionary change on Earth. One of Haldane's major achievements was to answer these skeptics definitively by demonstrating the power of natural selection to produce rapid change.[11] Not only was that successfully achieved, but the work of Haldane, Fisher, and Wright also demonstrated the irrelevance of orthogenesis and all other alternative theories of evolution that had risen to prominence at the end of the nineteenth century. Together, Haldane, Fisher, and Wright are taken to have founded the field of theoretical population genetics which continues to provide the foundation of evolutionary theory.

Fisher and Wright went on to propose global theories that were supposed to account for the history of the evolution of life on Earth. While Haldane was content to explore the consequences of a variety of different genetical models, Fisher argued that most of evolutionary history can be captured by natural selection acting on small fitness differences in large random-mating populations. Wright, in contrast, thought that small isolated structured populations were more important and that there were delicate interactions between selection, fluctuations due to finite population size (usually called *drift*), and other evolutionary forces. Fisher summarized his views in 1930 in *The Genetical Theory of Natural Selection*, still regarded by many biologists as one of the central works of evolutionary theory; Wright followed, in 1931, with a long paper, "Evolution in Mendelian Populations."[12] The dispute between Fisher and Wright, continued by their students, has been one of the driving forces of the development of evolutionary theory since the 1930s. Meanwhile, in 1932, Haldane published *The Causes of Evolution*, an integrative work that tied the mathematical models of population genetics to the empirical work of Morgan and his students (what is sometimes called *classical genetics*), and even proceeded to interpret the paleontological record in accordance to the theoretical results.[13] The result was what we have called the modern framework for the theory of evolution. It was assumed in all these developments that, though the models being constructed were explicitly only models of what happened within populations, that is, they were models of *microevolution*, they could also explain evolution at all other levels. In other words, they could model *macroevolution*. Macroevolution is simply microevolution writ large over geological time scales of millions of years.

The integration of the rest of biology with evolutionary theory was carried further by Dobzhansky in 1937, who brought empirical results from natural populations to bear upon the theoretical models of Haldane, Fisher, and Wright.[14] Dobzhansky also focused on speciation – the problem on which Darwin, in spite of the title of the *Origin*, had largely been silent. A major innovation of the 1930s was the widespread realization that geographical isolation was critical to many cases of speciation: subpopulations of a species that could not mingle and mate with each other due to physical separation deviated in different directions. Because of this, individuals from one sub-population eventually lost the ability to produce fertile offspring with individuals from the other. In 1938 Haldane announced that the new theory of evolution was a "synthesis" between biometry and Mendelism: from the former had come insights on how natural selection may be modeled; whereas the latter provided the theory of inheritance necessary for selection to do its work. Almost immediately afterwards, Julian Huxley's use of the "modern synthesis" as part of the title of his influential popularization of evolutionary theory in 1942 resulted in that theory often being called the "synthetic theory of evolution."[15]

Selectionism and Neutralism

Perhaps the most important innovation within the modern framework for the theory of evolution since the 1930s was the development of the "neutral" and "nearly neutral" theories of evolution in the 1960s and 1970s. The 1950s had seen the emergence of molecular biology and the growing physical characterization of organisms at the molecular level. In the 1960s a new technique, gel electrophoresis, enabled the detection of small differences between molecules which are a result of charge differences, for instance, in protein molecules (such as enzymes). Using this new technique, Lewontin and Hubby detected unexpectedly high levels of protein variation or polymorphism in natural populations of the fruit-fly, *Drosophila pseudoobscura*.[16] Almost simultaneously, Harris reported similar results for humans.[17] Given the degeneracy of the genetic code (because of which different sequences of DNA can code for the same protein), this observation implied that variation at the DNA level was even more pronounced. What maintains such a high level of variation?

In 1968 Kimura argued, on the basis of Haldane's thesis that there is a cost of natural selection,[18] that such selection could not maintain this degree of variation.[19] Much of this variation, he argued, must therefore be neutral. A year later, drawing on Kimura's calculation, King and Jukes provocatively announced the advent of a "non-Darwinian" model of evolution in which drift of neutral alleles replaced selection as the driving force of evolutionary change.[20] Partly because of King and Jukes' rhetoric, an acrimonious debate ensued about the etiology of molecular variation in natural populations. This debate has not ended. Besides the extensive – and unexpected – polymorphism mentioned above, further supporting evidence for the "neutral theory," as it came to be called, came from a high rate of amino acid substitution in proteins during evolution.[21] This rate appeared to be much higher than what is predicted from selectionist models. Over the years, Kimura and many collaborators have constructed a suite of elaborate mathematical models of neutral evolution at the molecular level. These constitute perhaps the most significant extension of evolutionary theory since the work of Haldane, Fisher, and Wright in the 1920s and 1930s.

The neutrality of a DNA sequence does not necessarily mean that it has no function. Rather, it means that the DNA sequence's product functions no better and no worse than the products of other DNA variants at that locus in the population. Thus neutrality at the molecular level is compatible with adaptedness of features of organisms at higher levels of organization. Nevertheless, Kimura acknowledged that neutrality at the molecular level presented a problem for significant fitness differences at higher levels of organization. To the extent that Kimura accepted that selection was the critical force shaping large-scale morphological (and behavioral) evolution, he remained partly bound by the traditional view that evolution is driven by natural selection.

As noted earlier, the neutral theory was roundly criticized when it appeared. Selectionists routinely tried to reinterpret the data that the neutralists produced in their favor, for instance, by invoking models with randomly fluctuating selection due to environmental fluctuations. These models mimicked the results of neutral models.[22] The dispute between neutralism and selectionism remains still unresolved though the vast data sets emerging from the various genome sequencing projects (see Chapter 11) should help decide the issue. Meanwhile, in the 1970s the neutral theory faced several recalcitrant difficulties. For instance, though the amount of observed polymorphism at the molecular level was higher than originally expected, the range of variability in many taxa seemed severely limited, for instance, about 12% in Drosophila and 5–6% in mammals. The narrowness of these ranges suggested the operation of natural selection.[24] For neutralists, the day may have been saved by the development of the "nearly neutral theory" of evolution.[25] This suggested that much of variation at the molecular level, if not strictly neutral, is only very slightly deleterious. This assumption helped maintain consistency with much of the data. However, most biologists today believe that selection has played a more important role in molecular evolution than what is allowed by the neutral or nearly neutral theories. With the new data from the genome sequencing projects, the next few decades should determine which of the competing claims is correct.

Reconstructing the Past[26]

Equally importantly, since the early 1970s, a lot of theoretical attention within evolutionary theory has turned to what the mathematical population geneticist, Warren Ewens, calls "retrospective" theories.[27] The models of population genetics so far discussed are "prospective" in the sense that, given the relevant initial conditions and parameter values, the models predict what will happen to a population in the future. However, in the context of evolution, we are often equally interested in reconstructing our past, the course that evolution has taken on Earth. Attempts to carry out such historical reconstructions lead to retrospective theories. Starting in the 1980s, mathematicians and biologists began developing techniques for inferring histories from the molecular data on variation that were becoming increasingly available. The result has been a set of inferences from molecular data about lineages (populations connected to each other by descent with modification) that complement and confirm what is inferred from the fossil record.

The crucial innovation came from the mathematician, J. F. C. Kingman, in the early 1980s.[28] Kingman's *coalescent* theory starts from the fact that the data we have available consist of samples of DNA sequences from a population. Sequences sampled from a single locus will be similar to each other because of common ancestry but not identical because of mutation. The differences allow the reconstruction of the evolutionary past. Each difference is the result of a mutation (a relatively rare event). The more different two sequences are, the more remote the common ancestor because more mutations were necessary to create the greater difference. Based on the number of differences and the size of a population, the coalescent theory allows the calculation of the time at which the most recent common ancestor of the existing sequences lived.

The simplest coalescent models assume no recombination (exchange of DNA segments between chromosomes during reproduction) and no selection.[29] In this case, predictions of the coalescent theory can even be used to devise sensitive tests of the neutral theory. These are the tests that may soon decide the neutrality–selectionism dispute. The coalescent theory can also be used to test whether population sizes have been constant through evolution, and whether these populations have been geographically subdivided. With it, retrospective evolutionary theory has moved far from the comparison of fossils to the comparison of DNA sequences of organisms living today.

Reconstructive work has already produced many surprises. For our context, one crucial development, though this still remains partly controversial, has been a significant challenge to a view once also held by the majority of evolutionary biologists, that all modern animal phyla, with different body-plans, evolved rather suddenly into their present forms during the so-called Cambrian "explosion" about 550 Mya. Reconstructions based on DNA sequences suggest a much earlier divergence of different animal phyla in many cases.[30] The molecular evidence was initially seen as being strongly contradicted by the fossil evidence but this problem has begun to disappear as fossils of structurally complex animals from earlier periods, similar to modern animals, have begun to be discovered. Perhaps the most interesting of these has been the discovery of microscopic bilateralian fossils (of the species, *Vernanimalcula guizhouena*) in southwestern China in 2004.[31] These fossils were dated to originate at least 40–55 million years before the Cambrian.

Though ID creationists often attempt to use a Cambrian "explosion" to suggest that the rather sudden emergence of the many complex body-plans could not be a result of natural processes, this has never been a respectable argument. The "explosion" took on the order of at least fifty million years (and this is a very low estimate), hardly a short time for the accumulation of changes. We now know that even changes in a single gene (that is, at a single locus) can make significant changes in body-plans. For instance, a major morphological change occurred in animal evolution about 400 Mya when six-legged arthropods diverged from crustacean-like arthropod ancestors with multiple limbs. In 2002 it was discovered that a change in a single gene (studied in *Drosophila melanogaster*) can account for such a radical transition.[32] Moreover, as the example of *V. guizhouena* shows, as more data are analyzed and more fossils unearthed, the Cambrian provides even less opportunity for plausible interpretation as special creation. This is unfortunate news especially for the creationist stalwart, Jonathan Wells, who, in *Icons of Evolution*, touted the Cambrian "explosion" as presenting an insurmountable problem for evolutionary theory. This supposed "explosion" also lies at the heart of Stephen Meyer's informational "challenge" to evolutionary theory which will be discussed in Chapter 7.

Contemporary Debates

Besides the major theoretical developments discussed in the last two sections, evolutionary biology has been host to many conceptual and technical innovations – and disputes – since the modern framework was launched in the early 1930s. The intellectual ferment in the field should be viewed as a sign of exciting progress, contrary to the claims of ID creationists who often try to use these disagreements to suggest that evolutionary biology is in trouble.[33] As we will see throughout this section, none of the internal disputes call into question the tenets of the modern framework for evolutionary theory, that is, evolution proceeds by mechanisms such as natural selection acting primarily on small blind variations produced at the genetic level. All evolutionary biologists agree on these essentials in spite of the debated issues discussed below.

Recall how, within that framework, there were disagreements even between Haldane, Fisher, Wright, and Kimura. Each of them can be regarded as constructing a different theory within the modern framework to explain the history of life on Earth: Haldane, a catholic one in which a variety of mechanisms are operating in different circumstances; Fisher, a theory in which populations are large and unstructured with genes producing only slight differences in fitness; Wright, one in which populations are small and divided into structured groups; and Kimura, one in which most mutations are neutral with respect to fitness. Thus, we can think of each of these theories as elaborating a basic framework in different ways. As prospective theories each makes predictions. As retrospective theories each makes a different historical claim about how evolution took place on Earth.

The innovations and disputes discussed in the rest of this section similarly elaborate the basic framework of evolutionary theory without calling it into question. In each of them what is at stake are different ways to add detail to that framework. Each thus represents an increase of our knowledge of the processes of evolution and the history of life on Earth, underscoring the continuing progress of evolutionary biology. The seven topics discussed below are undoubtedly partly idiosyncratic in the sense that others would have constructed a different list. This list is not supposed to be a definitive assessment of what are the central debated issues in evolutionary biology today. Rather, it is intended to illustrate how evolutionary biologists have gone about developing the field in the recent past. It gives a flavor of theoretical and conceptual research in contemporary evolutionary biology:

(i)   *What are species?* Ever since the early nineteenth century, biologists have been fascinated with the "species problem." As Ernst Mayr puts it, "[t]he so-called species problem can be reduced to a simple choice between two alternatives: Are species realities of nature or are they simply theoretical constructs of the human mind?"[34] Even after the theory of natural selection in the 1850s, biologists came to no agreement on the issue. Darwin himself took "the term species, as one arbitrarily given for the sake of convenience to a set of individuals closely resembling each other, and that it does not essentially differ from the term variety, which is given to less distinct and more fluctuating forms."[35] Even after the formulation of the modern theory of evolution, Haldane argued: "the concept of a species is a concession to our linguistic habits and neurological mechanisms[,] . . . a dispute as to the validity of a specific distinction is primarily a linguistic rather than a biological dispute."[36] For Darwin, Haldane, and many others who have continued to express such skepticism about the "reality" of species more recently,[37] that species are difficult to demarcate is what evolutionary theory predicts. This difficulty is yet another piece of evidence against creationists for whom species are unchanging types (the units of creation). That species are subject to such continuous transformations that the term can only be conventionally specified undercuts the fundamental claim of the creationist agenda.

Not all biologists agree with Darwin and Haldane.[38] However, those who believe in the "reality" of species are faced with the problem that the term has never been fully unproblematically defined. The most popular choice, the "biological species" definition, relies on the ability of conspecifics to interbreed with each other but not with individuals of another species: species are defined to be groups of interbreeding natural populations that are reproductively isolated from other such groups.[39] There are many problems with this definition. Among other things, the concept of species no longer applies to asexually reproducing organisms. But other attempts to define "species" fare no better. However, given that biological taxa are diverse and change over time, that is they evolve, it is also not clear why an inability to define "species" precisely should be cause for any concern. Rather, as noted above, the very fact of evolution suggests that boundaries between species should be murky.

(ii)   *What is the mechanism of speciation?* In the period after the emergence of modern evolutionary theory, Mayr argued forcefully that geographical isolation is critical for speciation.[40] As noted earlier, as local populations become geographically distinct and face different environmental challenges, selection encourages them to diverge further. As differences accumulate individuals from the different populations may lose the ability to breed together to produce fertile offspring (thus becoming different species, at least according to the biological species definition). This mechanism of speciation is called *allopatric*, in contrast to *sympatric* speciation which occurs without geographic isolation. Today most biologists still believe that allopatry is the major mode of speciation but it is also becoming recognized that sympatric speciation occurs fairly often (along with some less important modes).[41] Speciation that depends on changes in individual genes is probably largely driven by selection though chance factors may play a major role in speciation driven by chromosomal changes. This leads naturally to the next debated question.

(iii)   *How important is natural selection for evolution?* We have already encountered this question in the dispute between neutralism and selectionism. The debate runs even deeper. We will focus on only two issues here though there are many others. One issue is whether evolution should be modeled entirely as a process driven by natural selection. The claim that it should be so modeled is called *adaptationism*. Some ID creationists, such as Dembski (see Chapter 5), simply conflate evolution with adaptationism. Sociobiologists and Evolutionary Psychologists (see below) explicitly endorse adaptationism, while most evolutionary biologists are divided on the issue. In a justly famous critique of adaptationism, Lewontin and Stephen Jay Gould pointed out that the program is methodologically flawed since its practitioners always have available "just so" stories with which they can attribute new selective advantages of any trait should a given claim of adaptedness fail.[42] Others, including John Maynard Smith and Mayr, have tried to make adaptationism more palatable.[43] We will have to return to this issue in the next chapter where we will also question whether a belief in the importance of natural selection is identical to an endorsement of the models that adaptationists typically use. The modern framework for evolutionary theory neither endorses nor rejects adaptationism.

A related question is that of the role of contingency in evolution. The question can be very simply phrased: suppose we were able to return to some earlier stage of evolutionary history and start the process again. Would we end up with the same suite of organisms we have today? To some extent evolution must be a contingent process because it relies on blind variation for its raw matter. But how contingent is it? If selection is extremely strong, in spite of the blindness of variation, we should see the same – or, at least, very similar – organisms. This conclusion is supported by the many examples of convergent evolution in different areas of Earth. The now extinct marsupial Tasmanian tiger (sometimes called Tasmanian wolf, *Thylacinus cynocephalus*) had a skull uncannily similar to that of the placental wolf (*Canis lupus*). Other body parts are also strikingly similar. The marsupial moles of Australia (*Notoryctes typhlops* and *Notoryctes caurinus*), rare burrowing animals, are equally remarkably similar to the golden moles of Africa (family: Chrysochloridae) and placental moles in general. Antarctic notothenioid fishes (suborder: Notothenioidei) and several Arctic cods (belonging to the family, Gadidae) are phylogenetically distant. Yet, they have evolved almost identical antifreeze glycoproteins to survive in their respective environments.[44] Dendrobatid poison frogs in the neotropics (genus: Melanophyrniscus) obtain their toxin from a diet of myrmicine and formicine ants and the siphonotid millipede, *Rhinotus purpureus*. The poison frogs of Madagascar (genus: Mantella) obtain their toxin from three endemic Malagasy ant species and the same millipede, *R. purpureus*.[45] The convergent evolution of diet in these two groups was probably a prelude to subsequent convergent evolution of many other traits.

In contrast, if selection is weak, the effects of blind variation would dominate evolution which would be a highly contingent affair. If we restarted the process of evolution at some past point, we would obtain nothing like the organisms we see today. The issue of contingency divided Gould, who viewed contingency as central to the history of life on earth, and the paleontologist, Simon Conway Morris, who emphasized convergence.[46] No end to this debate is in sight. Both contingency and strong determination can be accommodated within the modern framework for evolutionary theory; contingency, however, is anathema to ID creationists who want to see evidence of transcendental design everywhere. Unfortunately for them, any evidence that they produce against contingency can equally and effectively be used as evidence for the power of natural selection.

(iv) *Is evolution always a gradual process?* Darwin and Wallace viewed evolution as a gradual process occurring at a uniform rate. During the last decades of the nineteenth century and the first half of the twentieth, there were many failed attempts to argue that evolution could take place through spurts, for instance, through large "macromutations." Nevertheless, in the 1970s, Gould and Niles Eldredge argued that the fossil record showed that there were short periods of rapid evolutionary change followed by long periods of stasis – they called this the punctuated equilibrium theory of evolution and presented it as an alternative to the gradualism accepted by most evolutionary theorists.[47]

More controversially, Gould and Eldredge suggested that macroevolution involves processes beyond those considered in the microevolutionary models of population genetics. Critics were abundant. Some doubted that the pattern of stasis and change really exists in the fossil record: the apparent evidence is merely an artifact of the uneven representation of fossils in the available data. If we also remember how long a billion years is, what appears to be a short burst of evolution in the fossil record may actually be gradual evolution over many millions of years. Many theorists pointed out that patterns of macroevolutionary stasis and change could be easily produced by standard microevolutionary models.[48] During the past decade controlled experimental work has also documented rapid morphological change in natural populations.[49] Thus, even if punctuated equilibrium is the pattern, the processes involved remain squarely within the modern framework of evolutionary theory. This is particularly important because ID creationists used to claim that the punctuated equilibrium model bolstered their claims for intelligent intervention into evolution, presumably during the episodes of rapid change.[50]

Punctuated equilibrium should probably no longer even be discussed as an ongoing controversy within contemporary evolutionary theory – it appears to have had a natural death. But the question of gradualism in evolution is of wider importance, as recent attempts to integrate developmental biology and evolution show.

(v) *What does development say about evolution?* Much of the recent excitement in evolutionary biology has come from attempts to open Morgan's black box and integrate development into evolutionary biology. This has resulted in the formation of the new field of evolutionary developmental biology.[51] The goal is to model evolution in phenotypic space, tracking changes in morphology and behavior. Two related issues are especially important. First, the relationship between phenotype and genotype may be complex, invalidating Morgan's heuristic. Second, there are features that are characteristic of higher taxa that cannot be studied by reference only to differences between individuals within populations. There are many puzzles here that we do not understand completely. For instance, all adult animals have bodies with two-fold symmetry (for instance, humans) or five-fold symmetry (for instance, starfish) but no other type. We do not know why. The evolution of animal body-plans, which distinguish the phyla, and which vary enormously, is in general poorly understood at present. Evolutionary developmental biology hopes to be able to explain these phenomena, whether they are due to natural selection, or due to physical constraints because of the nature of the materials out of which animals are constructed, or simply a matter of chance (or contingency).

Evolutionary developmental biology also tries to trace the evolutionary history of, and explain changes in, the developmental processes that bring about adult forms and behaviors. It begins by drawing on the many insights that developmental genetics has uncovered since the 1970s, especially the existence of a few genes (the *Hox* genes) that play a regulative role in morphogenesis in both invertebrates and vertebrates. But central to the new field are the many conserved features across all taxa at the cellular level. For instance, even though there are hundreds of molecules involved in inter-cellular signaling, there are only sixteen common mechanisms through which all such signaling takes place.[52] In the entire living world there are only six kinds of ion channels in cell membranes which can be structurally distinguished.[53] Evolutionary biology must go beyond Morgan's heuristic to understand these patterns; the black box of development is slowly but surely being opened to produce a much more detailed account of evolution than what the modern framework so far provides.

(vi) *What does genomics say about evolution?* The 1990s saw the initiation of the Human Genome and many other sequencing projects that have produced complete sequences for many species including scores of bacteria and other prokaryotes, yeast (*Saccharomyces cerevisiae*), mustard weed (*Arabidopsis thaliana*), rice (*Oryza sativa*), the fruit-fly (*Drosophila melanogaster*), and humans. When the HGP was initiated there was much scientific skepticism about its scientific worth.[54] But the stunning and unexpected results of the sequencing projects, particularly from the human sequence, have opened up new vistas for biology and converted most of the original scientific critics.[55] They have revealed a dynamic genome which is indicative of the breathtaking changes taking place in contemporary biology, including evolution.

Perhaps the most surprising discovery is that there is no correlation between the number of genes (loci) and organismic complexity. Humans have perhaps 30,000 or fewer genes while rice probably has around 45,000.[56] (Typically, "higher" plants have more genes than "higher" animals. If the recent past is any guide to the near future, all these numbers will likely be revised downwards as our knowledge accumulates.) When it comes to proteins, though, more complex animals seem to have more variety than simpler ones. This is achieved through a variety of mechanisms by which more than one protein is produced from the same gene. The most common mechanism is known as *alternative splicing*. The DNA of a gene produces a string of RNA through a process called transcription. In eukaryotes, these RNA transcripts contain both regions that are translated into proteins (exons) and regions that are spliced out (introns) before translation. If different regions are spliced out in different copies of the same RNA transcript (and thus, the name "alternative splicing") then the same DNA segment may encode several different proteins.

The ubiquity of alternative splicing in "higher" animals is not the only surprise from the sequencing projects. It has long been known that protein-coding genes form a tiny fraction of the total DNA of many species, about 2% in the case of humans. Sequencing has shown that these genes are unevenly distributed across the genome, with "cities" and "suburbs" separated by large swathes of "wilderness." We do not know why. There is also abundant evidence of the transfer of genes across species from widely divergent taxa though the extent of such transfers remains unknown. Evidence is accumulating that even though so little of the DNA gets translated into protein, a very large fraction of it is transcribed into RNA.[57] We have moved far from the molecular genetics even of the 1980s.

(vii)   *What does evolution say about the human mind and culture?* Recall, from Chapter 2, Darwin's hope of explaining human mental capacities by natural selection. He seems to have underestimated the difficulty of the task of understanding the evolution of mind and culture and we are probably not much closer to an answer than he was. The main trouble is that complex behavioral patterns (including mental behavior) do not leave fossil records in the way that physical traits do. Some biologists and some philosophers are skeptical that we will ever have plausible stories of the evolution of cognition and culture.[58] Meanwhile, others believe that the solution is already at hand. In the 1980s, human sociobiologists claimed to have explained much of human cultural behavior including the hierarchical gender structure of society, alleged universal xenophobia, and so on.[59] They even claimed to have found a basis in genetics and natural selection for human concern for nature.[60] Contemporary Evolutionary Psychologists claim to have shown that the mind is composed of a large number of modules each of which was selected during the Pleiostocene era (1.6–1.9 Mya–10,000 years ago) for a particular function such as syntax or detection of cheaters.[61] Some of them even claim that sexual jealousy and rape arose as adaptations.[62] By and large, evolutionary theorists reject these accounts, finding them fanciful adaptationist "fairy tales."[63] Whether or not these questions are central to evolutionary theory, there is no consensus that we have solved any of them in the way that we have consensus that we have solved many problems of the evolution of physical traits. If ID creationists suggest that claims of human sociobiology and Evolutionary Psychology should not be presented as hard scientific facts, they are correct, no matter whether their skepticism is generated by their religious beliefs. But these disciplines hardly belong to the core of evolutionary biology (which is why this debate is last on our list).

Creationists of every stripe often claim that evolution is a theory in crisis with no fertile research agenda and a treasury of recalcitrant data. In contrast, we have seen in this section how fecund the research agenda of evolutionary biology continues to be. There are, indeed, unsolved problems, but this a sign of health, not morbidity of its research program. So far the theory has adapted so readily to the wealth of new data over decades that its most basic claim, descent with modification through natural mechanisms, is no more questionable than the revolution of planets around the sun. The debates discussed in this section show that these are exciting times for evolutionary biology – readers are invited to join the enterprise.

Terminological Choices

ID creationists sometimes criticize what they call "evolution," sometimes what they call "neo-Darwinism," but most often what they call "Darwinism." It will, therefore, be useful to introduce and enforce some distinctions between these terms. If, by "Darwinism," we mean – as we should – the views that Darwin actually held, Darwinism is a pluralistic doctrine admitting a multiplicity of mechanisms of evolutionary change beyond natural selection. These mechanisms included ubiquitous use-inheritance and directional generation of variation. The term "neo-Darwinism" was invented in the 1890s to describe an emerging orthodoxy in which evolution was viewed as allowing only blind variation and no mechanism of change except natural selection, that is, the pan-selectionism of Wallace and (to a lesser extent) Weismann, as discussed in Chapter 2.[64]

Towards the middle of the twentieth century neo-Darwinism came to mean the modern framework for the theory of evolution with the added features that: (i) natural selection is a major, but not the only, force of evolution; and (ii) evolution is a continuous process. In this book we will use "neo-Darwinism" in this sense when it is used at all. Note that the neutral theory of evolution and the punctuated equilibrium theory are not neo-Darwinian in this sense. Thus the modern framework for evolution permits the formulation of evolutionary theories that are not neo-Darwinian.

By now, among biologists, "Darwinism" and "neo-Darwinism" are often used as synonyms to describe the conceptual framework of the modern theory of evolution. Nevertheless, we will not use the term "Darwinism" (and avoid the term "neo-Darwinism"). There are at least two reasons to avoid these uses. First, scientific frameworks identified with an "-ism" run the risk of appearing to be what they are not: ideological positions such as those normally associated with political or religious agendas. Indeed, ID creationists typically deploy "Darwinism" when speaking of evolution to suggest that their opponents are not defending a scientific framework rather than an ideology which is a counterpart to their own. It is a rhetorical ploy which should be resisted. If we do not resist this ploy, the dispute can be publicly presented as a conflict between two religions, or at least two ideologies, rather than what it is: one between a science and a religiously based doctrine masquerading as a scientific theory. What we should be defending is evolutionary theory, as it has emerged over the years, not Darwinism or any other doctrine suggesting that our allegiance is to some text rather than to whatever view that scientific work takes us.

Second, a mature scientific theory is not appropriately identified with a single individual no matter how critical that person may have been in its history. When a theory is proposed for the first time, it may perhaps be appropriately so identified: we speak without problems of Newton's mechanics, Dalton's atomic theory, Mendel's theory of heredity, or Einstein's theory of general relativity. But, as theories evolve in response to experiment and further theoretical work, the originator becomes increasingly less relevant in comparison to the ability of the theory to explain the phenomena in its domain. Moreover, in the case of evolution, in spite of acknowledging Darwin's and Wallace's crucial roles in first formulating that theory, the modern theory owes as much to others, including Mendel, Haldane, Fisher, and Wright. Again, in using "Darwinism" to describe our position ID creationists are trying to suggest, at least subliminally, that we are followers of some quasi-religious figure rather than defenders of science. Obviously, such suggestions should be resisted.

Finally, for expository simplicity, we will use "modern theory of evolution" for "modern framework for the theory of evolution" as we have already been doing in earlier chapters. In the dispute between evolutionary biology and ID creationism, the differences between the various theories formulated within the modern framework do not matter. Kimura is no more palatable to ID creationists than Haldane, Fisher, or Wright. Indeed, when we get to Chapter 7, we will see that, on his way to the neutral theory, Kimura inadvertently undercut one of the central claims of contemporary ID creationism by showing how natural selection leads to an accumulation of information.

5

The Cost of Lunch

According to the Central Argument of Intelligent Design (see Chapter 1), evolutionary theory does not have the conceptual resources to explain the biological facts we observe, in particular, the emergence of biological complexity. By and large, though ID creationists have not explicitly disavowed the flawed design inference in Dembski's early work (see Chapter 3), they largely ignore it today and, instead, rest their faith on three other claims: the limitations of what evolution-like processes can achieve as gleaned from some mathematical results from computer science, the irreducible complexity of biological systems, and an alleged law of the conservation of information. This chapter will assess the first of these claims; Chapters 6 and 7 will take up the other two.

The first claim constitutes an attempt to show that evolutionary theory is inconsistent with what we know of the biological world (thus deploying what was called the inconsistency option in Chapter 1) by interpreting evolutionary change as an algorithmic process and invoking supposed mathematical limitations of what various algorithms can achieve. An algorithm is a step-by-step procedure for solving a problem, sufficiently precise and detailed for it to be encoded in a computer program. Theoretical computer science studies the ability of various algorithms to solve different problems successfully and the resources it takes them to find such a solution (among many other things). This is done by formalizing the problems and the algorithms mathematically. For solving many problems, it has been found that algorithms that mimic evolution by natural selection perform very well. These algorithms start with an arbitrary set of rules to solve a problem, vary these rules at random, and continue to use those which perform well: this process mimics blind variation and natural selection. Dembski argues that such *evolutionary algorithms* cannot find solutions to problems any better than random search. Consequently, according to him, the actual process of natural selection on Earth could not have solved the adaptive problems that biological organisms are known to have solved. Unfortunately Dembski's argument is fallacious, a result of a shallow misunderstanding of both biological evolution and the mathematical results he uses. To see that will require us to understand evolutionary algorithms in some more detail.

Evolutionary Algorithms

Evolutionary algorithms were introduced by John Holland in the 1960s to solve optimization problems in a way that mimics evolution by natural selection.[1] In an optimization problem we are presented with a set of entities (sometimes called the "feasible" set or space). Each entity has a value which is a real number. Another way of saying the same thing is to say that there is a function (called the "objective" or "cost" function) which assigns such a number to each entity in the feasible set. Our problem is to find the entity that has the maximum (or minimum) value, or, equivalently, maximizes (or minimizes) the objective function. Without loss of generality we can only consider the maximization version of the optimization problem because of its obvious analogy to the evolutionary problem of maximizing fitness.[2]

Suppose that the function represents the height of a surface over the feasible space. This means that the height of a point on the surface is the value of the corresponding entity in the feasible space. Then optimization is the problem of finding the highest peak in this surface. On rugged surfaces with many local peaks and valleys, optimization can be a difficult computational problem. Suppose, for instance, that our algorithm consists of always climbing the surface, and never going downwards. Then, it would get stuck at the first local peak (or optimum) it encounters. It may never find the globally highest peak (or global optimum). Good optimization algorithms must get around such problems.

Such optimization problems are common in science. Consider, for instance, the protein-folding problem which is that of predicting the three-dimensional conformation of a protein molecule from its amino acid residue sequence (which is all that is specified by the gene encoding it). An almost infinite number of conformations are possible even for small proteins. In the 1960s, Cyrus Levinthal conceived of the problem as one of minimizing the energy of each conformation.[3] In this example, each conformation is one of the entities of the feasible set. The energy values, multiplied by −1, provide the surface.[4] The problem of finding the minimum energy conformation becomes that of finding the highest peak of this surface. (The protein-folding problem remains unsolved today though, by now, it is clear that a more complicated process than the one described here will be necessary.)

Genetic algorithms – the type of evolutionary algorithm introduced by Holland – search the feasible space for the optimal solution using a "population" of "individuals" consisting of modifiable "rules." The rules are modified in each generation based on their performance or "fitness" in finding higher peaks on the surface. Ultimately, the best rules that "evolve" in this fashion are used to solve the general problem – the procedure is described in some more detail in Figure 5.1. Genetic algorithms are empirically known to be good function optimizers in many contexts provided we always keep the best individual so far found, allowing it to go unchanged to the next generation.[5] For instance, one of the most successful applications of genetic algorithms has been in predicting the distribution of species' distributions from environmental

A typical genetic algorithm begins by selecting a population of rules (to solve the optimization problem) at random. Each rule is an individual in the population and possesses several sub-rules. These rules are used to try to find a solution to the optimization problem: they try to identify points in the feasible space with the highest value for the objective function. We now generate the population of rules for the next generation by creating new individuals by modifying (mutating) and recombining the sub-rules of the individual rules in the current population. But we do not treat all these individuals as equals. We allow some individuals to transfer their sub-rules to the next generation with a higher frequency than others depending on their performance. This performance is thus analogous to fitness, the sub-rules analogous to genes, and the individual rules analogous to biological individuals – the algorithm thus mimics the process of evolution by natural selection. Generation by generation, we usually end up with individual rules that identify entities in the feasible space with increasingly higher values for the objective function. The best rules are used to find optima in other similar data sets.

Figure 5.1 Genetic algorithms

parameters.[6] Other types of evolutionary algorithm draw analogies from other aspects of natural selection and are generally adept at function optimization.

The "No Free Lunch" Theorems

Creationists' excitement over evolutionary algorithms largely stems from two "No Free Lunch" (NFL) theorems proved by David Wolpert and William Macready in 1997.[7] Consider the set of all possible optimization problems. Then the NFL theorems state that no algorithm, on the average, outperforms any other over the whole set. The first theorem establishes this result for the situation in which an algorithm only tracks performance during the last generation (as is the case for the evolutionary algorithm described in Figure 5.1). The second theorem establishes the same result when there is temporal change in the optimization problem and we average over all possible such changes – the difference between the two theorems does not matter for our purposes. In the proofs of these theorems, it also does not matter whether an algorithm is deterministic or stochastic. The theorems have some startling consequences: Dembski harps on the fact that, since random search is also an algorithm, random search is just as effective as any other algorithm over the set of all optimization problems.[8] Hill-climbing through natural selection cannot do any better. In fact, the situation is even odder: even a algorithm that, on the average, climbs the surface downwards is, in this sense, just as good as one that climbs the surface upwards. Wolpert and Macready correctly conclude that, to devise an effective algorithm for a class of problems, we must obtain and exploit knowledge of the structure of these problems. The theorems thus confirm an intuition long shared by software designers: when we devise algorithms to solve problems we should use as much as we can of what we know of the nature of the problem.

The epistemological force of the NFL theorems is beautifully illustrated by a simple example due to Malcolm Forster (see Figure 5.2).[9] Consider a universe in which, on each day, only one of two objects exists: a sphere (S) or a cube (C). Suppose that this universe lasts for exactly two days. Then, this universe has exactly four possible histories (S, S), (S, C), (C, S), and (C, C). Our algorithm is supposed to predict what happens on the second day, given knowledge of the first. There are exactly four possible (deterministic) algorithms: (i) *Same* = "same on both

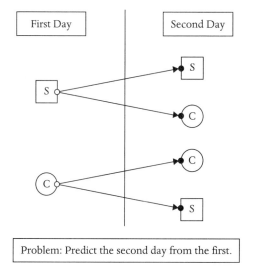

Figure 5.2   Malcolm Foster's toy universe

days"; (ii) *Diff* = "different on the two days"; (iii) *Sphere* = "sphere on the second day irrespective of the first"; and (iv) *Cube* = "cube on the second day irrespective of the first." If all four histories are equiprobable, and each, therefore, has a probability of ¼, then each algorithm has the same probability of ½ of predicting the second day correctly. This is what the NFL theorems mean, except that they establish the point for much more general scenarios rather than our depleted universe. (Figure 5.3 gives a slightly more technical description of the first theorem but it is not necessary for the development of our argument.)

But now suppose we make a correct "uniformity of nature" assumption, that the universe remains the same from day to day. Then the four algorithms no longer have the same probability of success; rather, that probability has values of 1, 0, ½, and ½, respectively. Now, *Same* is the best algorithm but only because of the uniformity of nature.

For Forster, the moral of the story is that we can devise an algorithm better than others only if we find out something about the world empirically, that is, we use what we learn from scientific investigation of the world – there is no a priori path to a successful epistemology. That epistemological practice should follow the path of science is a theme to which we will return in Chapter 9.

The NFL theorems will be stated here slightly more formally. We will restrict attention to the first theorem (the second is similar). Let Δ be our feasible set. Let the objective function (biologically, the fitness function) be f. Let Φ be the set of all fitness functions. Let α_i and α_j be two algorithms which attempt to find the maximum of f, exploring Δ one point at a time. Let A be the set of all algorithms. Suppose that each algorithm has carried out m steps. Each algorithm will then have produced a temporally ordered set or sample, d_m^Y, of m measured values of f within a range Y. For any algorithm, that is, for any $\alpha \in$ A, let $p(d_m^Y | f, m, Y, \alpha)$ be the conditional probability of obtaining the sample d_m^Y given f, m, Y, and α. Then, the first NFL theorem for optimization says that, for any two algorithms α_i, $\alpha_j \in$ A,

$$\sum_{f \in \Phi} p(d_m^Y | f, m, Y, \alpha_i) = \sum_{f \in \Phi} p(d_m^Y | f, m, Y, \alpha_j).$$

Because, in this equation, the summation is performed over all possible functions, $f \in \Phi$, we are measuring the average performance of the algorithm over all possible optimization problems. Thus, probabilistically, the result of the search are the same for any two algorithms at every stage of the search.

Figure 5.3   The first No Free Lunch theorem[1]
[1] The discussion here partly follows Perakh (2004a).

Dembski's Excitement

No one seems to have been as impressed with the NFL theorems as Dembski who adopts *No Free Lunch* as the title of his book which supposedly applies his design "theory" to the biological realm. But admiration does not lead to accuracy in interpreting the theorems. Dembski misinterprets them with aplomb. According to him, the NFL theorems are supposed to show that natural selection cannot lead to the evolution of biological complexity: in Dembski's own words, *No Free Lunch*

demonstrates the inadequacy of the Darwinian mechanism to generate complexity. Darwinists themselves have made possible such a refutation. By assimilating the Darwinian mechanism to evolutionary algorithms, they have invited a mathematical assessment of the power of the Darwinian mechanism to generate life's diversity. Such an assessment, begun with the No Free Lunch theorems of David Wolpert and William Macready . . . , will in this book be taken to its logical conclusion. The conclusion is that Darwinian mechanisms of any kind, whether in nature or in silico, are in principle incapable of generating specified complexity.[10]

Thus, this argument deploys the inconsistency option of ID's Central Argument (as elaborated in Chapter 1). The trouble is that the book presents no such technical result in spite of being replete with (generally irrelevant) mathematical formalism well designed to impress the book's likely readers, who are neither mathematicians nor evolutionary biologists.

To achieve the claimed result, Dembski would need to establish two independent claims. The first is that evolution can be viewed *formally* as an optimization problem: otherwise it falls beyond the domain of these NFL theorems. Now, it is almost trivially true that evolution cannot be viewed as an optimization of fitness simply because natural selection is not the only factor in evolution. Consequently, it would be reasonable to conclude that Dembski's book is a long exercise in irrelevance. But let us be charitable and ignore Dembski's blatant misunderstanding of evolutionary theory. Suppose that we restrict attention to evolution by natural selection because that mechanism is presumably involved in the evolution of many of the complex structures in which Dembski is interested. Even then, except in haploid organisms or for diploid traits controlled by exactly one gene (that is, at one locus), as we will see later in this chapter, it is a well-established mathematical result of evolutionary theory that natural selection does not optimize any biologically relevant mathematical function related to fitness. This leads to the conclusion that the NFL theorems are entirely irrelevant to evolution. However, the matter must be pursued further because, contrary to what Dembski seems to think, NFL theorems are not restricted to function optimization in this sense (see below).

It may perhaps be argued that the haploid case may be all that ID creationists need because their flagship example is the bacterial flagellum and bacteria are haploids. Let us, therefore, turn to the second claim that Dembski must establish to make his case: the evolutionary cases are exactly the type of problem for which the standard evolutionary algorithms cannot achieve the desired optimal result. After all, it is irrelevant how an evolutionary algorithm performs *on the average* over *all possible* optimization problems. What is relevant, for biological evolution, is how the algorithm performs in the particular optimization scenario that constitutes biological evolution on Earth.[11] The problems that organisms face on Earth do not remotely constitute a random sample of all possible optimization problems. For instance, most large animals have a feasible minimum and maximum size beyond which they cannot vary for simple physical reasons: if they are too small, they cannot function properly, and if they are too large, they break too easily.[12] They thus never encounter those problems in which they have to maximize or minimize their size without constraint.

Now, are evolutionary algorithms unsuited for the problems that organisms have encountered on Earth? Empirical evidence suggests they are not – that is what all the evidence for natural selection suggests. But Dembski is concerned with what we can *mathematically* show about them. But, it is at the mathematical level that Dembski's reasoning becomes embarrassingly vague, as we shall also see in Chapter 7. As Wolpert put it in his review of *No Free Lunch*: Dembski's book "is written in jello. There simply is not enough that is firm in his text, not sufficient precision of formulation, to allow one to declare unambiguously 'right' or 'wrong' when reading though the argument."[13] At best the reasoning runs as follows: we have independent evidence that complex biological structures cannot have evolved by natural selection because we have persistent empirical anomalies, unexplained exemplars of irreducible complexity.[14] Therefore, and this is all that there is to this argument, these must be the type of problem for which evolutionary algorithms cannot find the optimum. Note, as is typical of the discussion in *No Free Lunch*, the last claim is a leap of faith: it is not a valid logical conclusion from the given premises.

Utter Irrelevance

What is perhaps most odd about Dembski's excitement over the NFL theorems is that we do not need Wolpert and Macready's results as a basis for the claim that evolutionary algorithms may not, even on the average, find the optimum of a function in many situations. As early as 1993 Kenneth de Jong had pointed out that genetic algorithms are not general-purpose function optimizers even though they may be used to optimize functions fairly successfully in many contexts.[15] This conclusion generalizes to other types of evolutionary algorithm. The reason is quite simple: nothing guarantees that these algorithms, based as they are on blind search, will explore all regions of the feasible space. If, for instance, a very good solution – or high peak of the objective function – is surrounded by many inferior solutions, then it may well not be found depending on the history of the search and the time available for it. Biological evolution also exhibits the same pattern. We are thus forced to the following conclusion: to the extent that evolutionary algorithms are true to biological evolution, they are constrained by search history and may not be effective fitness optimizers.

That the NFL theorems for optimization say little about the process of biological evolution is also underscored by three related points, the last two of which have often not received the attention they deserve even from evolutionary biologists and philosophers of biology. The rest of the discussion in this section is somewhat technical, and not essential to the flow of the argument of this book. It can be safely skipped by those with no particular interest in the mathematics of evolutionary theory.

First, evolution by natural selection is not about finding a global optimum in a static environment. While average fitness may usually increase due to natural selection, selection may: (a) act disruptively leading to divergence of traits; (b) act weakly to allow some forms to persist indefinitely; (c) be in conflict at different levels of organization, leading to tradeoffs, etc. – there is no obvious limit to the ways in which selection may act. Extant organisms are not necessarily at local optima for many traits and almost certainly not at global optima for any trait. All we know is that the traits are functional enough for organisms we see around us to survive and reproduce, at least temporarily. It is far from clear that the NFL theorems – even for haploids – apply to all such circumstances.[16] More importantly, environments co-evolve with organisms, changing the "problem" to be solved at each stage. Now we are clearly out of the domain of the original NFL theorems. Wolpert and Macready have also recently proved results showing that, in many situations, there is a sumptuous free lunch available at the co-evolutionary table: some algorithms are systematically better than others (averaged across all possible problems).[17] To the extent that biological evolution can plausibly be viewed as optimization (doubts about which will be explained below), this result would come as no surprise to evolutionary biologists. However, it is unclear at present that these new results are directly applicable to biological cases: in the co-evolutionary free lunch results, a group first works together to produce a best-performing "champion" algorithm that then competes with other such "champions" from other groups. Wolpert and Macready do not claim that all these results are biologically relevant. However, it is possible that when populations are highly structured into small sub-populations and there is both selection between individuals within each sub-population and selection between different sub-populations, these co-evolutionary free theorems may describe some types of evolution by natural selection (once again, to the extent it can be modeled by optimization).

Second, evolution by natural selection does not even increase the mean fitness of a population uniformly in any except the simplest (what mathematicians call the degenerate) cases. In haploid organisms it is trivially true that the mean fitness increases in this way. In diploids, if selection is acting only on one locus, then, too, fitness increases in this way.[18] However, once selection begins to act at more than one locus, the situation changes dramatically. In 1964, P. A. P. Moran pointed out that the mean fitness of a population is now a function of gametic frequencies (roughly, the frequencies of different sperm and ova types) and not allelic frequencies (the frequency of the genes) alone.[19] The reason for this is that reproduction occurs through the formation of gametes containing an allele for each locus rather than the formation of units with individual alleles. One consequence of this organization is that the mean fitness of a population need not necessarily increase from one generation to the next due to selection and may, in fact, decrease – this is a mathematical result that has no other valid interpretation. If mean fitness increase is the target, evolution by natural selection cannot be accurately described as a hill-climbing process, contrary to many popularizations of that theory. Moreover, the equilibrium state of a population need not be a maximum of mean fitness.[20] Dembski seems to be unaware of these results of mathematical evolutionary theory.

Third, the last argument assumed that the quantity that should be maximized during evolution by natural selection is the mean fitness of a population. We concluded that no such maximization took place. This leaves open the possibility that some function other than mean fitness gets maximized in this way. If so, evolution by natural selection can still be interpreted as a hill-climbing process. (One could then even argue that the function that is being maximized should be interpreted as the relevant fitness function.) However, no such option is available: evolution by natural selection does not maximize any (mathematical) function which can in some sense be interpreted as a measure of fitness.[21] It is important that any such function have this kind of interpretation: the most basic fact about natural selection is that it increases the fit between an organism and its environment. The problem is usually called that of finding an optimum or maximum principle for natural selection.[22] Such principles are called variational principles in physics.[23] In 1972 Svirizhev found such a principle for the simplest one-locus model (with random mating and constant fitnesses).[24] Once we try to extend this result to multiple loci, we run into difficulty.[25] In the 1990s Behera showed that

Svirizhev's results can be extended to multiple loci only if there is no linkage (the tendency of genes on the same chromosome to be inherited together, as usually happens when they are physically close to each other), or epistasis (interactions between two or more genes to produce traits).[26] Otherwise no such variational principle is available. Linkage and epistasis are ubiquitous in the biology of all organisms: genes are physically organized on chromosomes and almost all traits depend on interactions between several genes. Moreover, once again, even in the simplest models, in which a variational principle is available, we must assume constant fitnesses. Again, Dembski seems to be unaware of these mathematical results.

The conclusion from all these negative results is that, in general, evolution by natural selection cannot plausibly be viewed as a mathematical optimization process leading to the maximization of any parameter that can be interpreted as a fitness. Consequently, the NFL theorems for optimization are irrelevant to biological evolution. Dembski's excitement over these theorems reveals little more than a lack of awareness of some basic results of mathematical evolutionary theory.

However, it still remains true that the NFL theorems can be viewed as applicable to more general search processes.[27] All we have to surrender is that fitness is what is being optimized. However, once we recognize that environments co-evolve with organisms, evolutionary processes fall beyond the domain of any version of these theorems. Mathematical critics of Dembski have routinely recognized the significance of this situation. As Jason Rosenhouse put it in his review of Dembski's book:

> NFL does suggest that selection's ability to ascend the fitness landscapes it actually confronts implies its inability to scale the different landscapes that no doubt exist in some alternate reality. Mutation and recombination, viewed as algorithms for searching genotype space, will be effective only when the landscapes they confront obey certain properties. This makes it reasonable to ask why nature presents us with just the sorts of landscapes that are searched effectively by these mechanisms . . . The answer, at least in part, is that fitness landscapes coevolve with organisms. This is the bedrock principle of modern ecology.[28]

Mark Perakh has observed, moreover, that even without co-evolution, the empirical evidence for natural selection shows that "the probability of some fraction of [possible evolutionary] algorithms being naturally fine-tuned to the existing landscapes is close to certainty."[29] Finally, all we need to add is that biological evolution does not even demand that these algorithms be particularly effective in the sense of taking us close to global optima. They just have to be effective enough to allow the persistence of the organisms bearing the relevant traits. It is plausible, as Fisher argued, to view evolution by natural selection as a continuous but never completely successful attempt of organisms to track an indefinitely changing environment.[30] Leigh Van Valen calls this the Red Queen hypothesis: like Alice and the Red Queen in Lewis Carroll's *Through the Looking Glass*, all the running keeps organisms at the same height on the fitness surface.[31]

Dembski partly admits these problems in the use of the NFL theorems in the context of evolution. He counters that evolutionary algorithms still face a "displacement" problem. The algorithms are supposed to require additional information, for instance, knowledge of a fitness surface, to solve the relevant problems:

> An evolutionary algorithm is supposed to find a target within phase space. To do this successfully, however, it needs more information than is available to a blind search. But this additional information is situated in a wider informational context . . . And locating that additional information within the wider context is no easier than locating the original target . . . I call this the *displacement* problem.[32]

These assertions are simply false. For one thing, evolutionary algorithms need not have targets specified in order for there to be systematic improvement of optimality. The NFL theorems remain applicable even in the absence of such targets.[33] What Dembski does not seem to understand is that neither evolutionary algorithms nor biological evolution is progression to some pre-determined point; rather, it is divergence from the past driven by selection and, in the case of biological evolution, the other mechanisms of evolutionary change. In biological evolution, there is, on the average, stepwise improvement in performance, or better "fit" or adaptation between an organism's features and its environment. That is all there is to it, no progress to a pre-ordained goal, and not even a guarantee of near optimality, let alone optimality.

Adaptationism

One implication to be drawn from the negative results discussed in the last section is one of some importance to the philosophical interpretations of biology: we should not view evolution as an optimization process. A critique of optimization arguments formed part of Gould and Lewontin's justly celebrated indictment of adaptationism, the "Panglossian paradigm" that led to the indefinite substitution of new adaptationist explanations when old ones failed to save the phenomena (recall the discussion of Chapter 4).[34] That adaptationism continues to have its defendants,[35] and that the status of natural selection is still debated, are signs of continuing vitality within evolutionary biology. However, the process of adaptation *per se* consists of changes driven by natural selection.[36] From a mathematical perspective, it does not require a function to be optimized at each step. Optimization is more restrictive, demanding that there exists a function that is being optimized. An adaptationist need not have a commitment to optimization as a model of evolution. This point deserves much more emphasis than it has traditionally received.

Now, evolution can be modeled in either the genotypic or the phenotypic space (or both). The standard view of evolution which was introduced in Chapter 4 assumed that evolution is best modeled in genotypic space, though recent advances in evolutionary developmental biology suggest that this will not always be sufficient (recall the discussion of Chapter 4). However, there has also been an extensive different tradition of modeling evolution in phenotypic space using the techniques of optimization theory. Efforts range from sociobiological models based on concepts such as inclusive fitness to evolutionary game theory.[37]

Consider, for example, two sexes in a sexually reproducing population. Assume that each parent can produce a fixed number of offspring during its lifetime. We will consider three generations. Let us suppose that there are f females and m males in the second generation. Let us suppose that n individuals are produced in the third generation. Then the average female from the second generation has n/f and the average male has n/m offspring in the third generation. If $f < m$, then $n/f > n/m$ and vice versa. Thus the minority sex will have an advantage. This means that a parent in the first generation which wants to maximize the number of its descendants in the third should try to maximize the number of its second generation offspring that are of the minority sex. The result is a self-regulatory dynamics resulting in an equal sex ratio at equilibrium. This informal argument, which goes back to Carl Düsing in 1884, is an optimality argument based on the assumption that what should be maximized by an individual is the number of grand-offspring.[38] It is supposed to explain why an equal sex ratio is often observed in nature in organisms in which parental biology – rather than, for instance, the environment – controls the sex of the offspring.

The argument may well be sound though it will not convince those who question adaptationism in evolutionary biology. However, even those who do not, in the sense that they believe that natural selection is by far the most important evolutionary mechanism, should be wary of such reasoning. What Moran's result shows is that, at the very least, fitness does not monotonically increase during evolution by natural selection and the equilibrium state need not be a maximum of fitness – hence, fitness need not be optimized. Behera's negative results show that there may not be any biologically relevant function[39] that is maximized. Optimization results in evolutionary theory require independent verification which goes beyond the principles of optimization theory alone.

Final Assessment

Returning to the cost of lunch, the most telling conclusion to be drawn from the discussions of this chapter is that Dembski presents a superficial account of evolutionary theory in *No Free Lunch* (and elsewhere). It is fairytale biology. (This may reflect a genuine lack of understanding or it may be a rhetorical ploy driven by political expediency – *No Free Lunch* suggests the former.) Now Dembski has available a response that some biologists, most notably Richard Dawkins, seem to accept his simplifications when writing for a popular audience. But this response, even if it were true of what Dawkins says (and it is not[40]), is inadequate. For the arguments of *No Free Lunch* to have any force, Dembski should have addressed what evolutionary *theory*, in all its gory detail, permits and does not permit. If he is going to deploy theorems from formal optimization theory (Wolpert and Macready's work), he must confront the *mathematical* theory of natural selection. Relying on popularizations, no matter by how competent a biologist, is simply not good enough.

Of all of Dembski's claims in *No Free Lunch*, the only one that cannot yet be dismissed out of hand is that there supposedly is a class of phenomena that evolution by natural selection systematically cannot explain: the irreducibly complex systems. Recall that, according to Dembski, these are supposed to pose precisely those problems that evolutionary algorithms cannot solve effectively because of the NFL theorems. We turn to these supposedly irreducibly complex systems in the next chapter. Note, though, that this marks a transition from the inconsistency option to the incompleteness option in the Central Argument of Intelligent Design, as pointed out in Chapter 1, when ID creationists try to show that evolutionary theory does not have the conceptual resources to explain all biological phenomena. ID's case has become markedly weaker: there is no longer any in-principle objection based on what the mechanism of natural selection can achieve in biological contexts. There is, instead, at most an objection based on what it has so far failed to achieve.

6

Complexity is Complicated

There is no biological star brighter than Michael Behe in the Reformed Creationists' cosmic firmament. To the extent that ID creationists have engaged any contemporary biological research, Behe must receive almost all the credit. Unlike Dembski's work, Behe's initial writings on design, especially the exquisitely written *Darwin's Black Box* from 1996, were intriguing because he seemed to pay attention to biological detail. Behe has also published at least one critique of evolutionary theory in a peer-reviewed journal though this piece makes no claim of Intelligent Design.[1] Moreover, in the 1990s, Behe was correct to point out that there are many biochemical mechanisms for which we lacked plausible detailed models of their evolutionary history. There still are.

Intelligent Design creationists – including Behe himself[2] – often claim that a close-minded academic community refuses to give critiques of evolutionary theory a fair hearing and tries to cover up the many alleged incompatibilities between that theory and empirical data. This is part of a rhetorical ploy to present themselves as a minority of embattled independent-minded seekers of the truth – "lonely pioneers laboring in a great and noble tradition of scientific outcastes," in Ken Miller's memorable words[3] – rather than religious zealots bent on inserting religious dogma into secular science. In the United States, with much of the population long pre-disposed to a paranoid fear of evolution, this strategy has been remarkably effective. Whether or not critics of evolutionary theory receive a fair hearing within biology is a question to which we will return in detail in Chapter 10.

However, contrary to the ID creationists' claim of bias and inattention, Behe's work has received serious scientific attention, perhaps more so than it has deserved. *Darwin's Black Box* generated widespread interest within the biological community when it first appeared in 1996. It was widely reviewed and though, without exception, scientists dismissed Behe's claim of having found evidence for design, they largely agreed with his assessment that biochemistry presented several as yet unresolved puzzles for the theory of evolution by natural selection.[4] Many of these critics – though Johnson and Behe try to deny this[5] – also questioned Behe's command of the relevant biology.[6] Behe's recent criticisms of evolutionary theory have also been met with serious – and devastating – response from biologists.[7] These issues will all be discussed later in this chapter.

To the extent that Behe may have been responsible for focusing attention on genuinely interesting puzzles, *Darwin's Black Box* may be viewed as a positive philosophical contribution to science: evolutionary theory, like any other scientific theory, should be confronted with recalcitrant facts. But it is very likely that problems of biochemical evolution were only beginning to receive serious attention in the 1990s because, until then, we did not know sufficient molecular detail to reconstruct evolutionary histories that were not largely speculative. This increase of knowledge, rather than Behe's objections, was the most important reason for the focus of research on biochemical evolution since the 1990s. For most biochemical systems we still do not have sufficient detail for all taxa we must consider to reconstruct complete evolutionary histories. It is only to be expected that many puzzles remain.

As this chapter will document, the conceptual issues that Behe raised, however intractable they may have seemed to him in the 1990s, have increasingly been resolved by empirical work in molecular evolution. What is troublesome – if the pursuit of knowledge is one of our salient goals – is that ID creationists have not modified Behe's original claims (at least in public). This attitude is not acceptable for any serious scientific claim, though it may be so if ID is to be taken as a theological thesis.

Irreducible Complexity?

Behe bases his claim that there are biochemical systems which cannot have evolved by natural selection on his definition of irreducible complexity: "By irreducibly complex I mean a single system which is composed of several well-matched, interacting parts that contribute to the basic function, and where the removal of any one of the parts causes the system to effectively cease functioning."[8] According to Behe the existence of such systems requires intervention by a conscious designer, natural or supernatural. Moreover, Behe argues, natural selection could not have fashioned such systems. They are supposed to be highly improbable because intermediate simpler stages of their evolution would be non-functional and, therefore, subject to negative selection. Like Kelvin a hundred and fifty years ago, Behe believes that there has not been sufficient time for evolution to have produced such systems. Behe's favorite example of an allegedly irreducibly complex system (ICS) is the bacterial flagellum though he also often harps on the blood clotting cascade.

Before we turn to the question of what evidence there is for Behe's claim, it is instructive to pay attention to the logic of the argument. First, it is trivially true that there are many biological systems, at all levels of organization, for which there are no reasonably complete evolutionary stories. In some cases this is simply because these systems have not been sufficiently studied. For instance, in 1995, a new species, *Symbion pandora*, belonging to an entirely new phylum, Cycliophora, was discovered in the bristles of the well-studied Norway lobster (*Nephrops norvegicus*).[9] *S. pandora* are minute (347 μm) bottle-shaped invertebrates that live in the mouthparts of the lobsters (see Figure 6.1). They have thread-like cilia in a ring for gathering food and an anus next to this mouth ring. They typically spend much of their time attached by an adhesive disc to the lobsters' mouthparts. They have a reproductive cycle consisting of both asexual and sexual stages. The cyclophoran's nearest known relatives are bryozoans. There are no very good evolutionary histories for almost any of *S. pandora*'s morphological features, for instance, why it has two penises. But that is no cause for surprise or worry about the abilities of evolutionary theory – we have been acquainted with *S. pandora* for barely a decade.

Second, there are cases for which the problem of evolutionary origins may be genuinely hard. We do not know what mechanisms were responsible for the evolution of the human mind or human language but this is not for want of attention. These puzzles are simply difficult. The point here is that the existence of these puzzles, by itself, is no reason to expect that no such explanation will ever be forthcoming. For instance, it was only in the 1990s that we began to understand how the left–right asymmetry of the vertebrate body-plan arose.[10] This is where the failure of Dembski's deployment of the NFL theorems most hurts ID:[11] it is not a serious objection to any scientific theory that it cannot yet account for

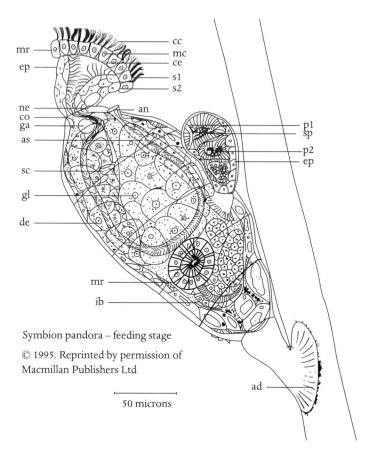

Symbion pandora – feeding stage

© 1995. Reprinted by permission of
Macmillan Publishers Ltd

50 microns

Figure 6.1 *Symbion pandora*
Key

ad – adhesive disc
an – anus
as – ascending branch of the
digestive system
cc – compound cilia
ce – ciliated epidermis
co – constriction (or "neck")

de – descending branch
of the digestive system
ep – epidermis
ga – ganglion
gl – gut lining cell
ib – inner bud
mc – myoepithelial cell
mr – mouth ring

ne – nerve
p1 – penis 1
p2 – penis 2
sc – stomach cells
sp – sperm
s1 – sphincter 1
s2 – sphincter 2

every phenomenon in its domain. As long as we can point to increasing
success at finding explanations, the present incompleteness of evolutionary explanations cannot count as an objection to that theory, let alone an
argument for design.

However, this incompleteness provides ID creationists such as Behe with the following argumentative strategy: should we provide a successful evolutionary explanation for one putative ICS, they can simply point to another that is as yet unexplained and continue to deny the claims of evolution. To prevent such a situation, we must establish standards of adequacy from the beginning: we must specify what is sufficient to establish that evolution by natural selection can produce ICSs. The criterion should be that, if natural selection suffices to produce a single ICS, then it is sufficient to produce all such systems. Otherwise, ID creationists would be making what is derisively called a "god of the gaps" argument: saving for God what science cannot presently explain. Besides not being convincing, as Henry Drummond pointed out in his Lowell Lectures, "The Ascent of Man," in the 1890s,[12] this is a poor defense of religion. It leads to the perhaps slow but inexorable circumscription of the domain left to the power of the "almighty."

In principle, Behe seems to accept the criterion that explaining one ICS by natural selection is sufficient. In his words: "If natural selection were shown to be capable of producing a system of a certain degree of complexity, then the presumption would be that it could produce any other system of an equal or lesser degree of complexity."[13] According to Behe, the complexity is sufficient if the system involves about forty gene products.[14] This is an important admission on Behe's part. It prevents recourse to the "god of the gaps" argument. Unfortunately, Behe's practice does not track his principles very faithfully on this and other points.

Pathways to ICSs

Let us return to Behe's definition of an ICS quoted earlier. All the plausibility of Behe's claim that ICSs cannot evolve by natural selection depends on the improbability that all the required beneficial mutations (or other relevant evolutionary changes) would occur simultaneously. But no evolutionary biologist has ever claimed that they would. They occur step by step, a necessarily slow process, which gave rise to the concern, from Darwin to Haldane (as was discussed in earlier chapters), about whether evolution by natural selection could have produced our extant organisms in the time that has been available to life on Earth. The point is that there are several pathways by which such step-by-step processes can generate ICSs. The most important of these are the *lost functional redundancy* pathway and the *structure co-option* pathway:[15]

(i)   *Lost functional redundancy.* In an article written in response to *Darwin's Black Box*, the evolutionary biologist H. Allen Orr succinctly explains the logic of the lost functional redundancy pathway:

> An irreducibly complex system can be built gradually by adding parts that, while initially just advantageous, become – because of later changes – essential. The logic is very simple. Some part (A) initially does some job (and not very well, perhaps). Another part (B) later gets added because it helps A. This new part isn't essential, it merely improves things. But later on, A (or something else) may change in such a way that B now becomes indispensable. This process continues as further parts get folded into the system. And at the end of the day, many parts may all be required.[16]

Part (A) may even drop out, for instance, when vestigial organs are lost during evolution. When, during the early evolution of cells, free-living mitochondria and other early cells formed symbiotic wholes, mitochondrial genes were transferred to the host cell genome and lost from the mitochondria itself. Meanwhile these symbiotic cells became dependent on energy production by the mitochondria. One consequence of these transitions is that return to the free-living state has become impossible for either – these systems thus satisfy the definition of an ICS. These symbiotic cells are the precursors of today's eukaryotes.

Behe may object that: (a) cells as a whole do not have single functions and, therefore, do not satisfy the definition of an ICS; (b) cells can lose some parts without losing their functions and thus again do not satisfy the definition; or (c) such evolution by symbiosis is not Darwinian evolution. Objections (a) and (b) are trivially met by considering highly specialized cells such as neuronal cells. Suggesting that these do not have single functions would make a mockery of their biology. Moreover, they do not have dispensable parts at least to the same extent as a bacterial flagellum does not have a dispensable part (see below). In both cases some small molecular structures are undoubtedly dispensable but, presumably, the larger ones that are typically of biological interest are not. Objection (c) is irrelevant: what ID creationists must address are the claims of modern biology which includes natural processes such as symbiosis, not some doctrine they invent as Darwinism.

But (a) and (b) were not part of Behe's response to Orr. Rather, he chose to modify his definition to read: "By irreducibly complex I mean a single system which is *necessarily* composed of several well-matched, interacting parts that contribute to the basic function, and where the removal of any one of the parts causes the system to effectively cease functioning,"[17] noting that, in *Darwin's Black Box*, he had written "[b]ecause the bacterial flagellum is necessarily composed of three parts – a paddle, a rotor, and a motor – it is irreducibly complex."[18] This appeal to necessity is supposed to invalidate Orr's argument because part (A) could perform the required action to some extent. Indeed, if one can even "imagine a different type of molecular system where a task can be performed by [fewer] part[s]" the definition of an ICS no longer holds.[19] Behe does not use his new definition consistently – even in the same paper he observes that "functions that are performed by irreducibly complex biochemical systems in humans can be performed by simpler systems"[20] and even that "the function of a mechanical mousetrap [one of his cherished ICSs] can be performed by a glue trap, which is not irreducibly complex."[21] This is inconsistent. Moreover, if the new definition is adopted, as we shall see below, we no longer have reason to believe that any ICS exists in nature[22] – as will be pointed out later in this chapter, Behe's bacterial flagellum will fail his new definition of an ICS. In what follows we shall stick with the old definition of an ICS which, at least, has non-vacuous scope.

Behe may also not wish to concede that the cell is an ICS because his focus is concentrated on the molecular level.[23] The next three sections will meet him at that level as we go through three examples that satisfy all conditions on an ICS that Behe has so far imposed. In each case their evolutionary history has been successfully reconstructed (though not always completely) during the past few decades. (Recall that Behe's official position is that even a single example is sufficient as an adequate defense of evolution by natural selection.[24])

(ii)   *Structure co-option.*[25] The logic of the structure co-option pathway is as follows: suppose that some feature A is present because of a function π for which it was selected along with many other features, including B. Now suppose that A also inadvertently potentially contributes, however slightly, to a different function μ for which there is as yet no specific selected feature. Let us assume that μ becomes increasingly important, for instance, because of environmental changes. There is now stronger and stronger selection on A to be modified to serve μ. (B continues to serve π adequately.) A and other functionally related features end up becoming part of an ICS because they have emerged by co-option, cobbled together for a new function because none was indispensable for the older functions for which it was selected.[26]

For this pathway, there is evidence from every level of organization, and not just the molecular level. Presumably the feathers of flying birds are part of an ICS: no feather-less bird is known to fly.[27] Feathers evolved from scales and evolutionary biologists agree with ID creationists that scale–feather intermediates offer no aerodynamic advantage. However, they do provide better thermal insulation and a wealth of evidence suggests that feathers were originally selected for this purpose. (For instance, they continue to function for insulation in juvenile birds today.[28]) Proto-feathers in fossils of Sinosauropteryx, a dinosaur that was only discovered in China in the mid-1990s,[29] consist of the same protein types as true bird feathers in Archaeopteryx (which was probably capable of flight – see Chapter 1) and the feather-like structures in the non-flying Caudipteryx and Protoarchaeopteryx.[30] The identity of molecular composition suggests stepwise linear evolution. Moreover, the thick distribution of proto-feathers in Sinosauropteryx strongly suggests the function of thermal insulation. Feathers arose to regulate heat, then became part of an ICS for flight. There are many other examples, as critics of creationism have repeatedly documented.[31] Figure 6.2 provides a molecular example of the structure co-option pathway in which the detailed evolutionary steps have all been worked out and the process of evolution has been remarkably fast.

Before we turn to some detailed examples, it is time to dispose of one subsidiary argument, not due to Behe, but one that Dembski makes to bolster Behe's claim of unevolvable irreducible complexity.[32] The evolutionary origin of ICSs by natural selection is supposed to be impossible because, according to Dembski, natural selection only selects for simplicity. Consequently, the emergence of complexity cannot be accounted for by natural selection. Dembski refers to Sol Spiegelman's experiments on the *in vitro* evolution of RNA sequences which showed the failure of one simple scenario for the evolution of longer sequences from shorter ones.[33] So what? The experiment does not show that natural selection can *only* select for simplicity, which is what Dembski's argument requires.[34] Moreover, no biologist has ever claimed that natural selection always selects for complexity. The evolutionary record is filled with fossils of lineages that have degenerated in the sense that forms appear less complex with time (for instance, in the case of the Ammonites which finally disappeared some 65 million years ago).[35] These were forms on the way

At the molecular level, the recent evolution of tolerance in bacteria to the highly toxic xenobiotic pesticide (that is, one that does not occur as a substance found in living organisms), pentachlorophenol (PCP), provides a striking example of the evolution of an irreducibly complex system. PCP does not occur naturally but has been used as a wood preservative since the 1930s; it is supposed to have been first introduced in the environment in 1936. It is now recognized as a dangerous pollutant. Some soil bacteria, such as *Sphinogomonas chlorophenolica* (also known as *Sphingobium chlorophenolicum*), have evolved a pathway to degrade PCP by the recruitment of enzymes from two other pathways in less than 70 years. Because PCP is xenobiotic it is unlikely that bacteria would already have had the capacity to degrade it before first exposure; moreover, because it is a highly chlorinated compound, degradation is not a trivial task.

PCP consists of a six-carbon ring with five chlorine atoms and one hydroxyl group (OH⁻) attached to the six carbon atoms. *S. chlorophenolica* uses three enzymes to degrade PCP. The first of these, PCP hydroxylase, removes one of the chlorine ions and replaces it with an OH⁻. The resulting compound, tetrachlorohydroquinone (TCHQ), though toxic, is not quite as harmful as PCP. The second enzyme, called TCHQ dehalogenase, next replaces two chlorine atoms by hydrogen atoms forming first the compound trichlorohydroquinone (TriCHQ) and second, 2,6-dichlorohydroquinone (DCHQ). TCHQ is produced in the cell constitutively (that is, at all times) and seems to have arisen from a duplicated gene of maleylaceto-acetate isomerase which is normally involved in degradation of tyrosine.[2] The third enzyme, DCHQ dioxygenase, breaks the ring. The PCP remnants may now even have nutritional value for *S. chlorophenolica*.

All three enzymes are required, along with the machinery for producing them – so this is clearly an ICS. The pathway was produced by cobbling together molecules from two other pathways. The first and third enzymes (PCP hydroxylase and DCHQ dioxygenase) were already present in a pathway by which bacteria degrade other naturally occurring chlorophenols. The production of both these enzymes is induced by the presence of PCP and other chlorophenols. The second enzyme, TCHQ dehalogenase, is produced in the cell constitutively. This wasteful produc-tion of TCHQ dehalogenase, presumably a result of a recent mutation, ensures that it is available to the pathway for PCP degradation. As it is an early evolutionary stage, the pathway as a whole is sub-optimal. PCP hydroxylase has poor catalytic effectiveness on PCP; the activity of TCHQ dehalogenase is inhibited by its own substrates, besides the fact that its continuous production is wasteful. Though obviously an ICS created by co-option, natural selection is yet to optimize its design.

Figure 6.2   The PCP degradation pathway[1]

[1] See Copley (2000) for the original report and Dunkelberg (2003) for a useful summary. Copley (2000) gives many other examples of biochemical pathway evolution by co-option including the urea and Krebs cycles – the latter will be discussed in the next section.

[2] Copley (2000); Anandarajah et al. (2000).

to extinction and, presumably, natural selection had an important role in that extinction. But phenomena such as these hardly pose a problem for evolutionary theory which only requires that complex systems can evolve from simpler ones through natural causes, not even that the evolution of complexity is necessarily driven by natural selection.

Finally, there are cases when natural selection prevents the evolution of simplicity from complexity. For instance, the formation of complex assemblages is often irreversible.[36] Return to the example of symbiosis between the early cells and free-living mitochondria to form the precursors of today's eukaryotic cells. Now that the simpler free-living state is impossible for either, no amount of ardent prayer will yield simplicity by natural selection.

We will turn to two examples favored by ID creationists and another that is biologically very important in the next three sections. These examples are treated in perhaps excruciating detail to emphasize the wealth of knowledge about molecular evolution that has emerged over the past two decades, and to underscore that we are well beyond merely plausible stories in our reconstructions of molecular evolutionary histories. However, the examples are not critical to the flow of the argument of this book and can be skipped by those who need no further convincing that molecular biology presents no insurmountable obstacle to the progress of evolutionary biology.

The Citric Acid Cycle

The citric acid cycle (also known as the tricarboxylic acid cycle and the Krebs cycle, after its discoverer, the refugee Jewish scientist, Hans Krebs, in 1937) is a metabolic pathway common to all aerobic cells by which carbohydrates, fats, and proteins are oxidized while generating energy for storage. The reactions all occur in the mitochondria. There is a fair amount of variation between species making it easier to reconstruct its evolutionary history.[37] At the first stage of the cycle, an initial enzyme catalyzes a set of reactions that eventually form citric acid. Subsequently there is a series of oxidation and decarboxlylation reactions altogether comprising an eight-stage cycle. At least nine enzymes and three co-factors are needed. In each turn of the cycle, two molecules of carbon dioxide are produced as waste products, along with three molecules of NADH (nicotinamide adenine dinucleotide), one molecule of GTP (guanine triphosphate), and one molecule of FADH$_2$ (a reduced form of flavin adenine dinucleotide). These molecules store energy. The cycle is essential for energy production through aerobic respiration. It is also an important source of biosynthetic building blocks used in many other cellular reactions. This cycle must have arisen early in evolution since it is common to all aerobic cells. No stage of the cycle can be removed without destroying its functionality – it satisfies Behe's definition of an ICS including his insistence that they be sufficiently complex.

How did such a complex cycle emerge? In words that would have fit smugly into a creationist text, Meléndez-Hevia and two collaborators write, "[t]he Krebs cycle has been frequently quoted as a key problem in the evolution of living cells, hard to explain by Darwin's natural selection: how could natural selection explain the building of a complicated structure in toto, when the intermediate stages have no obvious functionality?"[38] But they only raise this question after having effectively solved the problem, that is, by reconstructing a plausible sequence of stages leading to the full cycle. They began by considering the various possible chemical ways by which the citric acid cycle could have evolved. Then they imposed four simple rules:

(i)   any enzymatic reaction is chemically possible without the enzyme though not as efficient;[39]

(ii)   all intermediate molecular products in a sequence of reactions must be fairly stable;[40]

(iii)   any material used in the new pathway must exist in other reaction pathways;

(iv)   a new pathway must be thermodynamically and kinetically compatible with all previous ones.

Once these rules are imposed it is quite easy to see how the citric acid cycle arose by the opportunistic co-option of available processes which previously performed different functions. To get from these older reaction pathways to the full citric acid cycle required the emergence of only one new enzyme.

Some details of the reconstruction offered by Meléndez-Hevia and his collaborators will probably change with new research, as it often does in all types of historical reconstruction as new evidence accumulates. But the broad steps have been laid down: as these authors observe, "the cycle was built through the process that [the French molecular biologist, Francois] Jacob called 'evolution by molecular tinkering,' stating that evolution does not produce novelties from scratch: It works on what already exists."[41]

Reconstructing the evolutionary history of the citric acid cycle is important for three reasons. First, it is one of the most important biochemical pathways known and fundamental to almost all of life. Second, it arose very early in evolution – reconstructing its evolutionary history is much more difficult, and rewarding, than, for instance, reconstructing the history of PCP degradation pathway discussed in Figure 6.2. Third, it is complex, among the most complex biochemical cycles known. Lessons learned from an analysis of the citric acid cycle are likely to carry over to the evolution of most other cycles.

ID creationists have not been slow to respond to the new work on the citric acid cycle though their response has so far lacked intellectual merit. Gordon Mills, for instance, accepts the four rules mentioned above, but insists that the work of Meléndez-Hevia and his collaborators is not complete.[42] Mills demands that evolutionary biologists (a) prove that there be strong sequence similarity between the enzymes in the present citric acid cycle and their precursors; (b) that they construct a phylogenetic tree; (c) that they provide a mechanism for the incorporation of the citric acid cycle into the mitochondrial matrix; and (d) that they show how bacterial genes from plasmids (circular pieces of DNA) may be incorporated into the circular DNA of mitochondria. This is a curious mix: (c) may be an interesting question about the proximate mechanisms of the citric acid cycle but is not relevant to the question of evolutionary origins; (d) is easily envisioned, for instance, if mitochondrial ancestors entered into symbiosis with early ancestral cells – in any case, it is not a problem. As far as (a) and (b) are concerned, what is most odd is that Mills published these demands in 2002: in 1999 Huynen and two collaborators had already published a study of the genomes of nineteen unicellular species comparing the genes associated with the citric acid cycle.[43] The study found much variation, produced no surprises for existing evolutionary models, and paved the way for the reconstruction of a phylogeny. That there is a lot of variation is important because simpler variants – and several were found – show how the complex cycle may be sequentially assembled from simpler ones. Meanwhile, also in 1999, bringing new computational methods to bear on the problem, Forst and Schulten constructed explicit phylogenies of the cycle's evolution.[44]

The Blood Clotting System ─────────────────────

"Blood coagulation," writes Behe, "is a paradigm of the staggering complexity that underlies even apparently simple bodily processes. Faced with such complexity beneath even simple phenomena, Darwinian theory falls silent."[45] That silence had been broken long before Behe's book, mainly by the work of Russell Doolittle. While Behe considered a popularization of that work by Doolittle,[46] and found it wanting, once the technical details are taken into account, and we add what we know since the mid-1990s, the problem of the evolution of the blood clotting system (BCS) hardly appears insoluble. Because the BCS is an example given such importance by ID creationists, it will be discussed here in even more detail than the evolution of the citric acid cycle.

While Behe is correct that the vertebrate blood clotting system is complex (and he explicitly refers to it as an ICS), the core mechanism is simple: a fibrous, soluble protein called fibrinogen forms 2–3% of the protein part of blood plasma. A fibrinogen molecule has a "sticky" portion at its middle but this region is normally covered up. For clotting to occur, a protease molecule called thrombin removes this cover and the fibrinogen molecules begin to stick together to form a clot. But, like fibrinogen, thrombin itself exists in the blood in an inactive form, prothrombin, which must first be activated. Therefore, something must exist to activate the prothrombin.

Activation of prothrombin is carried out by yet another protease, Factor X (see Figure 6.3). But Factor X must itself be activated by yet another precursor molecule. There are two distinct pathways by which this is achieved. The right (extrinsic) pathway of Figure 6.3 shows what happens when clots form in response to internal hemorrhage (breakage of a blood vessel inside the body). Tissue Factor, a soluble protein naturally found in many tissues but not in blood, activates this pathway. The left (intrinsic) pathway of Figure 6.3 is stimulated by external hemorrhage which involves the damage of cell surfaces. This pathway consists of a cascade of activations. A simpler system may suffice but the cascade allows the amplification of an initial stimulus at every step. It thus enables a rapid concerted response even to mild cuts and bruises. Behe is probably not even correct in claiming that the BCS is irreducibly complex, that if we remove any part, the system probably collapses. Fish and whales, for instance, do not have the right (extrinsic) pathway.[47]

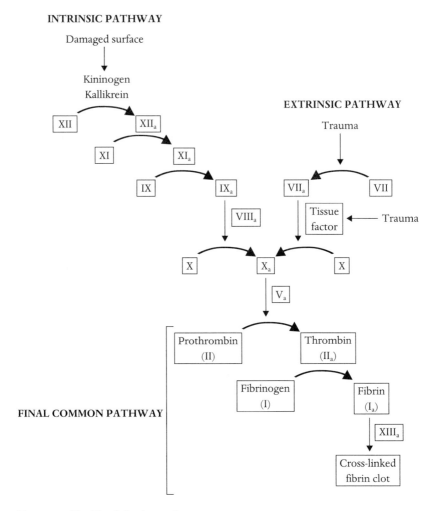

Figure 6.3 The blood clotting pathways
After Miller (1996b).

How can a system as complicated as the vertebrate BCS have evolved? Behe argues that it could not have evolved by natural selection: there just has not been enough time. Unfortunately for Behe there is a plausible relatively straightforward scenario, the details of which are being incrementally worked out. The description here will follow the treatment of Ken Miller who draws on the work of Russell Doolittle.[48]

We begin by noting that the evolution of clotting presumably began in the early vertebrates which, like the invertebrates, would have had a battery of sticky white cells to plug leaks. During hemorrhage, cells would typically be broken around a wound and the intra-cellular cell molecules would fall out and enter the vascular system. These molecules would include cyclic adenosine monophosphate (cAMP) which induces muscle contractions. These contractions would constrict blood vessels and reduce blood flow allowing the sticky cells enough time to plug the leak. The modern vertebrate BCS must have evolved from such a clotting mechanism.

Now, even in early vertebrates blood plasma would have been a viscous fluid full of various protein molecules. In contrast, the extracellular environment of other tissues is rich in proteases, enzymes that cut other proteins. The rupture of a blood vessel would result in the two types of molecules mixing, and the proteases would begin their decimation of the proteins. Some protein fragments would be insoluble and would help seal the wound, making the mechanism described in the last paragraph even more effective. Even today clotting in invertebrates follows this model: it is obviously good enough even though there is much room for improvement.

Gene duplication now comes into play. Gene duplication is a fairly common occurrence. For instance, in humans, 38–50% of genes have duplicates.[49] Duplication of a gene allows one copy to change freely without adversely affecting an organism's fitness because the other copy continues to perform the required function – this is called the duplication-divergence model of genetic function innovation.[50] Now, suppose that the gene that is duplicated specifies a serine protease, a digestive enzyme found in the pancreas. This gene has a regulatory region that prevents its expression elsewhere. Suppose that the regulatory region was damaged during duplication now allowing expression in both the pancreas and the liver. The result would be the release of an inactive form of the enzyme, a zymogen, into the bloodstream. These molecules are inactive unless a small piece near their active site is removed by a protease. But, following the rupture of a blood vessel, as the blood plasma seeps into the tissue, the proteases present would now activate the enzyme. This would result in even more cleavage of proteins at the site of the hemorrhage and the beginning of the cascade pathway that we see in the modern BCS.

The plasma serine protease gene would undergo a variety of random changes. Now suppose, these changes result in a DNA sequence called the EGF domain ("EGF" stands for epidermal growth factor) being spliced into the gene.[51] The EGF is a common small protein recognized by receptors in virtually all cells of the body. Consequently, the tissue surrounding a hemorrhage would have a large number of these receptors which would bind to the EGF domain which is now attached to the serine protease. The action of the serine protease now begins to be localized to such regions. The combination of a cell surface protein and the EGF domain is called Tissue Factor. Clots would now form faster and are more specific – there is little doubt that such an ability would be subject to positive natural selection.

Meanwhile, fibrinogen arose by modification of a soluble protein in the blood plasma, presumably by strong selection on a duplicate gene for a common plasma protein. The result is a rudimentary clotting system far more efficient than that of the invertebrates and produced by standard evolutionary processes. The more complicated cascade pathway was presumably generated by even more gene duplication using the fact that serine proteases are autocatalytic: they can activate themselves besides being activated by tissue proteases. Suppose the gene for it was duplicated, and the duplicate gene undergoes mutations that make it less likely to cut fibrinogen but more likely to activate the original serine protease. It will no longer matter whether the serine protease can continue to bind to the Tissue Factor by its EGF domain so long as the duplicated modified protein does so. We can see how the cascade can be iteratively built up step by step.

One final problem remains. The BCS that is being built up may become so efficient that clots form indiscriminately or continue to grow without control, killing the animal. Once again gene duplication is the key. Body tissues naturally contain a protein molecule called a1-antitrypsin which binds to the active site of serine proteases and inhibits them. Presumably the ancestral vertebrates would have some protease inhibitor that would evolve into antithrombin which inhibits thrombin and prevents it from cleaving fibrinogen indiscriminately.

How much evidence is there for this reconstruction? As with all historical reconstructions in the remote evolutionary past, there is an obvious sense in which not every detail can be fully verified. But there is plenty of evidence, better than the evidence we have for many historical reconstructions we accept. The reconstruction makes many predictions that can be tested and, so far, these have all been borne out. For instance, this reconstruction predicts that the clotting enzymes should be near duplicates of a pancreatic enzyme and each other (because of the iterative way in which the cascade is supposed to have evolved). That is exactly what we find. Moreover, if we reconstruct phylogenies using these molecules from one species, it should be consistent with what we get when we carry out the reconstruction using other species. That is again exactly what we find.[52]

If the modern fibrinogen gene was recruited from a duplicated ancestral gene with no clotting function, then we should find a gene similar to the fibrinogen gene in some animal which does not contain the vertebrate BCS. Had Behe done his homework, he would have found that Xun Xu and Doolittle had found such a gene in an echinoderm (a sea cucumber, *Parasfichopus parvimensis*), in 1990.[53] As more data come in, some parts of this reconstruction may be modified.[54] But we know enough of the story that we have no reason to suspect any inadequacy of standard evolutionary processes, let alone take recourse to extra-natural mechanisms.

The Bacterial Flagellum

Let us finally turn to the most cherished example with which ID creationists flagellate themselves into ecstasy, the bacterial flagellum. An image of this structure graces the cover of Dembski's *No Free Lunch*.[55] As Ken Miller has pointed out, the flagellum has acquired iconic status among ID creationists.[56] According to Behe, a flagellum consists of three parts: a motor, a paddle or shaft, and a propeller. Behe is correct in appreciating that it is a remarkable structure, producing rotary motion from an electrochemical gradient across the cell membrane. Now, recall Behe's modified definition of an ICS (which we have not been using): "By irreducibly complex I mean a single system which is *necessarily* composed of several well-matched, interacting parts that contribute to the basic function, and where the removal of any one of the parts causes the system to effectively cease functioning,"[57] and his additional claim that "[b]ecause the bacterial flagellum is necessarily composed of three parts – a paddle, a rotor, and a motor – it is irreducibly complex."[58] The second claim is false as we shall see below and, consequently, the bacterial flagellum would not even be an ICS according to the modified definition. In fact, it is doubtful that any multi-part biological system would be an ICS by that definition. As it will turn out, for ID creationists, choosing the bacterial flagellum as their icon has not been a very wise decision.

Flagella are primarily used by microbes for swimming. However, swimming is but one mode of locomotion for microbes.[59] For instance, the social bacterium, *Myxococcus xantus*, which hunts in groups, moves by slime secretion. Thus, if microbial locomotion is taken to be the relevant function, no microbial locomotory structure will satisfy Behe's modified definition of an ICS. But let us be charitable and take swimming itself to be the relevant function. Now, there are three main types of microbial organism: bacteria (or eubacteria), archae and unicellular eukaryotes. But, these use different swimming mechanisms, and within each group, there are significant differences between species. Some bacteria swim without any flagella. For instance, cyanobacteria, including Synechococcus species[60] and *Spiroplasma melliferum*,[61] swim using non-flagellar systems.[62]

Turning to archae, when they have flagella, these consist of only two components which may be described, if we choose to use Behe's terminology, as a motor and a combined shaft-propeller.[63] Thus, not only is a swimming function possible without three components, even a more specific flagellar swimming function can be achieved with fewer than three components. If necessity is part of the definition of an ICS, bacterial flagella fall outside its scope. David Ussery and Ian Musgrave have also pointed out that Behe's individuation of parts is questionable.[64] Almost all biologists would designate flagellar parts as proteins or as different functional components. As they show, even such an individuation also does not result in identifying irreducible flagella. But let us be charitable and drop the necessity component from Behe's definition.

The salient question, of course, is whether bacterial flagella could have evolved through standard evolutionary processes. Besides pointing out that we do not have a detailed evolutionary story (which is at best a "god of the gaps" argument, to the extent it is an argument at all), Behe offers no reason to disbelieve that flagella could have evolved. Moreover, we have a much better story than Behe admits. There are two critical strands of evidence that Behe ignores.

First, there is abundant molecular evidence that the bacterial flagellum evolved from simpler components. The paddle consists of flagellin molecules which can self-assemble to form that structure.[65] Flagellin sequences are known from a wide variety of species. There is considerable variation, as well as an underlying homology in the amino acid sequences. Whereas flagellin from the bacterium, *Escherichia coli* (the favorite model organism of molecular genetics), consists of 595 amino acid residues, that from another bacterium, *Salmonella enterica* (which can cause typhoid and food poisoning in humans), consists of only 359 residues, of which 193 are shared with *E. coli*.[66] Using molecular homologies, it is easy to reconstruct evolutionary histories which show how complexity among the flagellins arose incrementally. That there is so much variation as well as homology is important for evolutionary reconstruction because it shows how small incremental steps, one residue at a time, could have produced the more complex variants without loss of function in the intermediates. Turning to the rotor, a similar story of sequence variation and molecular homology emerges. The motor is less well understood at the molecular level and if Behe wants to suggest that there remains more to be discovered about the flagellum, he is correct. But the molecular picture so far does not suggest that there is any special problem here.

Second, there is a well-supported model of co-option. Some bacterial groups possess what are known as type III secretory systems (TTSS) which allow them to inject proteins into the cytoplasm of host cells. These proteins are often responsible for the virulence of these bacteria to their eukaryotic hosts (including humans).[67] Molecular studies have shown that the protein sequences of the TTSS are directly homologous to those of the bacterial flagellum.[68] About 80–88% of the proteins in the flagellum are now known to have homologs in other structures.[69] The homology between the TTSS and the flagellum is important for two reasons; (i) the TTSS shows that a fragment of the flagellum could be effective for a different function; and (ii) we can envisage an incremental step-by-step evolutionary process by which an ancestral form of the TTSS gives rise to the modern flagellum, besides the modern TTSS.[70] Musgrave, in particular, envisions a three-stage evolutionary scenario: (a) simple secretory systems powered by the same kind of motors that we see in modern flagella and TTSS; (b) then, gliding secretory systems powered in the same way; and (c) finally, rotating secretory systems such as those seen in modern flagella. A final stage would be the loss of the secretory function. It would be wise for the religious not to rest their faith on a bacterial flagellum.

Protein Evolution

Behe's response to critics has been to try to show that the duplication-divergence model of gene function innovation cannot work, that is, it cannot evolve the required new functions in the time available.[71] In 2004 Behe and David Snoke, a condensed matter physicist, published the results of simulations designed to prove this point. It constitutes perhaps the only positive research contribution that the ID creationists have so far made. Behe and Snoke were concerned with the evolution of proteins with new functions that required changes of multiple amino acid residues and, therefore, several mutations in the DNA. Essentially, their argument is that the requisite number of mutations cannot accumulate in the relevant gene in a plausible amount of time with plausible population sizes.

Their model is idiosyncratic.[72] They begin with two reasonable assumptions. First, they assume that there is no selective advantage conferred by a duplicated gene until it produces a fully functional protein with multiple residue changes. Second, they assume that there is also no selection against the organism while a duplicated gene undergoes changes so long as the original gene remains functional. Next they assume that all the mutations that must occur are independent of each other, which is not always plausible.[73] But they also assumed that: (i) a gene duplicates and then spreads through the entire population before it begins to accumulate mutations, which is highly unrealistic; (ii) that all the mutations that must occur should only occur after such a duplication event, which is again unreasonable; and (iii) that, after the first "desirable" mutation (that is, one which would go toward conferring the desired new function) occurs in the duplicated gene, all other mutations except other "desirable" ones are non-functional and result in the gene, along with the first desirable mutation, completely disappearing from the population. This is again an unreasonable assumption requiring in effect that multiple rare mutations occur virtually simultaneously. Every one of these unreasonable assumptions is biased towards slowing down evolution. They then found that the process of evolving new functional proteins requiring multiple residue changes will take 10^8 or more generations and populations with 10^9 or more individuals. But, once the unrealistic assumptions are removed, Michael Lynch found that the time taken can at most be about 10^6 years in populations $\geq 10^6$ individuals.[74] Given that we are dealing with microbial populations in most such cases, for which population size can easily exceed 10^{16}, even Behe's original constraints are not impossible to satisfy; Lynch's fall well within the scope of what is very likely to happen. Behe and Snoke's analysis hardly constitutes a serious objection to the evolutionary origin of new functional proteins.[75]

What Behe and Snoke did show is the relatively trivial result that it is easy to construct evolutionary models and scenarios in which change cannot occur very fast. It confirms another well-known fact about evolution: it is often highly conservative. Nevertheless, to end on a positive note, efforts, such as those of Behe and Snoke, to show the limitations of particular evolutionary scenarios fall squarely within the scope of useful research in evolutionary biology (but only because they make no mention of ID).

Irreducibility and Design

We may have lost the forest among the trees. One point has been ignored throughout the discussions of this chapter so far: why should irreducible complexity even be a sign of *design*? ID creationists, when they attempt to show that their views are scientific rather than religious, are careful not to specify who or what they take the designer to be. The nature of the designer is supposed to be a matter for future research. Critics of ID rarely fall for this ploy. ID creationists are being obviously disingenuous: they do claim that they know that the designer could not be any natural process, for instance, natural selection. And throughout, there is the unstated assumption that design is *good* design producing adequate function. That, presumably, is why it is supposed to be *intelligent* design.

But, is irreducible complexity good design? ICSs, if they exist in the natural world, would be incredibly fragile.[76] Functional redundancy, rampant in the living world, allows organisms to survive in the face of environmental caprice (or even systematic change). Human designers typically build in functional redundancy in almost anything complex they design: large planes almost always have more engines than they need, good building codes require multiple fire escapes, safe computer systems duplicate data – the list is virtually endless. Functional redundancy is easy to create by intelligent agents and by natural selection; unfortunately the unintelligence of blind chance sometimes gets rid of it, at least partially, to the detriment of organisms in many environments. Irreducible complexity is poor design. (Perhaps, following Miller's suggestion,[77] we should call it the hypothesis of Incompetent Design.)

Similarly, what is so special about the design of a system that takes a multiplicity of proteins for its construction? Now, if all the functions of a bacterial flagellum were performed by one protein molecule, that would be impressive and difficult to explain, given what biology says about the evolution of genes and proteins. Instead, the organic world is dominated by complex structures that, if they show any intentional analogy at all, show the handiwork of a cobbler limited by materials accidentally available rather than some grand design unfolding itself. Francois Jacob was right: evolution is tinkering.[78] Even if there were an argument for design from ICSs, it would hardly be an argument for *intelligent* design.

Behe may respond by saying that we do not know what a divine designer intended. He is right (assuming, of course, such a designer exists) but that adds weight to the arguments of Chapter 3 where it was pointed out that, because we know nothing of the features of a possible designer, we cannot assign a higher probability to design than evolution. Behe may also point to weighty theological speculation as to why organisms may have been created imperfect. But, if we are left with an appeal to likely (or unlikely) properties of divinity, we have left the realm of science for theology. It is for theologians to decide if ID is good – or even interesting – theology; it is beyond the scope of this book.

7

Questions of Information

On the back cover of Dembski's book, *Intelligent Design*, Robert C. Koons calls Dembski "the Isaac Newton of information theory" and adds, "since this is the Age of Information, that makes Dembski one of the most important thinkers of our time. His 'law of conservation of information' represents a revolutionary breakthrough."[1] As this chapter will show, rather than Newton, a comparison to Don Quixote would have been more apt, with Koons as Sancho Panza. The man from La Mancha would almost certainly have embraced what Dembski has so far presented as his greatest contribution: the "Law of Conservation of Information" that Koons mentioned. Of this "law" Dembski goes on to say: "I want to claim that the elusive fourth law of thermodynamics about which there has been sporadic and inconclusive speculation in the scientific literature is properly identified with the Law of Conservation of Information."[2] The law, moreover, "has profound implications for science."[3] No one should accuse ID creationists of false modesty (though, as this chapter will show, some genuine modesty would have served them well).

In the period since the publication of *No Free Lunch*, in spite of the title of the book and many remarks to the contrary within it, under criticism from Wolpert, Orr, and others, Dembski has muted his claim of significance for the NFL theorems for his project of demonstrating the impossibility of evolution by natural selection to produce complex structures (recall the discussions of Chapter 5).[4] Even in *No Free Lunch*, Dembski did not entirely rely on the NFL theorems to press the inconsistency option. Rather, he updated the explanatory filter (recall the discussion of Chapter 3) to produce a new account of specification through "specified complexity" or "complex specified information (CSI)." The alleged conservation law is supposed to hold for CSI. One version states that CSI cannot be generated by natural causes; another version precludes its generation by functions or random chance. In fact even the NFL theorems are supposed to be ultimately important because "they show that for evolutionary algorithms to output CSI they had first to receive a prior input of CSI."[5]

Now, provided that living organisms exhibit CSI, it follows trivially that they could not have emerged through natural processes, no longer even restricted to evolution by natural selection or any other evolutionary mechanism. In fact, if this law is true, then it is unclear why Dembski even needs an explanatory filter except perhaps as a mere heuristic for discovering the presence of CSI. It is even less clear why he needs the NFL theorems which are, at best, mere corollaries to his fundamental law. This great law would do all his work for him – but the structure and title of the book (*No Free Lunch*) becomes unclear. But, perhaps, Dembski was wise to hedge his bets. To the extent that there is any law of the conservation of information at all, it is trivially irrelevant.

What is Biological Information?

Molecular biology emerged as a distinct field of research in the 1950s during the same period in which digital computers and what came to be called the informational sciences also emerged. Consequently, it was probably inevitable that molecular biology borrowed informational metaphors from these other fields.[6] The physicist, Erwin Schrödinger (one of the founders of quantum mechanics), postulated the existence of a "hereditary codescript" as early as 1944.[7] By the 1950s the relationship between genes and proteins was widely viewed as one of coding because three DNA nucleotide bases combinatorially specified one amino acid residue.[8] This code was deciphered in the 1960s.[9] Meanwhile, in 1961, the evolutionary biologist, Ernst Mayr, and the molecular biologists, Francois Jacob and Jacques Monod, independently interpreted the genome as a program for the development of an organism.[10] From some perspectives what uniquely distinguished the new molecular biology from the biochemistry of the preceding decades was the use of informational concepts.

Informational metaphors in biology have been roundly criticized, but also occasionally defended, by both biologists and philosophers of biology.[11] The main criticism has been that the informational picture, though of didactic value, has not produced new biological models or other insight – it appears always as a *post hoc* description of results obtained by mundane chemical and biophysical reasoning. Moreover, the genetic program metaphor is far too static and deterministic, suggesting that embryological development is the unfolding of a pre-ordained plan, rather than being contingently produced by interactions between the embryo and its environment. Recent developments in eukaryotic genetics and, especially, genomics have also called into question the relevance of the coding metaphor. For instance, if almost all of the genomic DNA sequence (about 98% in humans) does not specify proteins at all, and the parts that do often have one sequence specifying several proteins (through a process called alternative splicing of the RNA), it is hard to see how the gene–protein relation is one of "coding."

These are serious but possibly not devastating objections. Nevertheless, it is incumbent upon those who think that informational concepts have theoretical value in biology (that is, they explain things rather than being merely metaphors) to produce an appropriate technical concept of information for biological contexts. Several formal strategies are available including the use of (i) semantic, (ii) statistical, or (iii) algorithmic concepts of information. We will ignore the algorithmic concepts here because none of Dembski's arguments make real use of them.[12] Semantic concepts of information are concerned with the specific content of a bearer of information, that is, a "message." The statistical concepts of information are concerned with the arrangement of parts of a message so that it can be faithfully transmitted from a source to a receiver.[13] In biological contexts, we are clearly more interested in semantic information showing how a given structure specifies a particular function. Unfortunately, even though there have been many attempts to develop a quantitative theory of semantic information, going back to the work of the philosophers Rudolf Carnap and Yehoshua Bar-Hillel in 1952,[14] we still do not have such a theory.

In contrast, there is a very well-developed theory of statistical information, going back to the pioneering work of Claude Shannon.[15] According to this theory, the amount of information in a string of symbols is measured (roughly) by the logarithm of the number of available choices during a transmission (or communication) process. This concept of information connotes uncertainty, its numerical value given by an "entropy" function (which has the same mathematical form as the physical entropy concept of statistical mechanics). Shannon considered a string constructed using n symbols. Let p_i be the probability of the occurrence of the i-th symbol. Then, the entropy, H, is given by $H = -\sum_{i=1}^{n} p_i \log_2 p_i.$[16] Shannon justified this function by proving a theorem showing that it is the only one[17] that satisfies three constraints: (i) that H be a continuous function of the p_i; (ii) if all the p_i are equal to $1/n$, that is, all symbols are equally probable, then H increases monotonically with n; and (iii) if a choice, such as the choice of symbols, can be broken up as a sequence of choices, H is a weighted sum of these successive choices. The intuitive reasonableness of these constraints, which serve as adequacy conditions for the definition, is the motivation of this form for the function that measures uncertainty. Information is a decrease of this uncertainty.[18]

Strangely, what Dembski means by "information" does not correspond to either of these two standard notions. Rather, he presents a simple formula, $I = -\sum_{i=1}^{n} \log_2 p_i$ with no explanation.[19] This function has no justification, for instance, in terms of uniquely satisfying appropriate adequacy conditions. Moreover, information merely becomes *surprisal*,[20] how surprising it is to see a particular symbol, measured by the inverse of the probability of its occurrence. Dembski's claim is that this entity cannot increase during evolution.

We will turn to what happens to information during evolution in the next section, though we will use both Dembski's and Shannon's measures.[21] But before that, an important caveat must be noted. All these information measures depend critically on the choice of alphabet, that is, what is taken to be the set of symbols with which the message is composed. This is another version of the old problem of choosing a reference class for computing probabilities, which we encountered in Chapter 3, and which prevented any reliable quantitative estimate of the probability of design. (The two problems are related because the reference class depends on the chosen symbols.) When we begin to use information measures in arguments, for instance, in the next section, we must make sure that appropriate symbols are chosen.

Information and Evolution

There have been many attempts to use information theory in evolutionary biology, of which two treatments stand out. What is common to both, and contrary to Dembski's assertions, is that evolution by natural selection easily leads to the accumulation of information in the genome.

In 1961, using a simplified haploid model, Kimura analyzed the difference between the probability that a mutation gets fixed in a population by chance (that is, genetic drift) because it is neutral and the probability that it is fixed by natural selection.[22] (Here, getting "fixed" means that it is the only allele left in the population.) Let p be the initial frequency of a mutant allele in a population. If the allele is neutral (that is, it does not make any difference to the fitness of the organism – recall the discussion of Chapter 4), the probability that it will eventually be fixed in the population is also p.[23] However, if the mutant allele is selected for, that probability is equal to 1. Thus, Kimura argued, the uncertainty removed by natural selection is measured by $1/p$. Using the same formula as the one used by Dembski, the information gained is $H = \log_2(1/p) = -\log_2 p = L/\ln 2$, where L is what is called genetic (or, more accurately, "substitutional") load. It measures the extent to which a population as a whole suffers due to selection because the less fit are weeded out.[24] L can be estimated directly from population data, and Kimura proposed using $H = L/\ln 2$ as the definition of the amount of genetic information accumulated in a population due to selection.

Kimura went on to estimate that 10^8 bits of information had accumulated in a typical genome since the Cambrian era. From the estimated size of chromosome sets in "higher" animals, he calculated 10^{10} bits as their information storage capacity. Redundancy due to repeated DNA sequences could explain this discrepancy but Kimura also noted the possibility that the "amount of genetic information which has accumulated [through natural selection] is small fraction of what can be stored in the chromosome set."[25] Historically, this was an important observation because it is the first inkling of his neutral theory (see Chapter 4), according to which evolution at the molecular level is largely due to chance factors rather than natural selection. Conceptually, what is important is that it shows that, if we use Dembski's formula and a natural choice of symbols, that is, the alleles present in a population, natural selection increases the information content of the genome.

More recently, using an even more natural symbol set, namely, DNA base pairs, Tom Schneider has constructed sophisticated models of the evolution of biological information.[26] Schneider simulated a genome consisting of 256 bases with 16 binding sites (functionally important regions). The idea was to compare the information content of the sequence of such a site with the amount of information required to detect a site in the genome, information being essentially measured by Shannon's formula.[27] Since the average distance between the sites is 16 bases, the amount of information required to find them is $\log_2 16 = 4$ bits. A small population ($n = 64$) was initialized with randomly generated sequences of bases (therefore, with an information content of 0 bits) and subjected to a cycle of mutation and selection regimes in which the half of the population that locates binding sites poorly was replaced by those making fewer errors in locating the sites. By about 700 generations (which is a very low number in evolutionary contexts) the information content at the binding sites reached the expected 4 bits per site and subsequently oscillated around it. The increase in information content was 0.006 ± 0.001 bits per site per generation. The amount of information generated through natural selection can be systematically increased in such models by increasing the number of sites and the size of the genome.[28]

Once again, it was easy to show how the information content of the genome increases during evolution. As Schneider points out, his results show "how this information gain comes about from mutation and selection, without any external influence, thereby completely answering the creationists."[29] ID creationists have never commented on the Kimura results. Dembski's response to Schneider has been that the No Free Lunch theorems discussed in Chapter 5 invalidate any claim that information could have been generated.[30] Moreover, according to Dembski, extra information was smuggled into Schneider's simulations because the number of mistakes due to mutations had to be determined. This is bizarre: the No Free Lunch theorems say nothing at all about an algorithm's performance on a given problem. Moreover, in nature, natural processes determine mistakes and remove them: the process is called natural selection.[31] Directional evolution will almost never occur unless there are patterns in the environment that evolving organisms track through natural selection, for instance, temperature and humidity regimes, resource availability, habitat suitability, and other interacting organisms. (The discussions of *No Free Lunch* entirely ignore this trivial fact about evolution.) There is thus no problem with evolving information in general but, perhaps, there is something special about what Dembski calls complex specified information (CSI). We now turn to that question.

Specified Complexity

The invocation of the no free lunch theorems (recall the discussions of Chapter 5) was one of three strands of the arguments of *No Free Lunch*.[32]

The second is an update of the explanatory filter (recall Chapter 3) to detect complex specified information (CSI). The third is the alleged law of conservation of information, which is supposed to hold for CSI, to which we will turn in the next section. Here we examine whether the concept of CSI is even coherent. Dembski has never defined the concept properly and his best examples are easily shown to be ones that may be generated through natural processes.

According to Dembski, the idea of specified complexity does not originate with him. Rather, it goes back to the noted origins-of-life researcher, Leslie Orgel, who used its presence as one of two criteria that distinguish living from non-living systems. The other criterion was reproduction. As Orgel put it in 1973: "living organisms are distinguished by their *specified complexity*" and explains further in a footnote, "[i]t is impossible to find a simple catch phrase to capture this complex idea. 'Specified and, therefore, repetitive complexity' gets a little closer."[33] Orgel's agenda was the creation of forms of life in the laboratory which reproduce and exhibit specified complexity and thus satisfy the biological criteria for being *life*. Dembski's creationist project was nowhere on this agenda.

Dembski does follow Orgel in trying to explicate the idea of specified complexity with informational concepts. But he never defines CSI. Presumably, by information he means surprisal, as before, rather than Shannon information. However, specification is only defined by a process similar to the explanatory filter and fares no better.[34] Roughly, we are supposed to observe some event, E. We find the class Ω of possible events to which E belongs. Next we find a pattern, T, to which E conforms, taking care that T is epistemically independent of E, that is, we did not use our knowledge of E to find T. (Dembski's concern for choosing T properly, guarding against fabrication, is appropriate – otherwise, he thinks, the process becomes circular.[35] Unfortunately, as will be seen below, his form of the requirement of epistemic independence leads to serious problems.) Finally we compute the probability that a random member of the class Ω would conform to the pattern P. We choose the largest k such that this probability is less than or equal to $1/2^k$. Then the event E has k bits of CSI. Notice that the procedure is similar but simpler than the explanatory filter discussed in Chapter 3, and that the move to compute an information value for the event is novel.

Beyond this procedure, Dembski does not give a definition of CSI though he can presumably respond to such a criticism by saying that the procedure operationally defines CSI. However, over the years, Dembski has provided a laundry list of entities that carry CSI though neither he nor any of the other ID creationists have explicitly carried out the identificatory procedure for any but a very few of them. The laundry list includes: 16-digit numbers on credit cards;[36] phone numbers;[37] other numbers on bills, credit slips, purchase orders, etc.;[38] the sequence of symbols comprising a Shakespearian sonnet;[39] most human artifacts;[40] DNA;[41] an error-counting function used while simulating evolution;[42] fitness functions that measure the activity of a catalyst;[43] the bacterial flagellum;[44] anthropic principles;[45] and fine-tuned cosmological constants.[46] However plausible these examples may seem, as will be seen below, choosing the proper reference classes and showing epistemic independence are not trivial tasks and it is a commentary on the lack of rigor on the part of ID creationists that these examples are presented without explicit analysis.

Attention will be restricted here to three of Dembski's best-known examples. The most important question is whether recognition of a fit to a pattern is plausible if epistemic independence is taken seriously. The three examples are:

(i)   the sequence "DDDDDDDDDDDDDDDDDDDDDDDDDRDDDDDD DDDDDDDDDDDDD";[46]

(ii) the sequence "110111011111011111110111111111011111111111 1101 . . ."

which is supposed to consist of all the prime numbers from 2 to 101 represented as strings of "1"s separated by a single "0" with extra "1"s added at the end to get to a string of a total size of 1,000;[47] and

(iii) the sequence "METHINKS•IT•IS•LIKE•A•WEASEL", taken from Hamlet, which can also be generated as output by an evolutionary algorithm due to Richard Dawkins.[48]

The first sequence is supposed to represent the decisions of Nicholas Caputo, a New Jersey County Clerk, to put a Democrat (D) or a Republican (R) ahead on the ballot in 41 successive years. But, by epistemic independence, this information is not supposed to be used to see if it fits a target. But, then, as Elsberry and Shallit have pointed out, there is a variety of natural processes by which such a sequence may be generated.[49] Here are three examples: (a) records of whether (represented by "D") or not (represented by "R") there was an earthquake of magnitude greater than 6 on the Richter scale in California on successive days; (b) records of whether (R) or not (D) the temperature fell below 0 °C in Austin, Texas, on successive days; or (c) records of whether (R) or not (D) Venus transited the Sun on successive years. If we choose a reasonable Ω as the reference class according to any of these possibilities, the sequence (i) will not have CSI. Epistemic independence has severe consequences.[50]

The second sequence is a variant of an episode in the 1997 movie *Contact* (based on a novel by Carl Sagan) in which the fictional radio astronomers receive this signal and infer the existence of extraterrestrial intelligent agents. Once again, Dembski does not say how the reference class, Ω, is to be selected.[51] The use of prime numbers in this example perhaps gives it psychological force but adds no epistemic weight: prime numbers are easy to compute algorithmically and are, therefore, not mathematically complex.[52] Now Dembski simply assumes that prime numbers cannot be generated by natural processes. Even this is false. Suppose that at the beginning of each year a regular signal, "1", representing, for instance, the quality of vegetation, is sent out from a habitat. But, whenever there is a cicada (genus: Magicicada) outburst, both that signal (because it was already sent at the beginning of the year) and another one, "0", representing changes in the vegetation due to the consumption of sap, is also sent out. Now, cicadas have prime number periods such as 7, 13, or 17. Consequently, it is possible for a natural process to generate a sequence such as (ii). Now, Dembski may argue that these prime number periods are themselves signatures of ID. The trouble is that relatively simple (and elegant) predator–prey models show how prime number periods emerge from natural selection.[53] Given the requirement of epistemic independence, even such SETI (Search for ExtraTerrestrial Intelligence) examples may not have probabilities low enough for Dembski's purposes. Choosing the reference class, Ω, properly is critical to probabilistic arguments and Dembski is embarrassingly vague on this point.

Turning to the line from *Hamlet*, Dawkins shows how it can be generated from an initially random 28-letter sequence by mutation and selection, as incorporated into an evolutionary algorithm. Dembski's main objection is that any fitness function used in such a simulation already has CSI (recall the discussion of the displacement problem in Chapter 5). This is a trivial objection: as noted earlier in this chapter, environmental regularities would always cause potential fitness "functions" to exist in nature, whether or not organisms exist. The outer planets of the Solar System are cold and potential organisms there will have to face that fitness "function" as they evolve, whether they like it or not. If this already constitutes the presence of CSI, then the question of specified complexity is not a question about biology, let alone evolutionary biology – we will turn to physics and design in the next chapter.

But what is interesting about this example is that Dembski falls afoul of his own vagueness on how to compute probabilities. At some points, he uses the assumption that all possible sequences are equally probable, which is reasonable given that Dawkins started out with a random sequence. He concludes that the probability of sequence (iii) is about $1/10^{40}$ which is correct.[54] But he also claims that the probability is 1 because Dawkins' algorithm ensures that evolution would converge to this sequence.[55] David Wolpert put it accurately: Dembski's book is "written in jello."[56]

The conclusion to draw from these examples is that Dembski's procedure – like the original explanatory filter (see Chapter 3) – is inadequate to decide whether some event is specified beyond chance and natural law. Couching the discussion in terms of information rather than raw probabilities only hides the problems with the original proposal and does not contribute towards their solution. Moreover, the inability to follow the procedure systematically and generate definite answers, a feature shared by all of these three examples, shows that, in this sense, the concept of CSI remains conceptually incoherent.

The Law of Conservation of Information

Let us finally turn to the achievement that has apparently makes Dembski the Isaac Newton of information theory, the Law of Conservation of Information. The argument is surprisingly simple:[57] consider two events, A and B, with B somehow arising out of A. Then the probabilities follow the equation:

$$\mathbf{Pr}(A \wedge B) = \mathbf{Pr}(A)\mathbf{Pr}(B \,|\, A)$$

where "$\wedge$" is the logical "and" and $\mathbf{Pr}(B \,|\, A)$ is the conditional probability of B given A. (This equation follows from the definition of conditional probabilities.) Using Dembski's definition of information (as surprisal) we get:

$I(A \wedge B) = I(A) + I(B \,|\, A).$

Now consider the deterministic case: if A occurs, B must occur. Then, $\mathbf{Pr}(B\,|\,A) = 1$ and, consequently, $I(B\,|\,A) = 0$. This means that:

$I(A \wedge B) = I(A).$

All this says is that deterministic processes do not change the probabilities of events. Presumably that is what we mean by "deterministic" and Dembski has managed to notice that fact. Note that the discussion so far does not depend on whether the information is CSI.

Now, Dembski's "Law" claims, additionally, that, if B is produced from A through natural causes, deterministic or not, it is generally true that:

$I(A \wedge B) \leq I(A) + 500.$

However, Dembski now explicitly insists that we must only consider CSI. How this is supposed to affect our computations (if at all) is left unstated. The number 500 is arbitrary. Leaving aside the number 500, what Dembski has succeed in showing, in an unfamiliar form, is the trivial fact that the joint probability of two events occurring cannot be higher than just one of them occurring.

All that the last form of the law says is that Dembski does not believe that an event with a probability lower than $1/2^{500}$ could occur due to natural causes.[58] This may seem plausible – in fact, it may seem plausible that events with that low a probability may not occur due to natural or extra-natural causes. But we are back to the problem of computing probabilities, and choosing reference classes properly, which was discussed in the last section and, earlier, in Chapter 3 during the discussion of Dembski's attempted resurrection of the design argument. There has been no progress; this putative law adds nothing to the discussion. If this is supposed to be the fourth law of thermodynamics, contemporary physics must be in very bad shape.

Besides the argument given above, Dembski also gives a "derivation" of his alleged law in elaborate mathematical notation that may impress non-mathematical readers but adds nothing substantive to the discussion. The derivation is supposed to show that neither functions nor chance can increase CSI content. Figure 7.1 disposes of that argument.

Dembski's technical argument is that neither changes in a system that can be described using a mathematical function nor changes due to chance can increase the amount of CSI in a system. There are two problems with this argument.

- The first problem is epistemic. According to Dembski, for any function f, if the string $y = f(x)$ has a certain amount of CSI, then x must have the same amount of CSI. For y to have CSI there must be an appropriate target T which provides its specification. Now, what is the specification of x? According to Dembski, it is $f^{-1}(T)$. But, for instance, if f represents transformation brought about from the remote evolutionary past by natural selection or whatever other natural process, we have almost no chance of knowing f in sufficient detail to compute f^{-1} and decide if the target for x is appropriately specified. We are being asked to accept Dembski's claims on faith.
- The second problem is conceptual and even more damaging. Let $y = xx$, that is, f duplicates x (or concatenates it twice). Such a function can be easily instantiated even by non-biological natural processes such as crystallization. Suppose that x is a string of "1"s and "0"s. Then, for example, f would take the string "010010" to the string "010010010010". Let us compute the information (surprisal) content of y and x using Dembski's measure. Following Dembski's usual practice in such situations, we will use a uniform distribution over strings of the length of x and y to fix our reference class. Suppose x is of length n. Then $\mathbf{Pr}(y) = 1/2^{2n}$ for any such string (because y will have length $2n$) and the information content, $I_y = 2n$. But $\mathbf{Pr}(x) = 1/2^n$ and $I_x = n$. Dembski's requirement, $I_x \geq I_y$, is obviously violated. Since $I_y - I_x = n$, if $n > 500$, the law of conservation of information is also violated. Roll over, Newton.

Figure 7.1   The law of conservation of information[1]

[1] The objections mentioned in the box are due to Shallit and Elsberry (2004).

The Cambrian "Explosion"

No discussion of the use of information by ID creationists will be complete without at least some mention of the first allegedly peer-reviewed paper mentioning ID that has so far been published.[59] As we will see below, if quality is the sole concern, this paper would not merit attention. But its publication was a sufficiently important event in the political controversy over ID creationism for it to be briefly discussed here in violation of this book's general practice of restricting political arguments to the Preface and Chapter 10. The paper in question, "The Origin of Biological Information and the Higher Taxonomic Categories," by

Stephen C. Meyer of the Discovery Institute, appeared in 2004 in the *Proceedings of the Biological Society of Washington*, a journal normally dedicated to taxonomic issues.[60] That journal was then edited by Richard von Sternberg, who also serves on the Editorial Board[61] of the *Occasional Papers of the Baraminology Study Group*[62] at Bryan College in Tennessee. Sternberg is also a signatory of the Discovery Institute's "scientific" dissent from "Darwinism." The Baraminology Study Group is a "research" group devoted to the determination of the created kinds of Genesis.[63] While ID creationists crowed about finally publishing a "peer-reviewed" paper, the Biological Society of Washington immediately issued a statement disclaiming as much responsibility as it could, given that the offending piece had appeared in its own journal. In particular, the statement made it clear that the paper had not gone through the normal reviewing process. It also correctly noted that Meyer's paper did not meet the journal's own scientific standards.[64]

Well, what does the paper say?[65] Meyer begins by noting, correctly, that there are many aspects of organic form for which we do not have reasonably complete evolutionary histories. In particular, as was also noted in Chapter 4, we do not fully understand the evolution of animal body-plans. Conveniently ignoring all recent work on fossils of the Cambrian and immediate pre-Cambrian eras, Meyer goes on to claim that almost all modern phyla originated during a 5–10-million-year period about 530 million years ago. This, according to Meyer, constituted an "information explosion" that could not have occurred through natural evolutionary processes. No measure of information – neither Dembski's nor anyone else's – is ever computed in the paper to justify this claim though Meyer claims to be using complex specified information (CSI). Rather, we are expected to accept Meyer's assertion on authority. There are some gems: "Many scientists and mathematicians have questioned the ability of mutation and selection to generate information in the form of novel genes and proteins";[66] therefore, Meyer concludes, the genes and proteins required for the Cambrian information explosion must have extra-natural origins. This "argument" is repeated several times with no evidence or further reasoning. There is no explicit discussion of even the connection between design and information. Strange as it may seem, there is very little other content to the paper and the little that there is reiterates standard creationist fare about the alleged inadequacies of contemporary evolutionary biology. We are told without argument, for instance, that higher taxa are real (rather than instrumental categories used for effective classification). All that is novel about this claim, compared to old-fashioned Creationism, is that it is embedded in a new-sounding discussion of information. The entire paper is a superb application of what Haldane used to call "The Bellman's Theorem: Say it three times and it becomes true."[67]

Taking Leave of Creation Biology

The alleged law of conservation of information is the latest attempt to date by ID creationists to show that biological evolution is inconsistent with some fundamental aspects of nature.[68] Its failure leaves the ball in the creationists' court. Given the rate at which our knowledge of biology is increasing, if intellectual merit decides the outcome of the debate, at least this version of Reformed Creationism has little time left.

The next two chapters will turn to more general issues, namely, to what ID creationism claims about physics, and the question of naturalism. So it is time to take stock of what we learned from its critique of evolutionary biology. From Behe we got some interesting problems of biochemical evolution on all of which we have made significant progress in recent years. This progress has been due both to work in structural chemistry and biochemistry, and because genomics and proteomics have begun to churn out large databases of DNA and protein sequences which can be compared to establish homologies and thereby reconstruct evolutionary histories. From Dembski we learned the importance of being surprised, how the degree of our surprise should be taken as the information we get.

Beyond that, from both we learned that they are very impressed by low probability events, and deeply believe that these cannot happen from natural causes. However, whatever plausibility this view could have disappears because of the gerrymandered way in which they, especially Dembski, choose reference classes to make any complex biological phenomenon appear highly improbable. But, even without this problem, what they offer us is what Miller has rightly called an "argument from personal incredulity":[69] because they are amazed at what evolution throws up, they cannot believe that evolution can occur by natural processes alone. For all the words and pseudo-calculations deployed by ID creationists, we have not made much progress from Paley. In fact, if intellectual integrity is one of our values, there has been regress: Paley wrote well before the work of Darwin and Wallace, let alone modern evolutionary theory.

8

Cosmic Coincidences

At the end of the *Origin* Darwin explicitly disavowed any claim to know how life began on Earth. His point was that the theory of natural selection was supposed to explain how life evolved after it originated, not how it began in the first place. Faced with the challenge from ID, today's biologists have the same option open to them – as we noted in Chapter 3, the origin of life is not a test case for biological theory even though almost all self-respecting biologists today believe that natural processes, as captured by models of prebiotic evolution, led to the first cells. However, ID creationists claim that some "intelligent" mechanism is operating during the history of life after it began: consequently, it is in that domain that ID must demonstrate that it does better than evolutionary theory. The last seven chapters have shown that no such demonstration is forthcoming.

In the same vein, questions about the origin of the universe, the values of the fundamental constants of physics, or the present laws of physics, and so on, are beyond the domain of evolutionary theory. Suppose, though only for the sake of argument, that some divine creator beyond the purview of natural study caused the Big Bang and stipulated the laws of physics. So long as this creator then takes a rest and does not subsequently influence the laws of matter responsible for the evolution of life on Earth, such an act of creation would be irrelevant to biological evolution, and ipso facto, to the dispute between evolutionary biology and ID.

Nevertheless, this chapter will turn to an argument for ID based on the alleged cosmic coincidences of the values taken by the fundamental constants of physics. This argument is based on the probably correct[1] – and intriguing – observation by physicists that only a certain limited range of values of the fundamental constants of physics would allow life as we know it (that is, carbon-based life) to exist and, not very surprisingly, our universe happens to have values for these constants within that range. This chain of reasoning provides various versions of what is called the "anthropic principle." The cosmic coincidences at the basis of this principle, so the argument goes, provide reason to believe that the universe has design, perhaps that there even is a designer. We will examine this so-called "fine-tuning" argument in this chapter. Here "fine-tuning" refers to the claim that all these constants must simultaneously have values within a very limited range for us to exist.

Physics and Biology

Indeed, even some strong proponents of evolutionary theory who are sharply critical of attempts by ID creationists to discredit that theory, nevertheless, accept the anthropic argument as evidence for the existence of a deity – among them is Ken Miller, the biologist whom we have already encountered in Chapter 6, who couples his belief in evolution with a theistic view of the universe. Though Miller acknowledges that the "ultimate purpose of the work of God may never be understood by the mind of man,"[2] he claims to know:

> Having decided to base life on the substance of matter and its fine tuned properties, a Creator who had already figured out how to fashion beauty and order . . . could easily have saved his greatest miracle for last. Having chosen to base the lives of His creatures on the properties of matter, why not draw the lives of His creatures on the properties of matter, why not draw the origins of His creatures from exactly the same source? God's wish for consistency in his relations with the natural world would have made this a perfect choice. As His great creations burst forth from the singularity of its origin, His laws would have set within it the seeds of galaxies, stars, and planets, the potential for life, the inevitability of change, and the confidence of emerging intelligence.[3]

Miller's warrant for any of these rather profound claims remains mysterious – luckily they are not presented as scientific hypotheses. Miller is correct to emphasize that his position poses no challenge to evolution and thus provides no support to creationists. However, it is hard not to sympathize with Niall Shanks' observation that he simply "wants creationists out of his own backyard and is happy to see them dumped on the hapless physicists and cosmologists."[4]

Though positions such as these do not challenge biological evolution, we will examine the fine-tuning argument below. Partly, we will do so for completeness of our arguments against design. But, mainly, our foray into physics is motivated by the concomitant purpose of this book to defend naturalism (the claim that we need not go beyond natural explanations to explain natural phenomena) and by the fact that addressing the fine-tuning argument does not require much beyond our earlier arguments, particularly those deployed in Chapter 3 to refute Paley's argument from design which, as we shall see below, turns out to be far more respectable. (However, given space limitations and the biological orientation of this book, we will not discuss every cosmological argument about the existence of God, ignoring those based on speculative interpretations of physical theory, including the many worlds and many minds interpretations of quantum mechanics.)

Anthropic Principles?

The laws of physics are dynamical laws, governing the temporal change of systems. These systems can range from something as simple as a pendulum to the entire universe. The fundamental laws of physics are those on which the rest of physical theories are supposed to be based – there are but few of these and they are supposed to govern all physical systems from sub-atomic particles to the universe itself. In principle, the future state of any such system depends on these laws and antecedent conditions. These conditions include several constants occurring in the fundamental laws of physics. At any stage of inquiry the values of these constants are postulated, as required, for accurate prediction. At later stages we hope that more fundamental theories fix these values but this is at present no more than a hope. It is possible that these values have no more fundamental explanation; it is also possible that they may vary from universe to universe – contemporary physics allows such a modality. Given what we now know, we must accept them as unexplained assumptions of fundamental physics.

In 1957, the physicist R. H. Dicke observed that certain numerical coincidences must obtain for life as we know it to exist in the universe. Over the years a cottage industry has grown around these coincidences.[5] Robin Collins, relying primarily on John Leslie, provides a list of five:[6]

(i)   if the initial strength of the Big Bang had differed by as little as 1 part in 10^{60}, the universe as we know it would not exist – it would have either collapsed or expanded too far for the formation of galaxies;

(ii)   if the strong force, which keeps the protons and neutrons in the nucleus together, had differed by 1 part in 20, life would have been impossible;

(iii)   if the strength of the gravitational interaction had been different by 1 part in 10^{40} then life-sustaining stars – so long as we must restrict our concept of life to the only kind of life we know, a point that Collins should, but does not, emphasize – like our Sun would not exist;

(iv)   were the mass of the neutron not about 1.001 that of the proton, neutrons would have decayed into protons or vice versa. Life – but, once again, provided that life must be as we know it – would have been impossible; and

(v)   if the electromagnetic force were slightly stronger or weaker, life – with the same proviso as before – would be impossible.

Others have other favorite lists[7] – an assessment of fine-tuning does not depend on which parameters are the ones that are used. No matter which list impresses us most, there is probably no gainsaying the point that these coincidences – and we must accept that they are coincidences given what we know of physics at present – must hold for us, humans, to exist. However, there are important skeptics, among them the physicist Steven Weinberg.[8] For the sake of argument, we will assume that fine-tuning holds. (If it does not, there is even less of an argument from design – the situation would be analogous to one in which the argument to functionality did not hold in the case of the biological argument from design [see Chapter 3].)

What should we make of this fact? Is it merely trivial, another way of describing the obvious fact that the world must be, and must have physically evolved into, what it is, for the world to be the way it is? Those who would believe that some deeper insight lurks behind these coincidences interpret them as pointing to an anthropic principle that is, at the very least, supposed to constrain all scientific theorizing. The constraint is that no scientific theory can violate the anthropic principle. In the canonical discussion of Barrow and Tipler, there emerge three versions of this principle:[9]

(i)   the *Weak Anthropic Principle (WAP)*: the observed values of the fundamental constants of nature are not equally probable;[10] they must take on values that are restricted by the requirement that carbon-based life may exist in some parts of the universe and the universe must be old enough to permit the emergence of such forms of life;

(ii)   the *Strong Anthropic Principle (SAP)*: the universe must have properties that allow the emergence of carbon-based life; and, rather ambitiously,

(iii)   the *Final Anthropic Principle (FAP)*: "intelligent information processing must come into existence in the universe, and once it comes into existence, it will never die out."[11]

Depending on how we interpret it, the second part of the WAP is unexceptionable but trivial. Barrow and Tipler interpret it as constituting "just a restatement, albeit a subtle restatement, of one of the most important and well-established principles of science: that it is essential to take into account the limitations of one's measuring apparatus when interpreting one's observations."[12] Even this is an inflated interpretation: all we are warranted in asserting is that the constants of nature must be such that they allow us to exist because we are part of the empirical evidence that the laws of physics must accommodate. Similarly, the constants of nature and the laws of physics must be such as to allow the existence of Sirius and of every other observed fact of the universe – otherwise, they would be empirically inadequate, especially if they are supposed to be the fundamental laws of physics. We are part of the physical world. Brandon Carter puts the *WAP* in a suitably deflated form: "what we can expect to observe must be restricted by the conditions necessary for our presence as observers."[13] By the time we get to the first half of the *WAP* we are in uncertain territory. How do we know that the particular values that we find for the fundamental constants are not more or less probable than the others? In particular, do we have any reason to believe that they have low probability? How are we supposed to assess these probabilities? What are the appropriate reference classes? One of our cosmological design arguments assumes that they do – we will turn to that question in the next section.

With the *SAP* we have left the realm of science and natural philosophy. We are supposed not to be able to imagine a universe similar to ours if it happens to exclude life as we know it. The universe is such that we (or some entities very much like us) must have happened. But our most fundamental physical theories, based on quantum mechanics, are indeterministic, allowing a multiplicity of possible universes that may have evolved from the Big Bang.[14] Solipsism is one way out – the universe exists in each of our minds; ipso facto, there could be no universe without us. But that would be far too high a price to pay. If the *SAP* were correct, unlike the *WAP* it would explain why fine-tuning holds. But the *SAP* has no justification.

The *FAP* is even stronger than the *SAP*. Given the absurdity of the *SAP*, no further discussion of the *FAP* is warranted. Additionally, all problems regarding the notion of information noted in the last chapter also return with full force here. Let us turn to the question whether the *WAP* leads to any defensible argument to a designer. (As we leave this topic, in fairness to Barrow and Tipler, we should note that they explicitly point out: "We should warn the reader once again that both the *FAP* and the *SAP* are quite speculative; unquestionably, neither should be regarded as well-established principles of physics."[15])

The Force of Improbability

The *WAP* lies at the basis of several popular cosmological design arguments though these generally can be, and sometimes are, formulated without any explicit reference to the *WAP*. One version of this argument begins with two premises:[16] (i) the fundamental constants of nature must fall within a small range of values for the universe to contain carbon-based life; (ii) we find carbon-based life in our universe. From these premises, we are first supposed to conclude: (a) our universe is improbable. Next, we are supposed to go on to the stronger theological conclusions: (b) the best explanation for an improbable universe is that it is designed; and (c) there exists an intelligent designer of universes. There is no reason here to question that the last conclusion (c) follows from the other two, (a) and (b). However, the inference to a designer (conclusion [b]) does not follow from the improbability of our universe (conclusion [a]) for the same reason that the argument to a designer does not follow from the conclusions of an argument to functionality in the case of the biological argument from design (recall the discussion of Chapter 3). We will return to this issue in the next section.

But, how improbable is the universe? Does the first conclusion (a) follow from its premises? Now, the value of each constant of nature is a real number. To say that a constant can take very few values, as indicated by fine-tuning, is to say that the observed value must lie in a finite, preferably rather small, interval on the real line.[17] What we have to estimate is the probability of this case. To do so we must assign probabilities to all intervals on the real line. Now, physical theory says nothing about how we should do this. Faced with this ignorance, some proponents of the cosmological design argument appeal to a principle of indifference: every interval of the same length should be the same probability.[18] The principle of indifference is controversial within probability but leave that aside.[19] This strategy will get nowhere. Since (roughly) the ratio of every finite interval to the infinite real line is 0, the probability of every fine-tuned constant to have an admissible value is also 0. And this is true on the hypothesis of design as well as on the hypothesis of an absence of design.

Other ways of trying to estimate these probabilities independent of physical theory also lead to bizarre conclusions. For instance, the number of observed universes is equal to 1.[20] Now, the number of observed universes with the given values of the fundamental constants is also 1. Dividing the latter number by the former, we find, as an empirical estimate, the probability that fine-tuned constants have their present values is equal to 1. Perhaps this argument can be used to justify the *SAP* but it will not take us to design via improbability.

The only alternative is to assume that physical possibility – as indicated by our best physical theories – provides a distribution of probabilities over the real line that gives the fine-tuned set an adequately low probability. The trouble is that we know no such distribution – we have no way of assigning the relevant probabilities. Proponents of the cosmological design argument are silent on this point or, more often, offer analogies instead of explicit recipes to compute these probabilities. They follow the same illegitimate strategy that Dembski did to justify his explanatory filter in its original and updated versions, namely, never clarifying how to identify the relevant reference classes and compute the probabilities (recall the discussions of Chapters 3 and 7).

For instance, Leslie writes: "Imagine that a bullet hits a fly surrounded by a large empty area. The bullet's trajectory needed fine tuning to achieve this result, which can help to show that a marksman was at work. It can help to show it regardless of whether distant areas are all of them so covered with flies that any bullet striking them would hit one. The crucial point is that the local area contained just one fly."[21] For this analogy to carry weight, we must be given a non-arbitrary criterion by which the local area is identified and, then, the analog for that criterion in the context of the laws of physics. Leslie offers no elaboration. At this point the fine-tuning argument becomes a purely verbal rhetorical ploy unrooted in any deep truth about physics.

A Cosmological Design Argument

But suppose that the relevant probabilities are sufficiently well defined in spite of our inability to assess them. (Such an assumption is question-begging: what does it mean to say that these probabilities are well defined when we know of no procedure, in principle, by which they could be assigned? Nevertheless, for the sake of argument, we will temporarily concede the point.) A more respectable comparative version of the cosmological argument can now be constructed in analogy to the biological inference to a designer considered in Chapter 3.[22] We will see that the same argument that we used there against that inference carries over to the cosmological context with very little modification – as Elliott Sober has recognized.[23]

Suppose that K is the claim that fine-tuning holds, and U is the claim that our universe exists, with carbon-based life, and so on. What the WAP asserts is: if U, then K. Given U – we know that our universe exists – we can infer, by *modus ponens*, that K. This fact will be useful later. Now, in the case of the biological argument for a designer, we considered three hypotheses, conscious design, blind chance, and blind chance coupled with natural selection. Here, since we know of no analog to natural selection, we will consider only two hypotheses: a design hypothesis and an absence-of-design hypothesis.[24] Now for the argument to a designer to work, what must hold is that the probability of the design hypothesis, given fine-tuning, that is, given K, is greater than the probability of the absence-of-design hypothesis, once again given K. Let us once again be charitable and assume that we assign the same prior probability to the two hypotheses, that is, prior to bringing the existence of fine-tuning to bear on the question. (Alternatively, we may choose to justify this assignment on the ground that assuming that one of the prior probabilities is greater than the other is question-begging.[25])

Now, elementary probability theory shows that these conditions require that the probability of fine-tuning, K, must be higher under the design hypothesis than the absence-of-design hypothesis.[26] Do we have any reason to believe this?[27] We are faced with at least as difficult a problem as the one we had earlier in the biological context: we have no basis for computing these probabilities. We have even less experience of any facet of universe design than some aspects of the design of functioning biological organisms. Why, for instance, would a designer desire a fine-tuned universe, rather than one that is more robust? We cannot even answer questions as basic as this.[28]

Faced with this situation, suppose we try to use all our existing knowledge to compute the probabilities. Our knowledge includes K (because we know the *WAP* and the fact that the world exists, as noted earlier). But then the probability of fine-tuning turns out to be 1, no matter whether we assume the design or the absence-of-design hypothesis.[29] The posterior probability of each hypothesis is equal to its prior probability – the evidence makes no difference. Fine-tuning is simply irrelevant to the choice between the design and absence-of-design hypotheses. Even if we concede the low probability of fine-tuning without knowing how such probabilities may be assigned we get no closer to the hypothesis of a designer.

This is where the biological design argument is superior to the cosmological: in that context, we would have no justification for assuming an analog of the *SAP* which would then allow us to infer that some feature is necessary because we know that biological organisms exist with that feature. Turning to physics from biology has produced nothing substantively different: we get stale wine in new bottles.

Is Fine-Tuning Surprising?

The discussions of the last two sections already suggest that fine tuning may not even be at all improbable, initial appearances to the contrary. We simply do not know enough to estimate the relevant probabilities. Nevertheless, there are good intuitive reasons to suggest that fine-tuning is highly probable – and remember that, because we cannot actually compute the relevant probabilities, the arguments in earlier sections for the improbability of fine-tuning are no more than intuitive. Cory Juhl considers a universe that is "sensitive," that is, it has some features which vary wildly when some of the fundamental constants change.[30] How probable is such a universe? Strictly speaking we cannot say because we have no way of computing such probabilities. But, given what we know of ordinary physical features, and even restricting attention to non-biological features, such sensitivity seems commonplace. It follows that sensitive universes may be highly probable. Now assume that a sensitive universe is complex enough that it contains "multifaceted" features, that is, features that depend on a lot of sensitive features. Now a sensitive universe need not contain multifaceted features: it may, for instance, contain exactly one hydrogen atom. But, if it does contain many multifaceted features, then the possible values of the fundamental constants must be severely constrained. We are on our way to discovering fine-tuning, and it is not very surprising. If we have a sensitive universe with many multifaceted features that have lasted a while, fine-tuning seems inevitable. So, the extent to which the force of anthropic and cosmological design arguments depends on the improbability of fine-tuning, these arguments now seem much less impressive.

A more technical gloss can be given to Juhl's argument though with some loss of generality. Suppose that the universe can be described by a set of coupled differential equations and their boundary and initial conditions. (In general, most physical theories make this assumption.) Suppose that the universe is stable in the sense that, if it is slightly disturbed, it tends to return to the original state. Then, it is a mathematical fact that such stability depends sensitively on the values of various constants occurring in the equations and boundary and initial conditions. Moreover, as the number of entities in the universe increases, the constants become more and more constrained. The mathematical ecologist, Robert May, used this argument in the 1970s to show that, contrary to expectations, as an ecological community becomes more complex (that is, has more species), it typically becomes less stable.[31] Here it shows that, if we have a relatively stable universe, finding fine-tuning of many parameters is almost inevitable.

A Concluding Note

The discussion of this chapter has largely been a detour from the central purpose of this book: ultimately, that cosmology does not provide an argument for design is not relevant to the question of whether evolution or design provides a better explanation of the history of life on Earth. But it does have some bearing on the question of naturalism to which we turn in the next chapter.

9

Naturalism and Its Discontents

When asked about his religious inclinations, J. B. S. Haldane is supposed to have quipped that when he designed an experiment he assumed that God, the Devil, and the angels would not interfere with it. Haldane's assumption embraces a minimal form of methodological naturalism. For Philip Johnson and many other proponents of ID and other versions of creationism, their ultimate target is not merely the theory of evolution; rather, it is naturalism itself, the denial of any divinity operating in nature. This chapter will take up the question of naturalism and whether ID creationists have offered any reason for us to consider abandoning it. Recall, in this context, a lesson we gleaned from the examples of scientific and metaphysical change discussed in Chapter 1: the reasons required for giving up our foundational principles must be very compelling. Moreover, except in the case of the theory of natural selection, even the radical conceptual changes discussed in Chapter 1 did not raise questions about methodological naturalism, and the theory of natural selection finally brought biological adaptation under its purview.

Both methodological and metaphysical naturalism will be defended in this chapter, but what is here called "metaphysics" will probably not excite many professional metaphysicians. In any case, the concerns of this chapter are strictly philosophical – scientists may well choose to skip it and proceed directly to the concluding chapter.

What Naturalism Is

There is a variety of views about what constitutes naturalism. For Michael Ruse, the "methodological naturalist is the person who assumes that the world runs according to unbroken law; that humans can understand the world in terms of this law; and that science involves just such understanding without any reference to extra or supernatural forces like God."[1] Almost all scientists, like Haldane, assume some form of methodological naturalism similar to this, no matter what their personal religious beliefs happen to be. Beyond methodological naturalism lies a more ambitious and ambiguous doctrine, metaphysical naturalism (sometimes also called ontological naturalism). For Ruse, "metaphysical naturalism . . . argues that the world is as we see it and that there is nothing more."[2] The contrast should be obvious: unlike the metaphysical naturalist, for the methodological naturalist, "[w]hether there are [supernatural] forces or beings is another matter entirely and simply not addressed by methodological naturalism."[3] In this book we will construe methodological naturalism in Ruse's sense though what we identify as metaphysical naturalism will be somewhat different.

Though Ruse is a critic of ID creationism, there is no substantive difference between this definition of methodological naturalism and those produced by most explicitly religiously motivated ID creationists. For instance, Johnson writes: "A methodological naturalist defines science as the search for the best naturalistic theories. A theory would not be naturalistic if it left something . . . to be explained by a supernatural cause."[4] Thus the definition of methodological naturalism we use on this book is not controversial in the sense that it will distinguish us from the creationists.

Most critics of ID creationism emphasize the *methodological* aspect of methodological naturalism more explicitly than Ruse. What they emphasize is a commitment to scientific method and, consequently, defeasibility. This is the possibility that accepted results may be shown to be wrong in the future in spite of satisfying every methodological stricture at present, and even the methods used to obtain results are subject to revision in the light of future experience. As Pennock puts it: "The Methodological Naturalist does not make a commitment directly to a picture of what exists in the world, but rather to a set of methods as a reliable way to find out about the world – typically the methods of the natural sciences, and perhaps extensions that are continuous with them – and indirectly to what those methods discover."[5] This description does not contradict Ruse's definition. Rather it presumes the former definition because the typical methods of the natural sciences assume humanly recognizable lawlike behavior of parts of the world, no matter whether those laws are deterministic or only statistical. Suppose that some hitherto unknown entity is discovered to influence observable events but does so in some lawlike fashion. This "lawlike" fashion may even be "random": there are laws – the laws governing stochastic processes – that regulate what random events may or may not do. Such entities become part of science, to be studied by scientific methods demanding, typically, a certain amount of precision and repeatability. The extent of precision and repeatability depends on the context. The methods used in science are flexible, and naturalism inherits that flexibility.[6] All it excludes is caprice and unintelligibility in the behavior of things which, given the paucity of the details that they are willing to furnish, is what ID creationists such as Johnson seem to suggest constitutes "creation."

Let us initially also assume that the distinction between methodological and metaphysical naturalism is cogent – we will question this assumption later. For some ID creationists, including Johnson, *methodological* naturalism, provided that we honestly stick to it, is unproblematic. For Johnson, trouble arises only because methodological naturalism slides inexorably to metaphysical naturalism.[7] Others are more critical. Alvin Plantinga, for example, will have no truck with methodological naturalism itself. We will consider both types of objection, but let us start with a more detailed look at what naturalism is.

Nagel's Legacy

The first point to note is that, during the twentieth century, critics of naturalism – methodological or metaphysical – included many who accepted the theory of evolution and even some who had no religious inclinations. Defenders of naturalism also did not form a homogeneous group. ID creationists – in particular, Johnson – present naturalism and creationism as if these were mutually exclusive and jointly exhaustive alternatives.[8] This is the same game as that played by Dembski in his attempt to resuscitate the design argument, where regularity, chance, and design were similarly presented as mutually exclusive and jointly exhaustive options (see Chapter 3). In both cases the claim that the alternatives are jointly exhaustive relies on logical skullduggery: one of the options (design, in Chapter 3, and creation, here) is defined to include everything that is left when the others are excluded. But the alternatives are not jointly exhaustive provided we take creation to have some teeth, that is, we assume that creationist epistemology claims something more is at stake than that there may be methods of gaining knowledge other than the methods of science.

We will not accept the claim that all those who are not naturalists are necessarily creationists. The reason for this is that most (probably almost all) philosophers who reject naturalism also reject creationism. Naturalists have been uncommon in twentieth-century epistemology but creationists, unreformed or Reformed, have been even rarer. Just as denying naturalism does not establish creationism, denying creationism successfully will also not establish naturalism, not even methodological naturalism, let alone metaphysical naturalism. For the naturalists, in the context of twentieth- and twenty-first-century philosophy, their most significant opponents were not creationists. Rather, they were the so-called "traditionalists" in epistemology.[9] Traditionalists, from this perspective, rely on intuition for epistemological insight, sometimes aided by armchair reflection, but with no serious concern for the details of empirical scientific knowledge or the methods required to obtain that knowledge.

Against these traditionalists, W. V. Quine is perhaps the best-known advocate of naturalism in twentieth-century philosophy. Nevertheless, the *locus classicus* of that position is the work of the philosopher of science, Ernest Nagel, who, perhaps more clearly than Quine, understood and emphasized how much it marks a departure from traditional Western epistemology.[10] Nagel's naturalism followed the sciences in being based on the epistemological primacy of experience: "naturalism . . . merely formulates what centuries of human experience have repeatedly confirmed . . . [It is] a generalized account of the world encountered in experience and in critical reflection, and a just perspective upon the human scene."[11] However, unlike a scientific theory, naturalism does not "specify a set of substantive principles with the help of which the detailed course of concrete happenings can be explained or understood." Rather, it depicts an attitude.

Four themes were central to Nagel's naturalism. Together they emphasize the point that naturalism is a thesis as much about the nature of epistemology as it is a thesis within epistemology:

(i)   naturalism requires a minimal ontological commitment to the primacy of the physical world, as Nagel puts it, "the existential and causal primacy of organized matter in the executive order of nature . . . [T]here is no place for the operation of disembodied forces." Here, this aspect of Nagel's naturalism is accepted but only because the laws of science we so far know also assume the primacy of physical matter (that is to say, physicalism);

(ii)   a recognition that no philosophical position or scientific theory is going to be a theory of everything. Thus, naturalism recognizes that "the manifest plurality and variety of things, of their qualities and their functions, are an irreducible feature of the cosmos . . . and that the sequential orders in which events occur or the manifold relations of dependence in which things exist are *contingent* connections, not the embodiment of a fixed and unified pattern of logically necessary links";[12]

(iii)   according to naturalism, a priori justification is neither required nor desirable for philosophical positions, and perhaps not even possible. It is also characteristic of naturalism that it does not exclude other philosophical frameworks on a priori grounds; experience, possibly including introspective reflection, is the arbitrator of disputes; and

(iv)   most importantly, since naturalism is derived from experience, it, as well as any other philosophical position, is fallible, just like the claims of science. The warrant for any epistemological proposition comes not from its being "self-luminous" or "self-evident," nor "from a faith in the uniformity of nature or in other principles with a cosmic scope. The warrant derives exclusively from the specific evidence available for that proposition, and from the contingent historical fact that the special ways employed in obtaining and appraising the evidence have been generally effective in yielding reliable knowledge."[13]

The last move, deriving support for philosophical positions from their success in the field, is central to our defense of naturalism. It was already invoked in Chapter 1 where it was pointed out that empirical success is ample and adequate motivation for our metaphysical conservatism in rejecting extra-natural causes.

On questions of detail, Nagel's is one type of naturalism. Naturalism comes in many varieties, as Nagel and others have explicitly noted.[14] Some of the more extreme versions of naturalism deny the existence of normativity in philosophy, that philosophy, whether it be in epistemology or ethics or aesthetics, concerns what we should believe or do, beyond what we do believe and do. Nagel makes no such claim. Quine and other behaviorists would deny the admissibility of introspection and self-reflection in our assessment of the success or failure of our views. Nagel places no such restriction.

Nagel's naturalism is particularly attractive because of its modesty. This modesty makes its defense relatively easy, especially when we restrict ourselves to methodological naturalism as an appropriate epistemology of science. A defense of evolutionary theory against the capricious and fantastic world of ID requires no more, though, as we shall see, much more can be said in favor of naturalism.

Perhaps what is most important about this version of naturalism is that all our empirical knowledge can be brought to bear upon our epistemological problems. Suppose that we are worried about the reliability of some inferential strategy. Then what can be brought to bear upon the discussion goes well beyond the merely logical or mathematical properties of that strategy: it includes not only empirical facts from psychology and cognitive science, but facts about our past experience with that strategy, most importantly, the history of science. Similarly, when we turn to normative questions of ethics, the history of human cultures has as much relevance as what we know of the biological origin of our emotions, desires, and ability to reason. Human cultural history can trump the claims of human sociobiology and Evolutionary Psychology. We may even choose to interpret and learn from our religious superstars – Moses, Lao-tze, Gautama Buddha, Christ, and so on. Naturalism does not prevent that. But it denies the authority of the text over that of our collective experience.

The Problem of Normativity

Naturalism in philosophy is not without its share of problems. In particular, normativity presents a problem for naturalism, one which prevents the contexts of epistemology and ethics from being entirely symmetrical. The discussion above assumed that we knew what constituted successful science; otherwise, we would not be in a position to judge which methods worked well and which did not. To know what constitutes successful science, the objection goes, we must go beyond naturalism because we are now broaching a normative question. At stake here is the assumption that we can never have sufficient empirical knowledge of norms to ground claims about the success of science.

How do we, as naturalists, ground these judgments? As Abner Shimony, Philip Kitcher, and others have pointed out, all we need is some minimal agreement about the ultimate goals of science.[15] These goals or "cognitive values," as Kitcher puts it, include understanding: "a structured account of nature"[16] besides many pragmatic goals such as prediction and control. (Prediction, control, and understanding comprise the nineteenth-century physiologist Claude Bernard's well-known trinity of the goals of science.[17]) Once we are given these goals, we can decide which of our epistemological practices have been successful in the past, and which have not. We need not have complete agreement about these goals; we merely need to have sufficient commonality. Where agreement is incomplete, we may have epistemological questions that continue to be debated. We may also change our goals over time, but we will do so because of empirical facts about the world. This type of argument offers no a priori certainty about our epistemological principles – but so be it. Naturalism never promised a single unified doctrine at the end of the day. Not only did it not promise a priori certainty, in fact, in Nagel's version, it explicitly denied it. There is no more certainty in philosophy than there is in science.

In ethics, at this point, it is not clear that we have a good analogy any longer. It is far less obvious that there is sufficient agreement about moral goals to ground our ethical principles and practices to the extent that we can resolve socially difficult cases such as euthanasia, abortion, and so on. Perhaps the only message to be taken from naturalism is a somewhat dispiriting one: we have to be modest about what degree of ethical certainty we can achieve in such cases. Luckily, ethical naturalism is not at stake here except insofar as it should be kept in mind that there is no claim here that ethical principles can be reduced to biological evolution, let alone natural selection acting on our individual ancestors in a distant past about which we can know very little. Naturalism, even in ethics, does not lead inexorably to human sociobiology or Evolutionary Psychology. There is more to the empirical world, including our cultural world, than what can be explained by the theory of natural selection.

Creationist Critiques

If naturalism is defeasible, then it is obviously legitimate to attempt to discredit it, as some creationists have done. Let us initially restrict ourselves to methodological – rather than metaphysical – naturalism. Philosophical arguments against naturalism in the context of the evolution–creationism debate have largely come from Alvin Plantinga who denies that science requires even methodological naturalism. What Plantinga means by "science" is worse than unclear – it evidently is much more than what we customarily take to be indicated by that term. But this largely linguistic issue need not detain us here. Plantinga has offered a variety of arguments – at least, what are intended as arguments – against methodological naturalism, some more scientifically respectable than others.

Among the less respectable moves is an exhortation – and not an argument – to Christian scientists to pursue "Augustinian" or "theistic science."[18] Christian scientists are supposed to view the world against the background of a presumed conflict between the "City of God" and the "City of Man," to interpret all intellectual life as episodes of this conflict, opt for those activities that are consistent with citizenship in Civitas Dei, and use categories such as original sin in the construction of the social sciences. Obviously, methodological naturalism is irrelevant to this enterprise which is more reminiscent of the Crusades than any episode in the history of the sciences.

But we do not need someone unsympathetic to religion to point out what is wrong with Plantinga's claims. As the Catholic priest – and noted philosopher of science – Ernan McMullin puts it:

> I do not think . . . that [Plantinga's] theistic science should be described *as* science. It lacks the universality of science, as that term has been understood in the Western tradition. It also lacks the sort of warrant that has gradually come to characterize natural science, one that points to systematic observation, generalization, and the testing of explanatory hypotheses. It appeals to a specifically Christian belief, one that lays no claim to assent from a Hindu or an agnostic. It requires faith, and faith (we are told) is a gift, a grace, from God. To use the term "science" in this context seems dangerously misleading; it encourages expectations that cannot be fulfilled, in the interests of adopting a label generally regarded as honorific.[19]

On this point, no further argument need be produced. Let us, instead, recall with reverence the spirit of the Enlightenment – which Plantinga explicitly dismisses – that took science and reason to be tools by which we can emerge from prejudice, from mere parochialism, to appreciate what is truly human in us.

Plantinga's various other arguments to show that methodological naturalism is conceptually incoherent are marginally more respectable.

The project, at least, is logically well conceived whether or not Plantinga realized it. Suppose, contrary to Plantinga's last exhortation, we take science to constitute what we ordinarily call science. If we also accept that the customary methods of science are naturalistic, as even Plantinga does, there are only two ways in which methodological naturalism can fail: (i) it may be leading science astray, barricading its frontiers and preventing progress; or (ii) it is conceptually flawed or incoherent which, ultimately, must be self-defeating. Given the advance of science during the past few centuries, and of the technology it has spawned, the first possibility is worse than implausible. So, only the second option remains and it makes sense that Plantinga should try to establish the incoherence of methodological naturalism.

The trouble is that the arguments deployed for this purpose make little sense. Plantinga offers two main arguments. The first begins with the observation that there are unique events postulated by science, for instance, the Big Bang. Now, methodological naturalism assumes that all events must be governed by laws, which, at the very least, must consist of observed regularities of nature. Therefore, Plantinga argues, unique events cannot be accounted for by a science that relies on methodo-logical naturalism. But why rely on the Big Bang? Every event in the universe is unique (unless we allow time travel). The fallacy lies in the assumption that such uniqueness presents any problem for governance by natural law: it is the laws of nature, referring to repeatable events, along with specified conditions of the universe at some given time, that predict the particular concatenation of circumstances that constitute the Big Bang, or any other event, whether it be in the past or the future.[20] Unique events pose no problem for naturalistic science.

Plantinga has other variations of this argument all designed to show that laws of nature should not be regarded as central to science. These include an argument that relies on the claim that there are no laws of nature because philosophers of science dispute the details of what consti-tutes such a law. The response is trivial and obvious: methodological naturalism asks that we deploy exactly the type of reasoning and infer-ence procedures we do every day when we do science. It is irrelevant whether we call these laws, regularities, or rules. The point is that we do not go beyond what is accessible to our experience and scientific reason when we try to explain features of the world.

Arguments of this type are unsophisticated enough about the nature of science and its epistemology that they do not merit serious attention.

But Plantinga has another apparently more sophisticated argument up his sleeve which is particularly important in our context because it dwells on evolution.[21] The essence of this argument consists of the following: naturalists are committed to the belief that our cognitive faculties arose because of evolution by natural selection. But the theory of natural selection, according to Plantinga, says that our cognitive faculties are not reliable. Therefore, since we arrived at the theory of natural selection through our cognitive facilities, it is not reliable. We should, therefore, abandon it – naturalism is self-defeating.[22] The trouble is that every premise in this argument is flawed.[23]

Naturalism, as we have construed it here, can deploy all the resources of the empirical sciences.[24] If it turns out that natural selection does not permit the evolution of sufficiently reliable cognitive faculties, and we have evidence to suggest that our cognitive faculties are so reliable, as naturalists we will simply look for other models of the emergence of our cognitive faculties. We will begin to study other biological mechanisms of evolutionary change, as well as social and cultural mechanisms. In fact, contrary to the more enthusiastic claims of human sociobiologists and Evolutionary Psychologists, there is ample reason to suspect that the evolution of our cognitive faculties requires more than natural selection among individuals competing with each other. But how unreliable does natural selection make our cognitive faculties? All Plantinga can do is point out, as Darwin did, that there are possible evolutionary scenarios in which unreliable features would be selected: for instance, natural selection cannot distinguish between adaptive behaviors produced by true beliefs and adaptive behaviors produced by false beliefs. (Ultimately, this observation is the lynchpin of Plantinga's argument.) But how likely is this? More importantly, how likely is it that, *typically*, false beliefs – and let us think of beliefs as internal representations of the world in the animal minds of our ancestors – would lead to adaptive behaviors? (Typicality is required because our cognitive faculties, and not merely some particular behaviors, are supposed to be unreliable.)

If we are careful to stick to what we actually know about human evolutionary history, at present we know very little about our cognitive evolution. Nevertheless, it seems odd to assume that we know that our cognitive faculties are unreliable if they are produced by natural selection. But that is what Plantinga's argument requires. But suppose, for the sake of argument, we concede the point to Plantinga. What does it show? Merely that, as with the rest of science, we must be modest about how much certainty we can claim about evolutionary theory. It does not follow from Plantinga's argument that, if our cognitive faculties are unreliable, all, or even the vast majority, of our beliefs must be incorrect. In particular, it does not follow that the theory of natural selection must be incorrect – purely logically, there is no paradox here. (As Fitelson and Sober have put it: "One lesson that should be extracted is a certain humility – an admission of fallibility."[25]) This argument is hardly a devastating objection to methodological naturalism.

There is yet another response to Plantinga, though one he will probably not appreciate. In contrast to the theory of natural selection, according to Plantinga, traditional theism confers a high degree of reliability on our cognitive processes. Now suppose that an evolutionary theorist believes, as is very likely, that these cognitive processes, along with the evidence discussed in earlier chapters, confer a high probability to evolutionary theory. Then, we should conclude that traditional theism confers a high probability to the truth of evolutionary theory. Now suppose, with Plantinga, that evolutionary theory (and, ipso facto, naturalism) denies theism. We have a self-defeating argument, now going against theism. The point is that neither of these arguments shows anything. Plantinga's attacks on methodological naturalism are at best innocuous or, more accurately, incoherent.

Where are we left? Not with any plausible critique of methodological naturalism within science. This is not surprising: even most theologians would probably not expect otherwise. Most critics of ID creationism would probably stop here, and political prudence would also dictate such a course, so as to avoid disagreements that are not necessary to defend science against creationism. But let us go further in the next section with the explicit proviso that it delves into an issue that is not necessary to develop and defend the other arguments of this book.

Metaphysical Naturalism

Let us finally turn to the much more troubling – and interesting – issue of metaphysical naturalism. The usual line of argument endorsed by most critics of ID and other forms of creationism is that science in general, and evolutionary biology in particular, makes no commitment to metaphysical naturalism. Metaphysical naturalism is typically construed as Ruse describes it (see above): as an ontological thesis, stated with a priori certainty, about the absolute non-existence of entities other than those posited by our current scientific theories. If this is what metaphysical naturalism is, then it is beyond what science can tell us. Evolutionary biology hardly needs any such assumption. In this sense, at least, the usual line of argument is correct. But there is no reason why naturalists should accept such a view of metaphysics, unless, of course, the ultimate purpose is to reject the very possibility of metaphysics. Such a rejection was a rather common desire among twentieth-century philosophers, though, as usual, with many antecedents in the empiricist tradition, most notably, Hume.

But this is not the only view of metaphysical commitment. It is, for instance, not the view of metaphysics adopted in Chapter 1 where metaphysics was taken to consist of a set of foundational assumptions supposed to be respected by all admissible scientific theories. Once we view metaphysics in this way, as Pierre Duhem – a practicing Catholic and superb philosopher of science – pointed out a century ago, science is never innocent of metaphysics.[26] This, presumably, is the kernel of truth in Johnson's claim that methodological naturalism necessarily collapses into metaphysical naturalism. Descartes, Huygens, and Leibniz assumed the mechanical philosophy as they pondered on the motion of planets. Newton, at least in practice, advocated more tolerance about permissible explanations, but put a much greater weight than Descartes on quantitative agreement between the predictions of a theory and the phenomena to be explained. (Newton, in this sense, was a positivist.) Duhem correctly pointed out that we will partly evaluate every theory, and thus, every explanation relying on that theory, on the basis of its metaphysical presuppositions. Huygens and Leibniz were justifiably skeptical of Newton's law of universal gravitation: it violated the mechanical philosophy's proscription of action-at-a-distance.

When we do evolutionary biology, we assume the metaphysics of that theory: the type of mechanisms it admits, that is, "blind" material interactions with no directionality built into them (recall the discussion of Chapter 4). We accept the role of chance and we accept the lawlike operation of natural selection and all principles of the physical science. When one such "blind" mechanism fails, we seek another that is equally "blind." This is all that metaphysical naturalism amounts to, no more and no less. Suppose, contrary to fact but for the sake of argument, that ID creationists had produced decent explanations of some phenomenon not well explained by evolutionary theory. Presumably such an explanation would invoke some directional or "intelligent" mechanism. Assume that these mechanisms did not obey natural laws (whatever that might mean). Even then we would, with some justice, be skeptical of such explanations because it would have violated metaphysical naturalism. Nevertheless, and this is where philosophical modesty and open-mindedness come to the front, naturalism demands that even metaphysical principles be subject to revision in the light of experience. In Chapter 1 we saw how that could happen.

The four examples of major scientific developments with which we started in Chapter 1 all underscore the value of metaphysical conservatism: as scientists, we do not trade our metaphysical principles in the market every day. Nevertheless, they also underscore that a naturalistic attitude towards metaphysics accepts the possibility of metaphysical revision. But such revision is not taken lightly. Let us return to evolutionary biology, and to the theory of natural selection. What Darwin and Wallace showed (recall the discussion of Chapter 3) was that the adaptedness of living organisms, that is, the appearance of design in nature, can be explained by appeal to natural selection acting on heritable individual variation. This move removed the necessity of any assumption of purpose or teleology in nature, let alone the operation of a sentient intelligent being. As emphasized in Chapter 3, it forced an unprecedented metaphysical revision.

Previous chapters have dealt fully with objections raised by ID creationists to the Darwin–Wallace solution to the problem of design. They have also dealt with the alleged lacunae of evolutionary theory. It should, by now, be uncontroversial that ID creationism's "no conceptual resources" claim about standard evolutionary theory cannot be sustained (recall Chapters 5 and 7). Even the most charitable account of ID creationism's arguments can point to no more than several partially solved biochemical and other problems that the theory of natural selection faces and none, yet, that bring into question the metaphysics of "blind" material interaction (recall Chapter 6). The contrast with the examples of metaphysical change in Chapter 1 could hardly be greater. We have no analog of action-at-a-distance, of the anomalous motion of mercury, or quantum jumps in the spectrum of light. We do not even have an analog of a new type of explanation for the apparent design of organisms. So far we have been provided with no reason to question, let alone abandon, metaphysical naturalism.

Philip Johnson will have to live with that. But he should take consolation from the fact that metaphysical naturalism, so construed, like its methodological counterpart, says nothing about the existence of God, the Devil, or angels, so long as they do not interfere with the more important scientific work of the laboratory.

10

Conclusions

There are some who doubt both the theory of evolution and naturalism. A recent book, *Uncommon Dissent*, edited by Dembski, records their increasingly strident cacophony.[1] But almost any far-reaching theory engenders both credible and not credible dissent. The former tends to dissipate if the theory satisfies the only unavoidable criterion of scientific acceptability: empirical success. The latter does not always disappear. Take general relativity, among the best established of physical theories and one, as we noted in Chapter 1, that significantly altered our metaphysical ideas about space, time, and matter. Recall that one important reason general relativity came to be accepted was the success of the 1919 eclipse expeditions in confirming the bending of light by the Sun's mass. Even general relativity continues to have its skeptics. Ian McCausland, an enthusiast of some now justly forgotten alternative theory of Paul Gerber, writes: "the confident announcement of the decisive confirmation of Einstein's general theory in November 1919 was not a triumph of science, as it is often portrayed, but one of the most unfortunate events of twentieth-century science."[2] According to McCausland, the acceptance of relativity closed people's minds, preventing other theories from being heard. The rhetoric is identical to that of ID creationists except that their target is the theory of evolution.

The real question is, what should we make of such claims? There is no question that they are legally protected. Beyond that, trying to censor them in the context of academic research would almost certainly do more harm than good besides being offensive to those of us who hold individual liberty as among our most cherished values. But, few scientists bother with dissent of as low credibility as McCausland's, and ID is no different in this respect. Typically such dissent makes no discernible difference to the practice of science or everyday life. This is why, until quite recently, few biologists have paid much attention to ID. What has changed is the political context of ID, especially in the United States, as ID creationists increasingly challenge the teaching of evolution in high schools (recall the examples mentioned in the Preface). As many commentators have documented, the ID movement is superbly funded,[3] which increases its political effectiveness beyond even what any conservative religious Christian movement would automatically have in the contemporary United States.

It has become a matter of social responsibility for biologists, who are the experts in the field, to ensure that correct science is taught to the next generation. Increasingly biologists are recognizing this fact, as seen by their increasing willingness to confront creationists, for instance, before State Boards of Education.[4] Similarly, since ID creationists routinely attempt to manipulate what should count as "science" (recall the discussion of the last chapter), philosophers of science also have the responsibility to respond to them publicly, and many have joined the fray.[5]

We will turn to the question of school curricula below and consider both whether ID should be taught and whether, at least, the ID creationists' criticisms of evolutionary biology should find a place in the curricula. But before that, let us dispose of the following two questions: (i) whether evolutionary biologists (or as the ID creationists like, inaccurately, to call us, "Darwinists") do not give critics of orthodoxy a fair hearing; and (ii) does ID constitute science? The answer to the first question will influence what we decide about the inclusion of the ID creationists' criticisms in biology curricula. An answer to the second is obviously important in determining the role of ID in science curricula.

Critiques of Evolutionary Theory

As noted in Chapter 6, ID creationists such as Behe routinely claim that there is a close-minded "Darwinian" scientific community that does not give critics of evolutionary theory a fair hearing.[6] When, in 1996, David Berlinski claimed (in an article in *Commentary* magazine entitled "The Deniable Darwin"[7]) that the scientific establishment stifled dissent about the status of evolution, readers enthusiastically endorsed his claim. But the claim is demonstrably false.[8] The attention bestowed by biologists on *Darwin's Black Box* is itself ample evidence against any such claim. Moreover, all available historical evidence goes against this claim: critiques of evolutionary theory, when they have any scientific merit, have been treated with full seriousness throughout the history of biology. Restricting attention to the twentieth century (because recent history is more relevant to our contemporary concerns than earlier periods), consider just four episodes:

(i)   in 1932 J. B. S. Haldane tried to synthesize all that was known about evolution in the light of the new population genetics of the 1920s in his seminal *Causes of Evolution*, an episode that has already been discussed in Chapter 4. By this point, there was hardly any reasonable doubt that natural selection acting on random (blind) variation suffices to explain known patterns of evolutionary change. But, Haldane realized that there was still a jump from micro-evolution, as modeled by population genetics, to macroevolution. So he explicitly identified and discussed all five evolutionary causes that had historically been suggested "for the deeper transformations of the geological record":[9] (a) basically random inheritable variation; (b) environmentally induced inheritable variation; (c) variation due to "internal causes" or orthogenesis; (d) variation due to hybridization; and (e) selection. Even Darwin had coupled selection with both (a) and (b) – recall the discussion of Chapter 2. But, experimental evidence had largely ruled out (b), that is, the inheritance of acquired characters or neo-Lamarckism. Even so, reports of the inheritance of acquired characteristics continued to be seriously investigated by biologists well into the late 1930s. Haldane took great pains to reinterpret phenomena that seemed to support orthogenesis in the light of the new population genetics. Only after such an examination was it clear that standard models of population genetics based on random mutation and natural selection sufficed as an explanation of all of organic evolution. There is no sign of a close-minded "Darwinist" community refusing to tolerate internal dissent or alternatives to the orthodoxy;

(ii) Kimura's neutral theory of evolution at the molecular level has been mentioned several times in this book (for instance, in Chapters 4 and 7). When it was first proposed in the 1960s, several of its best-known proponents, including King and Jukes,[10] explicitly called it "non-Darwinian" evolution. The neutral theory clearly challenged the consensus Haldane presented in 1932, and many others had since popularized,[11] because it denied the ubiquitous operation of natural selection. But it was neither ignored nor rejected without careful examination. Rather, it became the subject of an intense, and occasionally acrimonious, debate which has not entirely subsided to this day.[12] What was important was that it made definite quantitative predictions of data and its neo-Darwinian critics systematically confronted it with such data, just as good science demands. The result, as we saw in Chapter 4, was that the fully neutral theory was not viable: it did not fit the data. Neutralists then modified it to the nearly neutral theory and the debate between them and selectionists continues today. From some perspectives, there is a stalemate which can only be resolved with the type of data that are not yet available.[13] Most evolutionary biologists today probably prefer the selectionist models although it is also clear that neutral models are adequate for many aspects of molecular evolution, so much so that neutralist assumptions are often used to reconstruct evolutionary history from molecular data.[14] The salient point in the present context is that evolutionary biologists since the late 1960s have been perfectly willing to engage critics of the orthodoxy and, most notably, accept modifications of that orthodoxy when they are backed by definite claims with clear empirical consequences that are confirmed by the data;

(iii)   in Chapter 4 we discussed how, in the 1970s, Gould and Eldredge also went against the prevailing orthodoxy that evolution consisted of small, incremental changes by arguing for the punctuated equilibrium theory of evolution. According to them, the fossil record showed short periods of rapid evolutionary change followed by long periods of stasis. They even suggested that macroevolution involves processes beyond those considered in population genetics. There was substantial controversy over the punctuated equilibrium theory for several decades. For most biologists, the controversy ended when population geneticists showed that patterns of long macroevolutionary stasis and rapid change can easily be generated by standard models of population genetics.[15] Whether or not this resolution is correct – and if not, going by the history of science, the consensus will turn against it – the relevant point here is that, once again, there is no sign of close-minded resistance on the part of allegedly beleaguered "Darwinists";

(iv) turning to an even more recent episode, in the late 1990s, John Cairns and several colleagues suggested that mutations in bacteria were not always blind.[16] Rather, they were "directed" or "adaptive," more likely to occur in environments in which they were beneficial to the organism (that is, they increased fitness). Several other reports supported Cairns.[17] Heated controversy over these reports raged for over a decade mainly because they seemed to challenge the basic neo-Darwinian framework of random mutation and natural selection. Since such mutations appeared to be restricted to microbes, the ultimate significance of this challenge to the orthodoxy was far from clear. Nevertheless, neo-Darwinian skeptics were vehement in their criticism, repeating and extending the original experiments.[18] Once again, this is characteristic of good science. Some fifteen years after the original report, it is clear that some of the more sensational claims of adaptive mutation were based on faulty experimentation or interpretation.[19] By and large, the conservative neo-Darwinian defenders of the orthodoxy were correct, as conservatives usually are in the history of science. Nevertheless, the experimental and theoretical work spawned by the original claims made positive contributions. At the experimental level, in particular, it led to a widespread recognition that mutations in bacteria are not only due to copying errors during cell division. They also occur during the "stationary" phase when cells are not dividing, though these mutations only persist in the population if the cell divides and thus preserves it. At the theoretical level, we now have better techniques for estimating mutation rates. Once again, the salient point is that evolutionary biologists were willing to engage critics of the orthodoxy scientifically as long as they made definite claims subject to experimental tests.

It is not even surprising that challenges to orthodoxy appear within science and are typically seriously, though skeptically, examined. Probably no science, at any stage, has been entirely without anomaly. Consequently, changes from prevailing views, minor or major, are inevitable to maintain the empirical adequacy of a science. Theoretical scientists make their reputation by making such changes, and the more radical a change (provided, of course, it is correct), the greater the impact it is likely to have on that reputation and attendant benefits. If there were a new idea that has a slight chance of being correct and seriously challenges some fundamental tenet of evolutionary theory, there would be a cottage industry of biologists seriously pursuing that idea, at least part of the time, just as there is a cottage industry of theoretical physicists pursuing alternatives to quantum mechanics (see below). (This is exactly what happened with the neutral theory and during the controversy over directed mutations in bacteria.) Should any such biologist succeed in establishing such an idea, we would have our next Darwin or Mendel. It should be clear that this would provide ample motivation for any aspiring biologist. Unfortunately ID does not produce even a semblance of such an idea – this, along with the fact that it is largely vacuous (see the next section), rather than any bias on the part of biologists, is why almost all scientists find it scientifically irrelevant.

Is ID Science?

Philosophers of science have perhaps spilt an inordinate amount of ink trying to answer this question, usually in the negative. Typically the strategy has been to use some criterion that is supposed to distinguish science from non-science definitively (that is, in all cases), such as Popper's flawed criterion of falsifiability[20] or Hempel's more respectable criterion of testability, and argue that ID creationism fails to satisfy it. ID creationism does fail such tests, as will also be emphasized below. But this way of justifying a rejection of ID creationism as science may prove to be too glib for two related reasons:

(i)   most philosophers of science have long abandoned a sharp line of demarcation between science and non-science.[21] There is a distinction – no one would confuse Heidegger's *Being and Time* or Kripke's *Naming and Necessity* with a paper by Haldane – , just as there is a distinction between night and day. But it is not trivial, if at all possible, to adjudicate the boundary so clearly that entities near it are neatly put into one category or the other. The analogy with night and day is again appropriate. Speculative theories, especially at the early stages of their development, may well not satisfy criteria such as testability. Moreover, what is at stake is whether some claim is testable *in principle*, not merely in practice. Thus an evolutionary model predicting speciation in some population in a thousand years is testable in principle though not in practice. But there are situations where even the distinction between in principle and in practice claims is unclear. Suppose that, to test some physical theory, we require a cube of curium-247 with a mass of 10 kg. In principle there seems to be no problem, but physical law dictates that we can never assemble such a cube: curium-247 has a critical mass of 7 kg after which it blows up. Was our claim testable? The answer is far from clear; and

(ii) restricting attention to testability as the relevant criterion of demarcation, claims that appear not to be testable now may eventually be transformed into testable ones by the development of science. Our deepest physical theories today often hypothesize interactions at energies so high that we are sometimes at a loss to imagine how they can be testable in the laboratory. But the next generation may think very differently. Moreover, claims that are apparently untestable because they contain vague concepts may be made testable by operationalizing the concepts: in ecology, for instance, during the past fifty years, concepts such as complexity, diversity, and stability have been operationalized in a variety of ways, making claims about them testable. It is possible that some future intellectually honest version of ID will have an adequately operationalized concept of design.

We should, therefore, not base our objections to ID creationism as science entirely on a putative demarcation criterion between science and non-science which we present as definitive. It may not be fully intellectually respectable and thus open to credible objection from ID creationists.

At present the problem with ID runs much deeper than mere testability. The most important point, which was also noted at the end of Chapter 1, is that there is no positive account of design in the entire ID corpus – we are never told what design is. In *The Design Inference*, as part of the explanatory filter, Dembski simply defines it as the complement of regularity and chance. But no argument shows that this complement is non-empty (recall the discussion at the end of Chapter 3). Several years later, in *No Free Lunch*, the explanatory filter is updated and we are told to envision a process:

(1) A designer conceives a purpose. (2) To accomplish that purpose, the designer forms a plan. (3) To execute the plan, the designer specifies building materials and assembly instructions. (4) Finally, the designer or some surrogate applies the assembly instructions to the building materials.[22]

We still do not know what design is. (All we were ever told is that designed systems conform to specification – but, as Chapters 3 and 8 show, Dembski's concept of specification remains incoherent.) Consequently we have no method to investigate possible properties of designed systems. We are not even in a stage to determine whether claims involving design are testable. We do not know what they are with sufficient precision. Even the only two papers of "ID science" that have been published, at least allegedly after peer review, are of no help. The first, and the nature of its review, was already discussed in Chapter 7.[23] The second is a paper recently published by Jonathan Wells in the fringe journal, *Rivista di Biologia*.[24] Wells presents a hypothetical mechanism for the formation of cancer by malfunction of centrioles, which he compares to turbines, in animal cells. There is nothing special about that: this is typically how molecular biology proceeds. But where does design come in? Wells asks: "What if centrioles really are tiny turbines?" and proceeds to answer, "This is much easier to conceive if we adopt a holistic rather than reductionistic approach, and if we regard centrioles as designed structures rather than accidental by-products of neo-Darwinian evolution."[25] This is the only occurrence of "design" in the paper, and there is no further explanation. If this is what we get from a hypothesis of design, it is precious little after the tons of verbiage from its proponents. (Notice, also, Wells' disingenuous rhetorical strategy: he contrasts "design" with "accidental by-product" and not the legitimate "accidentally produced and *selected*" which is what a biologist would say. No biologist would claim that a complex structure is an accidental by-product.)

In other words, claims of "Intelligent Design" are so far from science that we cannot even have meaningful discussion of whether claims from ID creationism constitute science *no matter how we demarcate the boundary between science and non-science*. All that ID creationists have offered us is negative argumentation, in particular, the Central Argument of Intelligent Design that we examined in the first seven chapters of this book. It provides no credible objection to evolutionary theory. However, if we are inordinately charitable, we can extract from this negative argumentation one claim that *may* have some chance of being confronted with data: this is the claim that living systems exhibit more than a certain specified quantity of information and no system with such a quantity of information can be formed by natural causes. Two steps must be taken to make this claim amenable to experimentation: (i) the exact quantity must be specified, which is probably not implausible;[26] and (ii) a precise method must be given to determine what reference class must be used to compute all the relevant probabilities and, therefore, information content of such systems. This method must be such that it constitutes a protocol that requires no further disambiguation in all empirical cases. Until ID creationists produce these two minimal steps, any further discussion of whether ID creationism constitutes science is useless.

There is an even deeper reason to reject any attempt of ID creationism to masquerade as science. ID creationism includes a claim that the search for extra-natural explanations is part of the project. Science rejects that: naturalism is central to the pursuit of science. Recall that natural explanations require only that events conform to laws that can be discovered using empirical techniques (experiment and observation) and the standard ratiocinative methods (ordinary logic and mathematics) that science uses. This has been central to what has been accepted as the scientific method since the seventeenth century: to accept this aspect of scientific method requires no endorsement of even the mitigated version of metaphysical naturalism defended in Chapter 9. All that is required is methodological naturalism.

Now, it is legitimate to argue that science *may* change to embrace strategies beyond methodological naturalism but that will require changes as drastic as the conceptual revolutions discussed in Chapter 1: the acceptance of Newton's gravitational law with action-at-a-distance, Einstein's general relativity, quantum mechanics, or the theory of evolution. In each case, detailed agreement between the new theory and massive amounts of data forced a change of foundations. Meanwhile, the ID creationists have not come up with anything except two papers simply asserting design (Meyer on the Cambrian[27] and Wells on the centriole[28]). It is not exactly impressive. But, worst of all, these other conceptual revolutions still accepted naturalism: the laws embodying the new metaphysics were discovered using standard scientific methods. ID demands so much more, and offers nothing beyond vacuous objections to evolutionary theory in return.

Back to the Classroom

This book was not written because of some fascination with the intellectual merit of ID creationism – it has none. Rather it was written in response to the attempts, described in the Preface, to dilute the teaching of evolutionary biology in schools and to replace it with ID. We will deal with the second issue first. Should ID be taught? Four issues should be distinguished: (i) should ID be taught in public schools?; (ii) should ID be taught in private schools; and for each of these, (iii) should ID be taught in science classes?; and (iv) should ID be taught in other classes, for instance, in religion or philosophy classes? Obviously, the answer to (i) depends on the legal context of a school. With respect to this question, the discussion here will be restricted to the contemporary context of the United States. However, the arguments here will be philosophical, rather than legal.[29]

Let us consider non-science classes first. In the context of the United States, whether or not ID should be taught in public schools depends on whether ID should be viewed as science, religious doctrine, or, possibly, something entirely different. We will ignore the last possibility since there are no such proposals on the table though it is conceivable that someone could suggest that ID represents some new form of epistemology. Even then, epistemology is not part of the normal high school curriculum. Now the discussion of the last section shows that ID is yet to resemble anything like science. But is it religious doctrine? ID creationists insist it is not but their claims are not credible, as Judge Jones ruled in the Dover case in December 2005.[30] They also do not help their case by being remarkably inconsistent, depending on their intended audience: even Dembski calls ID the "bridge between science and theology."[31] In non-science classes, the relevant question now becomes whether teaching ID amounts to an endorsement of a religious doctrine. It need not, for instance, if it is taught as one view in a course devoted to comparative religions. But those are the only contexts in which it belongs. It is not a purpose of this book to examine whether or not ID is interesting and important enough to be included in curricula even in such contexts.

The situation is quite different for non-science classes in private schools, in particular, religious schools around the world in which religious instruction is accepted as part of the curriculum. Under these circumstances, there is no principled way in which ID can be excluded. If the Catholic Church can teach its doctrines in its schools, including such questionable ones as the non-practice of contraception, advocating ID hardly provides reason for complaint.

Turning to science classes, it should not matter whether a school is public or private: science classes should include only science in their curricula. Given what was said in the last section, ID does not belong in such curricula. But suppose we are charitable and accept that, very improbably, ID can eventually become science bereft of religious presuppositions. This makes ID *at present* speculations at the frontier of science. Should it be taught in science classes in *high schools*? If we use the same standards for biology classes as the ones we use for the other sciences, there is no question that ID should not be mentioned in the curriculum.

An important analogy should drive this point home. From Einstein onwards, a significant minority of unquestionably competent physicists have doubted the full validity of quantum mechanics on both philosophical and physical grounds.[32] Many of us believe that quantum mechanics will eventually be replaced by a more fundamental "stochastic" theory.[33] (There are others who believe that quantum mechanics must be modified in other ways.) But all of us admit that these are speculative claims and never suggest that they should enter school curricula. We all admit and take as a constraint to our speculations that standard quantum mechanics provides an overwhelmingly successful basic framework for physics, just as contemporary evolutionary biology does for biology. Now, while quantum mechanics is not usually taught in high schools, the chemistry that is taught depends on the correctness of quantum mechanics. It would be inappropriate to introduce skepticism about quantum mechanics and, indirectly, about chemistry. The same standard should be applied to ID. These arguments thus reject all attempts to include ID as part of state standards for science in the United States. Note that this argument does not depend on an ability to distinguish science from non-science.

Turning to the other issue raised at the beginning of this section, should the teaching of evolution be diluted in our biology classes? Obviously not, if we want our science standards to be high. The extent to which each topic should be covered in a curriculum is a valid (and common) topic for educational debate. But, there is no empirical evidence yet presented anywhere that suggests that too much evolutionary biology is being taught in schools at the expense of other equally or more important topics. If this is what ID creationists want to claim, it is incumbent upon them to set acceptable criteria to decide on the importance of various topics in the curricula and collect the data to support this claim.

But should criticisms of evolutionary theory be part of the curricula in school science classrooms? Science thrives on criticism. Without criticism from peers it is hard to imagine how scientific progress can take place. Moreover, controversies within science are commonplace and often exciting for students, perhaps inspiring them to enter research. Nevertheless, there is a difference between relevant criticism, based on empirical or conceptual problems recognized by the entire community as genuine, and vacuous criticism, sometimes originating from an extra-scientific agenda. Similarly, there is a difference between genuine controversy which is widely debated within a discipline by its practitioners (as in the case of the biological controversies discussed earlier in this chapter), and artificial controversy generated simply by claiming that there is a controversy.

It is instructive here to quote from a statement signed by a large number of biologists: while "there are legitimate debates about the patterns and processes of evolution, there is no serious scientific doubt that evolution occurred or that natural selection is a major mechanism in its occurrence."[34] Moreover, as the full statement makes clear, the basic framework for evolutionary theory (in the terminology from Chapter 4), is not in legitimate debate. Many of the debates alluded to in this statement have been discussed in this book, in Chapters 2, 4, and earlier in this chapter. If high school curricula include mention of the neutralism–selectionism debate, or the promise of the new evolutionary developmental biology, and the challenges posed by the structure of the genome, and the relevant teachers are conversant enough with contemporary biology to discuss these topics accurately, so much the better. It would be a major achievement, at least in the United States, if high school science instruction achieved such a level. However, in contrast, as this book shows, the criticisms leveled against evolutionary biology by ID creationists are vacuous and driven by their theological agenda. Moreover, the "controversy" within biology allegedly over evolution versus ID creationism is an artificial controversy generated by the claim that evolution is controversial. To the extent that this book helps resolve that artificial controversy, or at least remove it from debates about science education, it will have served its purpose.

Notes

Preface

1 See the book by Mooney (2005).

2 See http://www.cnn.com/2005/POLITICS/08/02/bush.education.ap/; accessed November 14, 2005.

3 For details on the story in Dover, PA, see the website maintained by the National Center for Science Education (http://www2.ncseweb.org/wp/; accessed December 12, 2005).

4 For details, see the website maintained by the National Center for Science Education (http://www.ncseweb.org/pressroom.asp?state=KS; accessed December 12, 2005).

5 For details, see the website maintained by the National Center for Science Education (http://www.ncseweb.org/pressroom.asp?state=CA; accessed December 12, 2005).

6 For details, see the website maintained by the National Center for Science Education (http://www.ncseweb.org/pressroom.asp?state=OH; accessed December 12, 2005).

7 For details, see the website maintained by the National Center for Science Education (http://www.ncseweb.org/pressroom.asp?state=OK; accessed December 12, 2005).

8 The last such assault was in the 1980s, also with attempts to introduce creationism into high school curricula. Those efforts were largely abandoned after a definitive verdict in the court case, *McLean v Arkansas*, against teaching creationism (Beckwith 2003).

9 Thus, they apparently believe, science and not only culture needs renewal in accordance with their religious credo.

10 For details and documentation, see Forrest and Gross (2004). The Discovery Institute, though not the Center for Science and Religion directly, is partly funded by a large grant from the Bill and Melinda Gates Foundation (see the Wikipedia entry: http://en.wikipedia.org/wiki/Discovery_Institute; accessed December 15, 2005).

11 See Pincock (2005).

12 Pincock (2005).

13 For details, see the website maintained by the National Center for Science Education (http://www.ncseweb.org/pressroom.asp?state=XX; accessed December 12, 2005).

14 For details, see the report in the *Catholic New Agency* (http://www.catholicnewsagency.com/new.php?n=4340; accessed December 14, 2005).

15 See the *Baltimore Sun* report (http://www.baltimoresun.com/news/nationworld/bal-te.worldlede19nov19,1,1998667.story?coll=bal-nationworld-headlines; accessed December 14, 2005).

16 See the report in the *Austin American-Statesman*, 6 January 2006 (http://www.statesman.com/news/content/news/stories/local/01/6perry.html; accessed January 6, 2006).

17 For details, see the website maintained by the National Center for Science Education (http://www.ncseweb.org/pressroom.asp?state=AK; accessed December 12, 2005).

18 For details, see the website maintained by the National Center for Science Education (http://www.ncseweb.org/pressroom.asp?state=UT; accessed December 12, 2005).

19 For details, see the website maintained by the National Center for Science Education (http://www.ncseweb.org/pressroom.asp?state=GA; accessed June 21, 2006).

20 Holden (2006a).

21 Mervis (2006). The elegant decision can be found at http://www.pamd.uscourts.gov/kitzmiller/kitzmiller_342.pdf (accessed June 21, 2006).

22 Holden (2006b).

23 For details, see the website maintained by the National Center for Science Education (http://www.ncseweb.org/pressroom.asp?state=AL; accessed December 12, 2005).

24 These are tracked by the National Center for Science Education (http://www.ncseweb.org/pressroom.asp?branch=statement; accessed December 12, 2005).

25 Gross et al. (2005), p. 25.

26 See, for instance, Johnson (1995).

27 See, for instance, Pennock (1999), Forrest and Gross (2004), and Scott (2004).

28 For more on this controversy, see Forrest (2001), Forrest and Gross (2004), and Menuge (2004).

Chapter 1

1 See Kitcher (2001) and Shanks (2004, "Introduction"). Kitcher (1982) and Ruse (1982) provide comprehensive critiques of old-fashioned Creationism. For a history, see Numbers (1992). Other useful criticisms of old-fashioned Creationism include Peacocke (1979), Newell (1982), Futuyma (1983), Montagu (1983), Young (1985), Strahler (1987), Berra (1990), and Eldredge (2000).

2 See Wilson and Wilson (2001), Gish (1992), and Woodmorappe (1996).

3 This is what Kitcher (2001) calls "born-again" creationism.

4 Philip Johnson may provide an exception to this moderating trend (see below).

5   See Mayr (1982), p. 510.

6   For details on this example, see Grant and Grant (1989).

7   On "deep time," see Gee (2001).

8   Johnson, Dembski, Behe, and others of their ilk do not endorse the "creationist" label because of its association with the unreformed past. But they rely on supernatural origins of biological features – "creationism" describes their position whether or not they endorse the term. As Judge Jones ruled in the 2005 Dover creationism case, their denials are not credible (see http://www.pamd.uscourts.gov/kitzmiller/ kitzmiller_342.pdf; accessed December 25, 2005).

9   See, for example, Perakh (2004b) for a logical analysis of ID's claims, and Shanks (2004) for a good scientific treatment. This book owes a lot to Perakh's work. Shanks provides some nineteenth-century historical background, though only with respect to Darwin. He also provides a much more detailed critique than what is attempted here (in Chapter 8) of the fine-tuning argument from physics which is supposed to show the presence of ID in the universe.

10 Miller (1999a).

11 Dobzhansky (1973).

12 For a history of the caloric theory, see Fox (1971).

13 For a history, see Eiseley (1958).

14 See Thomas and Garner (1998); the issue is further discussed in Chapter 6.

15 See Crompton and Jenkins (1973).

16 See Mayr (2001), Chapter 2. The discussion in the text draws heavily on that source.

17 Kirschner and Gerhart (2005), p. 29.

18 See Mayr (2001, pp. 62ff.) for a more detailed discussion of such phyletic series.

19 However, a well-differentiated Colombian subspecies is sometimes regarded as a separate species, M. magnirostris.

20 See Grant and Grant (1989), a record of a spectacular confirmation of the power of natural selection in the wild.

21 See Wallace (1876). On the basis of observed faunal distributions and the theory of natural selection Wallace divided Earth into the six biogeographical zones which we still accept today.

22 See Pourciau (2001).

23 For a history, see Roseveare (1982).

24 For historical detail, see Stachel (1995).

25 See Schrödinger (1944). The chemical mechanisms by which the stability of genes is maintained (essentially, the DNA repair mechanisms) do not require quantum mechanical principles except in the trivial sense that all chemical interactions are ultimately governed by quantum mechanics.

26 The claim that we must give up determinism is not altogether philosophically uncontroversial – see, for instance, Suppes (1993). However, most philosophers and physicists would accept the claim that quantum mechanics forces us to abandon determinism at least in the form it is interpreted in the text.

27 Ayala (1994), p. 4.

28 The argument here assumes that naturalism and science may not admit teleology. Somewhat strangely, ID creationists seem to accept this claim for science when they argue that embracing ID requires abandoning the customary principles of science.

(See, in particular, the position they defended in the Dover creationism trial [see http://www.pamd.uscourts.gov/kitzmiller/kitzmiller_342.pdf; accessed December 25, 2005).

29 Chapter 8 will examine some alleged objections from cosmology.

30 The case of natural selection also supports these principles, as should be evident from the discussion in the text.

31 This means that the disputants must all agree on the relevance of the evidence.

32 See Kuhn (1962) and Lakatos (1970).

33 See Johnson (1990) who criticizes scientists because they "impose a rule of procedure that disqualifies purely negative argument, so that a theory which obtains some very modest degree of evidential support can become immune to disproof until and unless it becomes supplanted by a better . . . theory." Whatever rhetorical force this "argument" has comes from the claim that the accepted theory has "some very modest degree of evidential support." In every one of our examples such modesty is strikingly lacking. Consequently, contrary to Johnson, rejecting purely negative argument is in no way "arbitrary." Rather, rooted as it is in the history of great science, it is a sound methodological dictum. See also Sober (2002).

34 See, for instance, Johnson's (1990, 1995) account of why biologists endorse naturalism.

35 Indeed, if Johnson's (1990) "purely negative arguments" have any value, it is only when they are used to bolster an inconsistency objection of this sort.

36 See Einstein et al. (1935).

37 See Bell (1964).

38 For more on this issue, see d'Espagnat (1976).

39 See, for instance, Dembski (1999) which is characteristically vague and says little more than that ID can be interpreted as a theory about information.

40 See, for instance, Dembski (2002); for a response, see Chapters 5 and 7.

Chapter 2

1 When, exactly, Darwin received the package – June 3–4 or 18 – is a matter of controversy. Those who believe that Wallace's input was critical to Darwin's completion of the argument for evolution by natural selection prefer the earlier date. Those who believe that Darwin had long developed but not published that argument prefer the latter; see Sarkar (1998b) and Shermer (2002) – among many other sources – for variant interpretations.

2 Wallace's brilliant travelogue from this trip was published as *The Malay Archipelago* (Wallace 1869).

3 This is sometimes called the "Sarawak Law" – see Wallace (1855).

4 See Wallace (1858).

5 Though this structure was clear to Darwin and Wallace and many later authors, it was first explicitly articulated in this form by Lewontin (1970).

6 The capitalization is to distinguish the controversial program, associated with figures such as David Buss, Lena Cosmides, Steven Pinker, Randy Thornhill, John Tooby, etc., from the non-controversial *evolutionary psychology* which views the human

mind as an evolved entity. For more on Evolutionary Psychology, see Chapter 4 and, especially, Buller (2005).

7 Darwin (1859), pp. 171–2.

8 See, for instance, Johnson (1990) and Berlinski ([1996] 2004).

9 Darwin (1859), p. 186; emphasis added.

10 See Land and Nilsson (2002), Fernald (2004), and also Chapter 3. Shanks (2004, Chapter 2) discusses the evolution of the eye – and the problems it poses for Creationists – in some detail.

11 Darwin (1859), pp. 186–7.

12 This can be put in another way: there is no claim that our contemporary most complex form arose from our contemporary simplest form or, for that matter, vice versa.

13 Darwin (1872), p. 395.

14 For instance, though they do not explicitly say it, such an interpretation is strongly suggested by Gould and Lewontin (1979) in their justly famous critique of adaptationism in evolutionary biology (that is, the assumption that natural selection is the sole guiding force of evolution).

15 Jenkin (1867).

16 For a history, see Burchfield (1990).

17 See Moorhead and Kaplan (1967).

18 Berlinski ([1996] 2004); Johnson (1991) and elsewhere. More examples will be given in Chapter 10. See, also, the so-called Discovery Institute's "Scientific Dissent from Darwin" (at http://www.discovery.org/articleFiles/PDFs/100ScientistsAd.pdf; accessed November 15, 2005).

19 See Vorzimmer (1963) on this point.

20 See Johnson (1991), the title of which is "Darwin on Trial."

21 Wilkins (2004) has recently emphasized this point.

22 Note that this is the later Wallace. In the 1860s Wallace, too, espoused a naturalistic account of the origin of mental and moral qualities on the basis of group selection, similar to Darwin (see below). See Wallace (1864).

23 Here, Wallace conveniently ignores the counterexample of Archimedes who was involved in the defense of Syracuse against Roman sieges during the First and Second Punic Wars (264–241 BCE, 218–202 BCE) supposedly using war machines of his own design.

24 This assessment of Genghis Khan is also inaccurate – see Weatherford (2005).

25 Wallace (1889), pp. 466–77.

26 Wallace (1889), p. 474.

27 Wallace (1889), p. 476.

28 Wallace (1889), p. 476.

29 See Weismann (1889).

30 Wallace (1889), p. 473n.

31 Following Julian Huxley (1942), Bowler (1983) has called these developments the "eclipse of Darwinism."

32 See Endler (1986) for a discussion and a survey up to the 1980s.

33 See Weldon (1893).

34 For details of both neo-Lamarckism and orthogenesis, see Bowler (1983).

35 See Haldane (1932) and Chapter 4.

36 See Landman (1991) for a review.
37 Darwin (1871), p. 65.
38 Darwin ([1872] 1965), p. 12.
39 For more details, see Richards (1987).
40 John Wilkins (personal communication) has argued that what is really at stake here is that Darwin did not distinguish between biology and culture. This suggests a slightly different interpretation of his views than what is suggested in the text. The text suggests that culture is being reduced to biology; Wilkins' interpretation would not go quite that far.
41 See, for example, Wells (2000).

Chapter 3

1 See Raup (1991). Newman and Palmer (2003) review recent theoretical work.
2 This fact does not receive the emphasis it deserves: it underscores how much progress evolutionary biology has made in the last 150 years. (The *Origin*'s lack of emphasis on speciation has, however, been explicitly noted in Coyne and Orr's [2004] recent synthesis of what we know about speciation.)
3 For a discussion, see Sulloway (1979).
4 See Coyne and Orr (2004).
5 See Waterton (1973). Among other things, during his South American travels, Waterton transported a 14-foot "Coulacanara" snake in wreaths around his body and rode a cayman along the bank of a river – for more on Waterton's eccentricities, see Barber (1980), Chapter 7.
6 Waterton (1973), pp. 5–6.
7 Waterton (1973), p. 93.
8 See Goffart (1971).
9 For historical details, see Ruse (2003) and Shanks (2004, Chapter 1).
10 Paley (1802), p. 1; emphasis in the original.
11 Ruse (2003), p. 42.
12 Paley (1802), p. 19.
13 It has been called by many other names, for instance, the argument to "apparent organized complexity" (Ruse 2003, p. 16).
14 The philosophical literature on functions is huge. Buller (1999) and Garson (2007) provide good entries.
15 Ruse (2003), p. 6.
16 This is sometimes called the etiological view of functions. It has been elaborated in slightly different ways by many philosophers – the most systematic, though often ignored, account is that of Wimsatt (1972).
17 See Strickberger (2000, p. 382).
18 See Baker (1992) for more detail.
19 See Sober (2004) for this "likelihood approach" which is an alternative to the approach used here. This section draws extensively on Sober's careful analysis. The reason for using the Bayesian argument is not because the likelihood framework is inadequate; in fact a Bayesian approach also requires the computation of likelihoods.

Rather, the choice made here is designed to underscore the fact that the argument against a designer is not dependent on some arcane assumptions about the nature of scientific inference. Dembski (2002, pp. 101–10) attempted to answer Sober's earlier criticisms (see Fitelson et al. 1999) by suggesting that the likelihood approach was flawed. Generating the same criticism from a different approach shows that the salient problems with Dembski's argument remain whether or not we are wedded to the likelihood framework. Moreover, it is Dembski's response to Fitelson et al. (1999) that is flawed: he argues that we need not compare two hypotheses to judge the validity of one of them. However, in this case, when we are given two hypotheses (design and selection), if we are intellectually honest, we have no option other than to consider and compare both.

20 This point has been emphasized by both Kitcher (1983) and Sober (1999).

21 See Sober (1999) and Kitcher (1983).

22 Darwin (1859), p. 188.

23 Darwin (1859), p. 202.

24 Sober (2004) emphasizes this important point. The Maynard Smith example discussed below is also from this source.

25 Discovered in 1901, this clockwork bronze machine was used to calculate the motion of stars and planets – see de Solla Price (1974) for details of the story.

26 See Newman (1973), p. 97.

27 See Futuyma (1983).

28 Huxley (1893), p. 82. For an extended discussion of the fate of teleology among Darwin's followers, see Ruse (2003).

29 Huxley (1893), pp. 82–3.

30 Huxley (1893), p. 84.

31 See Gray (1876), p. 237.

32 Shallit (2002) and Perakh (2004b) have correctly emphasized this point. Dembski's mathematics is designed to impress the less mathematical reader, not develop any new facet of his argument.

33 Dembski (1998), p. 9.

34 See Dembski (1998), p. 37ff. The reconstruction here is partly based on Fitelson et al. (1999) and is more detailed than Dembski's more cursory treatment. It is also consistent with Dembski (2002), p. 13. For a slightly different – but ultimately logically equivalent – reconstruction, see Perakh (2004b). Wilkins and Elsberry (2001) provide a reconstruction designed to allow chance to emerge again after design is rejected. Their reconstruction is supposed to correct Dembski's in an attempt to generate an explanatory filter that is similar to his but not absurd.

35 In *The Design Inference*, all this means is that the probability that C assigns to E does not change when we include our background knowledge (that is, there is conditional independence of this probability from that knowledge) and that we have a "tractable" description of E. Essentially all that tractability means is that we can recognize a pattern in the event. In later work Dembski and other ID creationists move to a somewhat different definition of "specified" – we will turn to it in Chapter 5. The motivation for conditional independence is to ensure that the background knowledge we use to identify a pattern does not affect the computation of the probability of the event.

36 Dembski uses parsimony – or, roughly, simplicity – as the criterion by which the three hypotheses are ordered. But, as far as the logic of this argument goes, it does not matter what criterion is used.

37 However, as Fitelson et al. (1999) have noted, Dembski is not clear as to whether we should ever accept R or C, or merely not reject them. The latter option would let us maintain that every event is a result of design, even if we cannot reject regularity or chance. This is a happy theological option, though of little scientific interest.

38 Dembski (1998), p. 36.

39 See BBC, "Lightning Kills Football Team" <http://news.bbc.co.uk/1/hi/world/africa/203137.stm>; accessed February 20, 2005.

40 Our description ensures that events of this type cannot have occurred in the universe before the invention of soccer.

41 For a detailed development of this argument, see Fitelson et al. (1999). We show that Dembski's procedure produces false positives, which is all that is required to reject any claim of ID. However, Fitelson et al. also show that it generates false negatives – logically, the filter is even worse than it looks.

42 We also easily see that the conditional independence claim in the definition (see note 37) is satisfied.

43 See http://www.forteantimes.com/articles/118_sdays.shtml; accessed November 17, 2005.

44 Perakh (2004b), pp. 40–3. There are many other such examples. Ratzsch (2001, p. 166) gives one in which he was driving along a deserted road bordered by a long fence with exactly one small hole in it. A gust of wind happened to drive a tumbleweed across the road in front of Ratzsch's car and into the small hole in the fence. This event, too, had a very small probability – there was just one small hole in a long fence. It was specified in the sense any target on a wall is specified. So, if Dembski is correct, it is yet another example of design, though this example suffers from the problem that the event witnessed by Ratzsch may not (intuitively) be highly improbable.

45 Details are from Bell Burnell (2004).

46 Fitelson et al. (1999) have also emphasized this point.

47 See Oakley and Cunningham (2002).

48 See Land and Nilsson (2002), p. 4; Land and Nilsson give ample detail to show that – contrary to beliefs popular among creationists – intermediate stages in the evolution from light-sensitive cells to both simple and compound eyes are likely to be adaptive. See, also, Shanks (2004), Chapter 2.

49 See Nilsson and Pelger (1994). This estimate is pessimistic in the sense that it is a conservative over-estimate of the number of generations required.

50 Wilkins and Elsberry (2001) also make this point.

51 See, for instance, Crick (1981).

52 Dembski (1998), p. 26.

53 Dembski knows that. *The Design Inference* was supposed to be a work devoid of any explicit religious agenda setting the stage for his future theological excursions.

54 Dembski (1998), p. 36. The complement is the remainder of the set; this is a privative definition.

55 Dembski's use of the filter justifies reading "or" here as an exclusive disjunction, not allowing chance and design to act together.

56 This means that the disjunction is being interpreted as an inclusive one, allowing the truth of both disjuncts.

Chapter 4 ──────────────────────────

1   See Dembski (2002).

2   Mendel (1866).

3   For a history of the developments discussed in this section, see Provine (1971).

4   Many of the themes mentioned in this paragraph have been previously explored by Bowler (1989). There is occasionally heated dispute among historians about the timing of the emergence of the modern framework for evolutionary theory; some would date it to the late 1930s or even the 1940s – see Sarkar (2005) for a detailed discussion.

5   See Johannsen (1909).

6   The crucial experiments were those of Avery, MacLeod, and McCarty (1944).

7   Watson and Crick (1953a, b).

8   Morgan (1926), p. 26.

9   Muller ([1926] 1962), p. 195; a decade later, Dobzhansky (1937, p. 11) would echo the same sentiment, defining evolution to be a "change in the genetic [allelic] composition of populations."

10 See Haldane (1924), which was the first of a series of ten papers published between 1924 and 1934.

11 McOuat and Winsor (1995) and Sarkar (2005) reconstruct this history in some detail.

12 See Fisher (1930); Wright (1931).

13 Haldane (1932).

14 Dobzhansky (1937).

15 Huxley (1942).

16 Lewontin and Hubby (1966).

17 Harris (1966).

18 The thesis is that, for natural selection to operate, a population must pay a cost in terms of the elimination of the less fit individuals (Haldane 1957b).

19 See Kimura (1968).

20 See King and Jukes (1969), titled "Non-Darwinian Evolution."

21 See Takahata (2000).

22 See Gillespie (1991) for a review.

23 See Ohta (2000).

24 See Lewontin (1974) for an elaboration of this and other arguments against the neutral theory.

25 See Ohta (1973) for the original statement and Ohta (1996) for a historical reappraisal.

26 This is the title of Sober's (1988) excellent philosophical analysis of these problems.

27 See, for instance, Ewens (1993).

28 Kingman (1982).

29 Here, by no recombination we mean that there is no recombination within the sequence at that locus, which is often plausible, and not that there is no recombination between different loci.

30 For more discussion, see Valentine et al. (1999) and Bromham (2003).

31 See Chen et al. (2004). For earlier fossil evidence also supporting pre-Cambrian origins for metazoan animals, see Xiao et al. (1998), with a commentary by Thomas (1998).

32 Ronshaugen et al. (2002).

33 See, for instance, Denton (1996).

34 Mayr (1982), p. 285.

35 Darwin (1859), p. 52.

36 Haldane (1956), p. 96.

37 See, for example, Raven (1976), Mishler and Donoghue (1982), and Nelson (1989).

38 For an up-to-date survey of the state of the discussion, see Coyne and Orr (2004).

39 This definition goes back to Dobzhansky (1935) though it is most commonly associated with Mayr (1942).

40 Mayr (1963).

41 For details, see Coyne and Orr (2004).

42 See Gould and Lewontin (1979).

43 See Maynard Smith (1978) and Mayr (1982).

44 Chen et al. (1997).

45 Clark et al. (2005).

46 See Gould (1989) and Conway Morris (1998, 2004).

47 See Eldredge and Gould (1972).

48 See, for example, Maynard Smith (1983), Newman et al. (1985), and Williams and Sarkar (1994).

49 See Reznick et al. (1997); Gingerich (1983) reviews earlier evidence supporting the same conclusion.

50 Miller (1999a) discusses this issue in detail.

51 Kirschner and Gerhart (2005) offer an exciting new precis.

52 Gerhart and Kirschner (1997, pp. 102–3).

53 Gerhart and Kirschner (1997, p. 100). However, within each kind there is a large amount of variation.

54 See, for example, Tauber and Sarkar (1992).

55 For details of this discussion, see Sarkar (2005, Chapter 14).

56 There are other surprises. For instance, the tiger pufferfish (*Fugu rubripes*) genome has only about 365 million base pairs, less than a tenth of the human genome, but roughly the same number of genes as in the human genome – see Mulley and Holland (2004).

57 See, for example, Mattick (2004).

58 See, for instance, Lewontin (1998) and Kitcher (1985).

59 See Wilson (1978).

60 See Wilson (1984).

61 See Barkow et al. (1995).

62 See Buss (2000) and Thornhill and Palmer (2000).

63 See Coyne (2000); Buller (2005) provides a nuanced critique. Dennett (1995) provides what is perhaps the most sustained philosophical defense of Evolutionary Psychology.

64 See Romanes (1896).

Chapter 5

1 See Holland (1975).

2 Restricting attention to maximization can be done without loss of generality because, if our problem is that of minimizing some function, f, we can convert it to that of maximizing the function, $g = -f$.

3 For a history, see Honig (1999).

4 The multiplication by -1 is required only to convert the minimization problem to a maximization one.

5 See de Jong (1993).

6 See Stockwell and Peters (1999).

7 Wolpert and Macready (1997); for an accurate accessible account, see Perakh (2004a).

8 Mihai Oltean (2004) has recently even constructed explicit objective functions in which random search performs better than evolutionary algorithms. Ironically, finding such functions itself involved evolutionary computation.

9 See Forster (1999).

10 Dembski (2002), p. xiii.

11 A similar point was made by Perakh (2003, 2004a).

12 See Haldane (1928), pp. 20–8.

13 Wolpert's (2003) review is aptly titled "William Dembski's Treatment of the No Free Lunch Theorems is Written in Jello."

14 Note, also, we have now moved from the inconsistency option to the incompleteness option of the Central Argument.

15 See de Jong (1993).

16 The same point is made slightly differently by Orr (2002).

17 Wolpert and Macready (2005). Note that Dembski cannot be held responsible for not discussing this work which was done after the publication of No Free Lunch. However, it will be instructive to see the response from him and other ID creationists.

18 This explicit result goes back at least to Scheuer and Mandel (1959). They discuss all the other assumptions besides one-locus control that must hold for this result to be correct – these complications are being left out here for the sake of expository simplicity. They only underscore the point being made in the text that selection may be viewed as optimization only in very restricted situations.

19 See Moran (1964). For a response, see Wright (1967).

20 At most, as Warren Ewens has argued, only that part of the change in mean fitness that may be interpreted as due only to changes in allele frequencies may be so interpreted. Once again we must assume that fitnesses are constant, that is, time-independent and frequency-independent. See Ewens (1989, 1992); this is Ewens' interpretation of Fisher's (1930) so-called "fundamental theorem of natural selection."

21　This means that the function is question must be one of the fitnesses and frequencies of the alleles, gametes, genotypes, etc. (For details, see Sarkar [2006].)

22　See, for instance, Crow and Kimura (1970), pp. 230–6.

23　See Lanczos (1959) for a detailed discussion, including the history of such principles.

24　Svirizhev (1972).

25　The mathematical framework for the multi-locus case, which requires the use of an abstract Riemanninan space, was developed by Shahshahani (1979).

26　See Behera (1996).

27　See, for instance, Wolpert and Macready (1995). For a general introduction to NFL theorems, visit the site <www.no-free-lunch.org> (accessed: February 18, 2005).

28　Rosenhouse (2002), p. 1721.

29　Perakh (2004a), p. 168.

30　Fisher (1930).

31　Van Valen (1973).

32　Dembski (2002), pp. 203–4; emphasis in the original. Dembski may be being misled by his analogy with the archer firing an arrow. The point is that evolutionary processes (or algorithms) are unlike arrows: they do not have pre-specified targets.

33　Recall that the theorems (see Figure 5.3) state the equality of performance over two samples, and not with respect to a target.

34　See Gould and Lewontin (1979).

35　See, for instance, Mayr (1983).

36　See, however, Lewontin (1978) who points out that there are situations in which adaptation, understood as fit with the environment, is not the same as what is brought about by natural selection. This complication will be ignored here – it is largely a matter of how one defines "adaptation."

37　See, for instance, Oster and Wilson (1978) and Maynard Smith (1982).

38　See Düsing (1884).

39　Once again "function" is being used to indicate a mathematical function.

40　As many commentators (e.g., Orr [2002]) have pointed out, Dembski misrepresents the arguments presented by Dawkins (1996).

Chapter 6

1　See Behe and Snoke (2004). The arguments of that paper will be addressed later in this chapter.

2　See Behe (2001). For other examples, see Chapter 10.

3　Miller (1999a), p. 62.

4　Behe (2001) lists many of these reviews, duly noting that many of them also accused him of exaggeration. Behe's work has also been subject to searching examination in the *Journal of Theoretical Biology* – see Thornhill and Ussery (2000).

5　See Dembski and Kushiner (2001), pp. 38, 100, for Johnson's and Behe's self-congratulatory remarks.

6　See, for instance, Coyne (1996), Orr (1996–7), Dorit (1997), and Ussery (1999).

7　See Hermodson (2005) and Lynch (2005).

8　Behe (1996), p. 39.

9   Funch and Kristensen (1995); Conway Morris (1995).

10 See Miller (2004).

11 The same point is applicable to Dembski's claims about complex specified information to which we will turn in the next chapter.

12 Drummond (1894), p. 333.

13 Behe (2001), p. 697.

14 Behe (2001), p. 697.

15 These were distinguished (though not with these names) by Thornhill and Ussery (2000).

16 Orr (1996–7).

17 Behe (2001), p. 694.

18 Behe (1996), p. 72.

19 Behe (2001), p. 694.

20 Behe (2001), p. 700. This is a typical example of Behe's practice of not tracking his principles faithfully.

21 Behe (2001), p. 699.

22 Berlinski's (1998) attempt to give a mathematical gloss to Behe's definition falls apart for the same reason. He assumes that if any component of an ICS is ever missing, the organism cannot survive – for details, see Rosenhouse (2001).

23 In his response to Orr (1996–7), Behe (2001) explicitly suggests that his arguments are only intended at the molecular level.

24 See Behe (2001).

25 This section draws heavily on Thornhill and Ussery (2000) and Dunkelberg (2003).

26 Gould and Vrba (1982) call such features exaptations to distinguish them from adaptations which were selected for their present functions.

27 The discussion here is limited to feathers, rather than the entire flying apparatus, mainly because, out of charity, Behe (1996) is being indulged in his desire to have all discussions occur at the molecular level. Thus this chapter gives short shrift to evolution at other levels of organization. Gishlick (2004) provides an illuminating discussion of the entire avian flying apparatus as an ICS. He – and not any of the creationists – also describes how a test for an ICS can be carried out, this time with a chicken wing and kitchen knife.

28 Brush (2000); Prum and Brush (2002, 2003). Gishlick (2004) discusses other possibilities for the early function of feathers.

29 See Unwin (1998).

30 See Thornhill and Ussery (2000) and Kundrát (2004) for the original references. Ascription of feathers to dinosaurs and the theropod origin of birds are not entirely uncontroversial – see Thomas and Garner (1998), Lingham-Soliar (2003), and Feduccia et al. (2005).

31 See, in particular, Miller (1999b), Chapter 5.

32 See Dembski (2002).

33 See Mills et al. (1967).

34 In fact, the experiment was explicitly designed to show that shorter sequences would develop in the scenario that was used (Mills et al. 1967).

35 For a famous discussion of this example, see Haldane (1932).

36 See Maynard Smith and Szathmáry (1995) for a development of this argument.

37 Huynen et al. (1999).

38 See Meléndez-Hevia et al. (1996), p. 302.

39 This is trivially true because enzymes are catalysts speeding up a reaction that would already occur in their absence.

40 This assumption was motivated by the view that, at early stages of evolution, the reactions would not be very efficient and the chain of reactions would be broken if an intermediate degenerated rapidly.

41 Meléndez-Hevia et al. (1996), p. 302.

42 Mills (2002) incorrectly claims that the "authors [Meléndez-Hevia et al. 1996] do not deal with whether these compounds [molecules in the citric acid cycle] were selected by chance or chosen by a designer." Leaving aside the fact that "selected by chance" is creationist rhetoric designed to make evolution look implausible, Mills deliberately ignores the fact that Meléndez-Hevia et al. (1996) explicitly try to reconstruct the history of the *evolution by natural selection* of the citric acid cycle.

43 Huynen et al. (1999).

44 Forst and Schulten (1999).

45 Behe (1996), p. 97.

46 See Doolittle (1993).

47 That fish would not have this pathway was predicted by Doolittle (1993) on evolutionary grounds, and subsequently confirmed (Jiang and Doolittle 2003).

48 See Miller (1999b) who draws on Doolittle and Feng (1987), Doolittle and Riley (1990), Xu and Doolittle (1990), and Doolittle (1993).

49 See Zhang (2003). Plants such as *Arabidopsis thaliana* (a mustard weed) have much higher proportions.

50 For a review, including a smattering of the history, see Taylor and Raes (2004).

51 This requires no more than the well-known mechanism of exon shuffling – see Gerhart and Kirschner (1997), pp. 220–222.

52 See, for instance, Jiang and Doolittle (2003).

53 Xu and Doolittle (1990).

54 The current situation is summarized by Davidson et al. (2003).

55 Dembski (2002).

56 Miller (2004).

57 Behe (2001), p. 694.

58 Behe (1996), p. 72.

59 For a review, see Bardy et al. (2003).

60 Samuel et al. (2001).

61 Trachtenberg et al. (2003)

62 Musgrave (2004).

63 See Thomas et al. (2001) and Musgrave (2004).

64 Ussery (2004); Musgrave (2004).

64 Yonekura et al. (2002); Ussery (2004).

66 Ussery (2004).

67 Heuck (1998); Büttner and Bonas (2002); Miller (2004).

68 McNab (1999); Aizawa (2001).

69 Aizawa (2001); Musgrave (2004).

70 Thus, contrary to Dembski (as cited by Musgrave [2004, p. 82]), it is irrelevant that modern TTSS specialize in eukaryotes which evolved later than prokaryotes. (By that argument, we should not see modern bacteria that are specific to eukaryotic hosts!)

71 The discussion of Behe's views in this section is based entirely on Behe and Snoke (2004, 2005).

72 This is pointed out by Lynch (2005) who responds to Behe and Snoke by modeling the same situation using more standard techniques of theoretical population genetics.

73 See Hermodson (2005) and the references therein.

74 Lynch (2005). Moreover, if we admit digital organisms into the discussion – and our arguments do not require their use – recent results of Richard Lenski and several collaborators (Lenski et al. 2003) have shown that it is fairly easy to evolve complexity dependent on multiple mutations.

75 For microbial population sizes, see Finlay (2002).

76 Dawkins (1995, pp. 82–3) uses "brittle" to make the same point.

77 Miller (1999a), Chapter 4.

78 Jacob (1977).

Chapter 7

1 See Dembski (1999). Koons repeated the assertion in 2002 – see Shallit and Elsberry (2004), p. 129. In 2005, according to *Mathematical Reviews*, Dembski had not published a single peer-reviewed paper in information theory.

2 Dembski (2002), p. 167.

3 Dembski (2002), p. 163.

4 See Perakh (2004a) for references. Here are some of the things Dembski once said of these theorems: "The No Free Lunch theorems dash any hope of generating specified complexity via evolutionary algorithms" (2002, p. 196); or "The No Free Lunch theorems show that evolutionary algorithms, apart from careful fine-tuning by a programmer, are no better than blind search and thus no better than pure search" (2002, p. 212).

5 Dembski (2002), p. 223.

6 Several studies have highlighted these developments – see Sarkar (1996) and Kay (2000).

7 Schrödinger (1944).

8 This means that the sequence of bases, rather than their detailed chemistry, sufficed to specify which nucleotide residue occurred in the corresponding protein.

9 For an excellent readable history, see Judson (1979).

10 Mayr (1961); Jacob and Monod (1961).

11 Sarkar (1996, 2000, 2004); Maynard Smith (2000); Sterelny (2000); Griffiths (2001); Godfrey-Smith (2004).

12 Dembski (2002) also seems not to understand what complexity is according to algorithmic information theory: an inability to compress a message. Rather, he claims: "It is CSI that within the Chaitin-Kolmogorov-Solomonoff theory of algorithmic

information identifies the highly compressible, nonrandom strings of digits (p. 144)." This is exactly incorrect, as pointed out by Elsberry and Shallit (2003).

13   The explicit distinction goes back to Claude Shannon's (1948) seminal paper of 1948.

14   Carnap and Bar-Hillel (1952). For important recent work towards this goal, see Floridi (2004a, b).

15   See Shannon (1948).

16   The choice of a base for the logarithm is conventional. Using base 2 lets the information content to be measured in the familiar bits.

17   The uniqueness claim is correct only up to multiplication by a constant factor. The choice of the base of the logarithm fixes this constant.

18   Shannon (1948).

19   Dembski (2002), pp. 127, 174 n.4, Dembski seems not to realize that he is using something very different from Shannon measure. The formula, $I = -\sum_{i=1}^{n} \log_2 p_i$, is sometimes used within information theory when, in contrast to Shannon (1948), n is the length of the string comprising the message – it is sometimes called "self-information" (see Reza 1961; Brillouin 1962; Abramson 1963). However, this formula still has questionable theoretical justification. If each unit is independent of the others, it merely computes the logarithm of their joint probability as the logarithm of the product of their individual probabilities. Using an information measure rather than the raw probabilities contributes nothing. If this is how Dembski intends his formula to be interpreted, we have nothing more than the battered probabilistic arguments of *Design Inference* (Dembski 1998; see Chapter 3) paraded in new clothes. We are back to the "Law of Small Probability."

20   Tribus (1961).

21   Using Shannon's formula is a valid move because Dembski (2002), p. 174 n.4, accepts the Shannon measure as the appropriate definition of information.

22   Kimura (1961).

23   The calculations assume an infinite population for simplicity.

24   Haldane (1957b).

25   Kimura (1961), p. 135.

26   See, for instance, Schneider (2000).

27   The qualification "essentially" is required because Schneider corrects the value to take into account the small sample size.

28   If we admit digital organisms to the discussion, Christoph Adami and colleagues have shown that they evolved to more complex forms in spatially explicit models. Adami et al. (2000) measure the complexity of the genome using a formula based on Shannon's measure. Using the same simulation platform (called "Avida") Lenski and his collaborators, as previously noted in Chapter 6, also found that complexity evolves easily though they do not interpret complexity in terms of information. There are other such results – we will not harp on these in case it is objected that artificial life modes are inadmissible to the debate. We do not need them.

29   Schneider (2000), p. 2797. In the model the sequence for a recognizer gene co-evolves with its binding sites in such a way that a mutation in either leads to the elimination of the entire organism. This system is irreducibly complex in Behe's (1996) sense – see Chapter 6.

30 Dembski (2002), p. 215.

31 It is also unhelpful that none of these claims is backed by quantitative estimates of how much information, if any, was "smuggled" in. If ID creationists want to engage scientists, they have to do better. This is where Behe and Snoke (2004) were far more respectable.

32 Dembski (2002).

33 Orgel (1973), p. 189.

34 Dembski (2002), pp. 140–142.

35 Even here Dembski has not always been consistent, at one point saying that T can be "read off an event E" (1998, p. 146) though, later, he seems to abandon any such hope (Dembski 2002).

36 Dembski (1999), p. 159; Elsberry and Shallit (2003) provide a more complete list.

37 Dembski (1999), p. 159.

38 Dembski (1999), p. 160.

39 Dembski (2002), p. xiii.

40 Dembski (2002), p. 207.

41 Dembski (2002), p. 151.

42 Dembski (2002), p. 217.

43 Dembski (2002), p. 221.

44 Dembski (2002), pp. 289–302; recall the discussion of Chapter 6 where it was pointed out that this example has iconic status among ID creationists.

45 Dembski (2002), p. 144. These will be discussed in detail in the next chapter. What is particularly peculiar to this claim is that a particular scientific principle, rather than all those we have formulated, is singled out as a repository of CSI.

46 Dembski (2002), pp. 55–8.

47 Dembski (2002), p. 7; apparently, according to Dembski, 59 is not a prime number – it does not occur in his list. As Shallit and Elsberry (2004) observe, the crucial point is not that Dembski made a trivial mistake but that, without recourse to knowledge about what E is supposed to be, it is implausible to be able to decide whether it fits a given T.

48 See Dawkins (1986); Dembski (2002), pp. 179–87.

49 The discussion is based on Elsberry and Shallit (2003).

50 Technically, Dembski's requirement is the following: let B be the background knowledge. Then epistemic independence says that $\mathbf{Pr}(E|H \wedge B) = \mathbf{Pr}(E|H)$ where H is the hypothesis that E occurred by chance. But this requirement is violated by the Caputo example and the others that will follow in the text.

51 Recall (from Chapter 3) that the same problem bedevils the explanatory filter of *The Design Inference* (Dembski 1998). This is a recurrent problem for ID creationists.

52 Elsberry and Shallit (2003) also make this point.

53 See Goles et al. (2000, 2001).

54 Dembski (2002), pp. 188–9, 194.

55 Dembski (2002), p. 183.

56 Wolpert (2003).

57 The discussion is based on Dembski (2002), pp. 159–66. We will not follow Dembski in his idiosyncratic use of the mathematical operator "mod".

58 If $I(a) = -\mathbf{log}_2 p(A) = 500$, then $\mathbf{log}_2 p(A) = -500$, which gives $p(A) = 1/2^{500}$.

59   The only other such paper, Wells (2005), published in the fringe journal, *Rivista di Biologia*, will be discussed in Chapter 10.

60   Meyer (2004).

61   See: http://www.bryancore.org/bsg/opbsg/index.html; accessed December 19, 2005.

62   See: http://www.bryancore.org/bsg/aboutmain.html; accessed December 19, 2005.

63   This is *not* a joke.

64   The full statement reads: "The paper by Stephen C. Meyer, 'The origin of biological information and the higher taxonomic categories,' in vol. 117, no. 2, pp. 213–239 of the *Proceedings of the Biological Society of Washington*, was published at the discretion of the former editor, Richard v. Sternberg. Contrary to typical editorial practices, the paper was published without review by any associate editor; Sternberg handled the entire review process. The Council, which includes officers, elected councilors, and past presidents, and the associate editors would have deemed the paper inappropriate for the pages of the Proceedings because the subject matter represents such a significant departure from the nearly purely systematic content for which this journal has been known throughout its 122-year history. For the same reason, the journal will not publish a rebuttal to the thesis of the paper, the superiority of intelligent design (ID) over evolution as an explanation of the emergence of Cambrian body-plan diversity. The Council endorses a resolution on ID published by the American Association for the Advancement of Science (http://www.aaas.org/news/releases/2002/1106id2.shtml), which observes that there is no credible scientific evidence supporting ID as a testable hypothesis to explain the origin of organic diversity. Accordingly, the Meyer paper does not meet the scientific standards of the Proceedings." From http://www.biolsocwash.org/id_statement.html; accessed December 19, 2005.

65   Gishlick et al. (2004) provide an excellent commentary.

66   Meyer (2004).

67   John Maynard Smith (personal communication). The closest published version is Haldane (1957a).

68   Recall that this is the use of the inconsistency option of ID's Central Argument from Chapter 1. Thus, it follows the same strategy as Dembski does when he deploys the no free lunch theorem (Chapter 5), but is different from Behe's strategy (Chapter 6) of following the incompleteness option.

69   Miller (1999a), p. 111.

Chapter 8

1   Weinberg's (1993) skepticism will be duly noted below.

2   Miller (1999a), p. 253.

3   Miller (1999a), p. 252.

4   Shanks (2004), pp. 211–12.

5   Dicke (1957, 1961).

6   Collins (1999); Leslie (1989).

7   Rees (1999), for instance, presents six magic numbers: N, measuring the ratio of electromagnetic and graviational forces; ε, measuring how firmly atomic nuclei bind

together; Ω, measuring the amount of matter in the universe, λ, measuring a force that controls the expansion of the universe; Q, which represents the ratio of two fundamental energies; and D, the number of spatial dimensions. Note that Rees does *not* conclude that a deity exists from the fine tuning of the universe; he prefers the existence of multiple universes.

8   See Weinberg (1993). Physicists have also provided other types of skepticism about anthropic principles. For instance, Kane et al. (2002) argue that if string theory is correct, there is no room for anthropic arguments in cosmology.

9   See Barow and Tipler (1986). The discussion here partly follows the excellent treatment of Shanks (2004, Chapter 6).

10 This is supposed to mean that not all possible values have equal probability of being observed by conscious observers. For expository convenience we will formulate all our arguments in terms of the admissible values of fundamental constants. However, the same arguments – and objections to them – can be formulated just as well in terms of any boundary or initial conditions for the existence of the universe.

11 The formulation is due to Shanks (2004), p. 209.

12 Barrow and Tipler (1986), p. 23.

13 Carter (1974).

14 This argument ignores the fact that classical general relativity – should it be regarded as a fundamental theory – is deterministic in most important respects. This qualification does not matter since, for the argument in the text, all that is required is that some of our fundamental theories be indeterministic.

15 Barrow and Tipler (1986), p. 23. It is important to note this qualification to distinguish between this work and Tipler's later efforts, including what he takes to be a scientific proof of the resurrection of the dead (see Tipler [1995]).

16 The argument is reconstructed from the discussions of Leslie (1989, 1997) and Swinburne (1990, 1991). However, the former usually does not offer precise probabilistic discussions and the reconstruction may not be entirely faithful to his intent. The treatment here largely follows Colyvan et al. (2005).

17 This argument is due to Colyvan et al. (2005) which should be consulted for technical details about probability measures that are glossed over in this paragraph.

18 See, for instance, Collins (1999).

19 For a discussion of these controversies, see, for instance, Fine (1973).

20 This argument is due to Stenger (1998, 2000).

21 Leslie (1998).

22 This version of the argument has been considered by Colyvan et al. (2005) though analyzed differently than here. Collins (1999) gives a version using the odds ratio that falls foul of the same technical considerations as the one explicitly considered here.

23 Sober (2004). The last point, that the biological arguments carry over to the cosmological context, deserves more recognition than it has obtained among those who deploy the cosmological design argument for the existence of God.

24 In the context of epistemological arguments, this choice has the advantage of making our hypotheses logically exhaustive and mutually exclusive, a luxury we did not enjoy in the biological context.

25 However, this amounts to an endorsement of the principle of indifference which, as noted earlier, is also problematic.

26 Let h be the hypothesis of design; then $\neg h$ is the hypothesis of absence-of-design. Let $p(h)$ and $p(\neg h)$ be the two prior probabilities and $p(h \mid K)$ and $p(\neg h \mid K)$ be the two posterior probabilities. Let $p(K)$ be the probability of fine tuning, and $p(K \mid h)$ and $p(K \mid \neg h)$ be the probability of fine tuning given each of the two hypotheses. Bayes' theorem says that

$$p(h \mid K) = \frac{p(K \mid h)p(h)}{p(K)} \text{ and } p(\neg h \mid K) = \frac{p(K \mid h)p(\neg h)}{p(K)}.$$

Therefore, for $p(h \mid K)$ to be greater than $p(\neg h \mid K)$, $p(K \mid h)p(h)$ must be greater than $p(K \mid \neg h)p(\neg h)$. If $p(h)$ is equal to $p(\neg h)$, then what is required is that $p(K \mid \neg h)$ is greater $p(K \mid \neg h)$.

27 Some critics of the cosmological design argument – for instance, Sober (2004) – concede this point but then argue that we assign such unequal probabilities only because of observational bias (or sampling bias): in principle, we cannot sample situations in which we do not exist. How we obtain samples must have a role in how we calculate probabilities. Consequently, according to them, what we should have been computing are the probabilities given all that we know, that is, the computation discussed in the next paragraph of the text. Moreover, Sober (2004) considers a specific hypothesis of chance, rather than absence-of-design, which makes the required inequality between probabilities somewhat more plausible.

28 We are left with the same situation even if we did not assume that the prior probabilities of the design and absence-of-design hypotheses are equal. The computation of the probabilities at least to the extent that we can assert the relevant inequality is unavoidable.

29 Thus, $p(K \mid h \wedge K) = p(K \mid \neg h \wedge K) = 1$. Essentially, Sober (2004) makes the same argument.

30 Essentially, the same argument appears in Juhl (2006).

31 May (1973).

Chapter 9

1 Ruse (2001), p. 365.
2 Ruse (2001), p. 365.
3 Ruse (2001), p. 365.
4 Johnson (1995), p. 208. Strangely, Johnson still asks: "The key question raised by the qualifier *methodological* is this: What is being limited – science or reality (p. 212)?" The obvious answer is the one he had given earlier – science; not only that, there is no claim on the part of a methodological naturalist that there necessarily is even a way to speak of a reality independent of all our descriptions of it. Methodological naturalism makes no commitment to the claim that there is only one description available of the world, viz., the scientific description.
5 See Pennock (1996). This formulation is slightly unfortunate insofar as it suggests that naturalism is being prescriptively *defined* using the methods of contemporary science, rather than being *described* by those methods.
6 Accusing naturalism of dogmatic inflexibility as Johnson (1990, 1995) does – probably very self-consciously for rhetorical purposes – is simply inaccurate.

7 Johnson (1996).

8 In referring generally to creationism, rather than more specifically to ID creationism, this chapter follows the lead of religious critics of naturalism such as Johnson and Plantinga.

9 See Feldman (2001). The terminology used here will follow that source though the accounts of the various positions will be sometimes different.

10 Rosenberg (1996) has also emphasized Nagel's significance.

11 All quotations from Nagel, except when explicitly indicated otherwise, are from Nagel (1956), pp. 6–7.

12 Nagel (1956), pp. 7–8; emphasis in the original.

13 Nagel (1956), p. 15.

14 See, in particular, Kitcher (1992). In contrast to Nagel and the view presented in the text, Kitcher finds naturalism generally prevalent in Western philosophy until the twentieth century when Frege's allegedly pernicious influence on epistemology replaced concern for empirical facts about human cognitive goals and capacities by an a priori analysis of the use of language.

15 See Shimony (1981), Kitcher (1992, 1995).

16 Kitcher (1992), p. 105.

17 See Bernard ([1865] 1957). Kitcher (1992) places the same emphasis.

18 See, for instance, Plantinga (1996), excerpted in Pennock (2001) and elsewhere.

19 See McMullin ([1991] 2001), p. 167.

20 Past prediction is sometimes called retrodiction – the distinction does not carry any relevant epistemological weight.

21 See Plantinga (1993).

22 Plantinga intends this as a formal argument, partly constructed in a Bayesian framework. But once the argument is so reconstructed carefully, it falls apart under minimal sustained formal scrutiny and the details are not particularly illuminating. This was shown by Fitelson and Sober (1998; reprinted in Pennock [2001]). Dretske (1971) made a similar argument against Shimony (1971) with equally little success. (Note that Dretske was only presenting a case against naturalized epistemology and *not* a defense of creationism.)

23 For an interesting analysis, see Fales (1996; reprinted in Pennock [2001]).

24 Plantinga, however, believes that naturalists have no option other than natural selection in their repertoire. Strangely, even his critics often accept this claim (e.g., Fales [1996]).

25 See Fitelson and Sober (1998).

26 See Duhem ([1906] 1954).

Chapter 10

1 See Dembski (2004).

2 McCausland (1999), p. 290. This was published in a peer-reviewed journal but the peers seem largely to consist of those who believe in telepathy, reincarnation, folk reports of animals unknown to zoology, and so on.

3 See, especially, Forrest and Gross (2004).

4 See, for instance, the list maintained by the National Center for Science Education at http://www.ncseweb.org/resources/articles/3541_project_steve_2_16_2003.asp (accessed December 18, 2005). There will be more on this list below.

5 These include Branden Fitelson, Peter Godfrey-Smith, Philip Kitcher, Robert Pennock, Michael Ruse, Niall Shanks, Elliott Sober, Chris Stephens, John Wilkins, and William Wimsatt – and this is not an exhaustive list.

6 See Behe (2001). Chapter 6 has detailed the seriousness with which biologists have responded to every relevant criticism that Behe has made. For other examples of the creationists' rhetoric see, for instance, Stephen C. Meyer's claim: "The numbers of scientists who question Darwinism is a minority, but it is growing fast. This is happening in the face of fierce attempts to intimidate and suppress legitimate dissent. Young scientists are threatened with deprivation of tenure. Others have seen a consistent pattern of answering scientific arguments with ad hominem attacks. In particular, the [2001 PBS (Public Broadcasting Service) Evolution] series' attempt to stigmatize all critics – including scientists – as religious 'creationists' is an excellent example of viewpoint discrimination" (http://www.reviewevolution.com/press/pressRelease_100Scientists.php; accessed December 19, 2005). Elsberry and Thomas (http://www.antievolution.org/wre_dogdar.html; accessed December 20, 2005) collect many other examples.

7 Berlinski ([1996] 2004).

8 Miller (1999a), p. 20.

9 Haldane (1932), p. 11.

10 See King and Jukes (1969).

11 Most notably, Huxley (1942) was instrumental in presenting this consensus to a wide audience.

12 For an early analysis from the selectionist camp, see Lewontin (1974); for the neutralist account, see Kimura (1983).

13 See, for instance, Lewontin (1991).

14 Recall the discussion of the coalescent model in Chapter 4.

15 See, for example, Maynard Smith (1983), Newman et al. (1985), and Williams and Sarkar (1994).

16 See Cairns et al. (1988) for the original report, and Sarkar (1991) and Keller (1992) for early commentary.

17 Foster (1993) provides a sympathetic review.

18 These are reviewed by Sniegowski and Lenski (1995).

19 The situation is reviewed by Sarkar (2005), Chapter 13. The rest of this paragraph draws heavily from that source.

20 This criterion is also very popular among biologists but it is flawed: it makes any existential claim unscientific because it is unfalsifiable (in a universe with an arbitrarily large number of entities). For instance, the claim, "there is a common ancestor of humans and chimpanzees" is logically impossible to falsify.

21 Laudan (1983, p. 349) puts this point forcefully: "If we would stand up and be counted on the side of reason, we ought to drop terms like 'pseudo-science' and 'unscientific' from our vocabulary; they are just hollow phrases which do only emotive work for us."

22 Dembski (2002), p. xi.

23 This is Meyer (2004).

24 Wells (2005).

25 Wells (2005), p. 75.

26 Recall how Dembski (2002) harps on 50 bits – see Chapter 7.

27 Meyer (2004), which was discussed in Chapter 8.

28 Wells (2005), as discussed earlier in this chapter.

29 For a consideration of the legal issues, see Brauer et al. (2005). Judge Jones' verdict in the Dover case is shorter, and perhaps even more pointed (see http://www.pamd.uscourts.gov/kitzmiller/kitzmiller_342.pdf; accessed December 25, 2005). Fitelson (2006) makes similar distinctions.

30 See the Preface.

31 Dembski (1999).

32 The philosophical grounds range from quantum mechanics' rejection of determinism to its rejection of locality – see, for instance, d'Espagnat (1976). Physical grounds include the insolubility of the measurement problem and the inability of making a smooth transition from the microscopic to the macroscopic level – see Stein (1972) and Leggett (1987).

33 See, for example, Ghirardi et al. (1986), Pearle (1986), Gisin (1989), Sarkar (1997), and Ghirardi (2002) for an entry into the extensive literature on the subject.

34 The statement is the one endorsed by Project Steve (see http://www.ncseweb.org/resources/articles/3541_project_steve_2_16_2003.asp; accessed December 18, 2005), a parody organized by the National Center for Science Education (NCSE). Since the Discovery Institute takes pride in publishing lists of very charitably defined "scientists" who dissent from evolution, the NCSE launched its own list but restricted it to genuine scientists named "Steve" (to honor the late Stephen Jay Gould).

References

Abramson, N. 1963. *Information Theory and Coding*. New York: McGraw-Hill.

Adami, C., Ofria, C., and Collier, T. C. 2000. "Evolution of Biological Complexity." *Proceedings of the National Academy of Sciences (USA)* **97**: 4464–8.

Aizawa, S.-I. 2001. "Bacterial flagella and type III secretion systems." *FEMS Microbiology Letters* **202**: 157–64.

Anandarajah, K., Kiefer, P. M., and Copley, S. D. 2000. "Recruitment of a Double Bond Isomerase to Serve as a Reductive Dehalogenase during Biodegradation of Pentachlorophenol." *Biochemistry* **39**: 5303–11.

Avery, O. T., MacLeod, C. M., and McCarty, M. 1944. "Studies on the Chemical Nature of the Substance Inducing Transformation of Pneumococcal Types: Induction of Transformation by a Deoxyribonucleic Acid Fraction Isolated from Pneumococcus III." *Journal of Experimental Medicine* **79**: 137–57.

Ayala, F. J. 1994. "Darwin's Revolution." In Campbell, J. H. and Schopf, J. W. Eds. *Creative Evolution?!* Boston: Jones & Bartlett, pp. 4–5.

Baker, P. T. 1992. "Sweating – the Human Response to Heat." In Jones, S., Martin, R., and Pilbeam, D. Eds. *The Cambridge Encyclopedia of Evolution*. Cambridge: Cambridge University Press, p. 48.

Barber, L. 1980. *The Heyday of Natural History, 1820–1870*. New York: Doubleday.

Bardy, S. L., Ng, S. Y. M., and Jarrell, K. F. 2003. "Prokaryotic Motility Structures." *Microbiology* **149**: 295–304.

Barkow, J. H., Cosmides, L., and Tooby, J. Eds. 1995. *The Adapted Mind: Evolutionary Psychology and the Generation of Culture*. Oxford: Oxford University Press.

Barrow, J. D. and Tipler, F. J. 1986. *The Anthropic Cosmological Principle*. Oxford: Oxford University Press.

Beckwith F. J. 2003. "Science and Religion Twenty Years after *McLean v. Arkansas*: Evolution, Public Education, and the New challenge of Intelligent Design." *Harvard Journal of Law and Public Policy* **26**: 455–499.

Behe, M. J. 1996. *Darwin's Black Box: The Biochemical Challenge to Evolution*. New York: Free Press.

Behe, M. J. 2001. "Reply to My Critics: A Response to Reviews of *Darwin's Black Box: The Biochemical Challenge to Evolution*." *Biology and Philosophy* **16**: 685–709.

REFERENCES

Behe, M. J. and Snoke, D. W. 2004. "Simulating Evolution by Gene Duplication of Protein Features the Required Multiple Amino Acid Residues." *Protein Science* **13**: 2651–64.

Behe, M. J. and Snoke, D. W. 2005. "A Response to Michael Lynch." *Protein Science* **14**: 2226–7.

Behera, N. 1996. "Variational Principles in Evolution." *Bulletin of Mathematical Biology* **58**: 175–202.

Bell, J. S. 1964. "On the Einstein Plodosky Rosen Paradox." *Physics* **1**: 195–200.

Bell Burnell, S. J. 2004. "Pliers, Pulsars and Extreme Physics." *Status: A Report on Women in Astronomy* (June 2004): 1–7.

Berlinksi, D. [1996] 2004. "The Deniable Darwin." In Dembski, W. A. Ed. *Uncommon Dissent: Intellectuals Who Find Darwinism Unconvincing.* Wilmington, DE: ISI Books, pp. 263–82.

Berlinski, D. 1998. "Gödel's Question." In Dembski, W. A. Ed. *Mere Creation: Science, Faith, and Intelligent Design.* Downers Grove, IL: Intervarsity Press, pp. 427–45.

Bernard, C. [1865] 1957. *An Introduction to the Study of Experimental Medicine.* New York: Dover.

Berra, T. M. 1990. *Evolution and the Myth of Creationism.* Stanford, CA: Stanford University Press.

Bowler, P. J. 1983. *The Eclipse of Darwinism: Anti-Darwinian Evolution Theories in the Decades around 1900.* Baltimore: Johns Hopkins University Press.

Bowler, P. J. 1989. *The Mendelian Revolution: The Emergence of Hereditarian Concepts in Science and Society.* Baltimore: Johns Hopkins University Press.

Brauer, M. J., Forrest, B., and Gey, S. G. 2005. "Is It Science Yet?: Intelligent Design Creationism and the Constitution." *Washington University Law Quarterly* **83**: 1–149.

Brillouin, L. 1962. *Science and Information Theory.* New York: Academic Press

Bromham, L. 2003. "What Can DNA Tell us about the Cambrian Explosion?" *Integrative and Comparative Biology* **43**: 148–56.

Brush, A. H. 2000. "Evolving a Protofeather and Feather Diversity." *American Zoologist* **40**: 631–9.

Buller, D. J. Ed. 1999. *Function, Selection, and Design.* Binghampton, NY: State University of New York Press.

Buller, D. J. 2005. *Adapting Minds: Evolutionary Psychology and the Persistent Quest for Human Nature.* Cambridge, MA: MIT Press.

Burchfield, J. D. 1990. *Lord Kelvin and the Age of the Earth.* Chicago: University of Chicago Press.

Buss, D. 2000. *The Dangerous Passion: Why Jealousy Is as Necessary as Love and Sex.* New York: Free Press.

Büttner, D. and Bonas, U. 2002. "Port of Entry – The Type III Secretion Translocon." *Trends in Microbiology* **10**: 186–91.

Cairns, J., Overbaugh, J., and Miller, S. 1988. "The Origin of Mutants." *Nature* **335**: 142–5.

Carnap, R. and Bar-Hillel, Y. 1952. *An Outline of a Theory of Semantic Information.* Research Laboratory of Electronics, Massachusetts Institute of Technology. Technical Report No. 247.

Carter, B. 1974. "Large Number Coincidences and the Anthropic Principle in Cosmology." In Longair, M. S. Ed. *Confrontation of Cosmological Theories with Observational Data*. Dordrecht, Germany: Reidel, pp. 291–8.

Chen, J.-Y., Bottjer, D. J., Oliveri, P., Dornbos, S. Q., Gao, F., Ruffins, S., Chi, H., Li, C.-W., and Davidson, E. H. 2004. "Small Bilaterian Fossils from 40 to 55 Million Years Before the Cambrian." *Science* **305**: 218–22.

Chen, L., DeVries, A. L., and Cheng, C.-H. C. 1997. "Convergent Evolution of Antifreeze Glycoproteins in Antarctic Notothenioid Fish and Arctic Cod." *Proceedings of the National Academy of Sciences (USA)* **94**: 3817–22.

Clark, V. C., Raxworthy, C. J., Rakotomalala, V., Sierwald, P., and Fisher, B. L. 2005. "Convergent Evolution of Chemical Defense in Poison Frogs and Arthropod Prey between Madagascar and the Neotropics." *Proceedings of the National Academy of Sciences (USA)* **102**: 11617–22.

Collins, R. 1999. "A Scientific Argument for the Existence of God: The Fine-tuning Design Argument." In Murray, M. Ed. *Reason for the Hope Within* (Grand Rapids, MI: Wm. B. Eerdmans), pp. 47–75.

Colyvan, M., Garfield, J. L. and Priest, G. 2005. "Problems with the Argument from Fine Tuning." *Synthese* **145**: 325–38.

Conway Morris, S. 1995. "New Phylum from the Lobster's Lips." *Nature* **378**: 661–2.

Conway Morris, S. 1998. *The Crucible of Creation: The Burgess Shale and the Rise of Animals*. Oxford: Oxford University Press.

Conway Morris, S. 2004. *Life's Solution: Inevitable Humans in a Lonely Universe*. Cambridge: Cambridge University Press.

Copley, S. D. 2000. "Evolution of a Metabolic Pathway for Degradation of a Toxic Xenobiotic: The Patchwork Approach." *Trends in Biochemical Sciences* **15**: 261–5.

Coyne, J. A. 1996. "God in the Details." *Nature* **383**: 227–8.

Coyne, J. 2000. "Of Vice and Men: The Fairy Tales of Evolutionary Psychology." *New Republic*, 3 April, pp. 27–33.

Coyne, J. A. and Orr, H. A. 2004. *Speciation*. Sunderland, MA: Sinauer Associates.

Crick, F. H. C. 1981. *Life Itself: Its Origin and Nature*. New York: Simon and Schuster.

Crompton, A. W. and Jenkins, F. A. 1973. "Mammals from Reptiles: A Review of Mammalian Origins." *Annual Review of Earth and Planetary Sciences* **1**(1): 131–55.

Crow, J. F. and Kimura, M. 1970. *An Introduction to Population Genetics Theory*. Minneapolis: Burgess.

Darwin, C. 1859. *On the Origin of Species*. London: John Murray.

Darwin, C. 1871. *The Descent of Man and Selection in Relation to Sex*. London: John Murray.

Darwin, C. 1872. *On the Origin of Species*. 6th. Ed. London: John Murray.

Darwin, C. [1872] 1965. *The Expression of Emotions in Man and Animals*. Chicago: University of Chicago Press.

Davidson, C. J., Tuddenham, E. G., and McVey, J. H. 2003. "450 Million Years of Hemostasis." *Journal of Thrombosis and Haemostasis* **1**: 1487–94.

Dawkins, R. 1986. *The Blind Watchmaker*. New York: W. W. Norton & Co.

Dawkins, R. 1995. *River Out of Eden*. New York: Basic Books.

Dawkins, R. 1996. *Climbing Mount Improbable*. New York: W. W. Norton.

de Jong, K. 1993. "Genetic Algorithms are NOT Function Optimizers." In Whitley, L. D. Ed. *Foundations of Genetic Algorithms*. San Mateo, CA: Morgan Kaufmann, pp. 5–17.

de Solla Price, D. 1974. "Gears from the Greeks: The Antikythera Mechanism – a Calendar Computer from *ca*. 80 BC." *Transactions of the American Philosophical Society* **64**: 1–70.

Dembski, W. A. 1998. *The Design Inference: Eliminating Chance through Small Probabilities*. New York: Cambridge University Press.

Dembski, W. A. 1999. *Intelligent Design: The Bridge between Science and Theology*. Downers Grove, IL: InterVarsity Press.

Dembski, W. A. 2002. *No Free Lunch: Why Specified Complexity Cannot be Purchased without Intelligence*. Lanham, MD: Rowman and Littlefield.

Dembski, W. A. Ed. 2004. *Uncommon Dissent: Intellectuals Who Find Darwinism Unconvincing*. Wilmington, DE: ISI Books.

Dembski, W. A. and Kushiner, J. M. Eds. 2001. *Signs of Intelligence: Understanding Intelligent Design*. Grand Rapids, MI: Brazos.

Dennett, D. C. 1995. *Darwin's Dangerous Idea*. New York: Simon & Schuster.

Denton, M. 1996. *Evolution: A Theory in Crisis*. Bethesda, MD: Adler and Adler.

d'Espagnat, B. 1976. *Conceptual Foundations of Quantum Mechanics*. 2nd Ed. Menlo Park, CA: W. A. Benjamin.

Dicke, R. H. 1957. "Principle of Equivalence and Weak Interactions." *Reviews of Modern Physics* **29**: 355–62.

Dicke, R. H. 1961. "Dirac's Cosmology and Mach's Principle." *Nature* **192**: 440–1.

Dobzhansky, T. 1935. "A Critique of the Species Concept in Biology." *Philosophy of Science* **2**: 344–55.

Dobzhansky, T. 1937. *Genetics and the Origin of Species*. New York: Columbia University Press.

Dobzhansky, T. 1973. "Nothing in Biology Makes Sense Except in the Light of Evolution." *American Biology Teacher* **35**: 125–9.

Doolittle, R. F. 1993. "The Evolution of Vertebrate Blood Coagulation: A Case of Yin and Yang." *Thrombosis and Haemostasis* **70**: 24–8.

Doolittle, R. F. and Feng, D. F. 1987. "Reconstructing the Evolution of Vertebrate Blood Coagulation from a Consideration of Amino Acid Sequences of Clotting Proteins." *Cold Spring Harbor Symposia in Quantitative Biology* **52**: 869–74.

Doolittle, R. F. and Riley, M. 1990. "The Amino-Acid Sequence of Lobster Fibrinogen Reveals Common Ancestry with Vitellogenin." *Biochemical and Biophysical Research Communications* **167**: 16–19.

Dorit, R. 1997. "Molecular Evolution and Scientific Inquiry, Misperceived." *American Scientist* **85**: 474–5.

Dretske, F. I. 1971. "Perception from an Epistemological Point of View." *Journal of Philosophy* **68**: 584–91.

Drummond, H. 1894. *Ascent of Man*. New York: James Pott & Co.

Duhem, Pierre. [1906] 1954. *The Aim and Structure of Physical Theory*. Princeton, NJ: Princeton University Press.

Dunkelberg, P. 2003. "Irreducible Complexity Demystified." http://www.talkdesign.org/faqs/icdmyst/ICDmyst.html (accessed December 8, 2005).

Düsing, C. 1884. *Die Regulierung des Geschlechtverhältnisses*. Jena, Germany: Gustav Fischer.

Einstein, A., Podolsky, B., and Rosen, N. 1935. "Can Quantum-mechanical Description of Physical Reality Be Considered Complete?" *Physical Review* **47**: 777–80.

Eiseley, L. 1958. *Darwin's Century: Evolution and the Men Who Discovered It.* Garden City, NY: Doubleday Anchor.

Eldredge, N. 2000. *The Triumph of Evolution and the Failure of Creationism.* New York: W. H. Freeman.

Eldredge, N. and Gould, S. J. 1972. "Punctuated Equilibria: An Alternative to Phyletic Gradualism." In Schopf, T. J. M. Ed. *Models in Paleobiology.* San Francisco: Freeman, Cooper, pp. 82–115.

Elsberry, W. and Shallit, J. 2003. "Information Theory, Evolutionary Computation, and Dembski's 'Complex Specified Information.'" http://www.antievolution.org/people/wre/papers/eandsdembski.pdf; accessed December 18, 2005.

Endler, J. A. 1986. *Natural Selection in the Wild.* Princeton, NJ: Princeton University Press.

Ewens, W. J. 1989. "An Interpretation and Proof of the Fundamental Theorem of Natural Selection." *Theoretical Population Biology* 36: 167–80.

Ewens, W. J. 1992. "An Optimizing Principle of Natural Selection in Evolutionary Population Genetics." *Theoretical Population Biology* 42: 333–46.

Ewens, W. J. 1993. "Beanbag Genetics and After." In Majumder, P. P. Ed. *Human Population Genetics.* New York: Plenum, pp. 7–29.

Fales, E. 1996. "Plantinga's case against Naturalistic Epistemology." *Philosophy of Science* 63: 432–51.

Feduccia, A., Lingham-Soliar, T., and Hinchliffe, J. R. 2005. "Do Feathered Dinosaurs Exist? Testing the Hypothesis on Neontological and Paleontological Rvidence." *Journal of Morphology* 266: 125–66.

Feldman, R. 2001. "Naturalized Epistemology." In Zalta, E. N. Ed. *Stanford Encyclopedia of Philosophy* (Fall 2001 Edition) URL = <http://plato.stanford.edu/archives/fall2001/entries/epistemology-naturalized/>; accessed December 19, 2005.

Fernald, R. D. 2004. "Evolving eyes." *International Journal of Developmental Biology* 48: 701–5.

Fine, T. L. 1973. *Theories of Probability: An Examination of Foundations.* New York: Academic Press.

Finlay, B. J. 2002. "Global Dispersal of Free-Living Microbial Eukaryote Species." *Science* 296: 1061–3.

Fisher, R. A. 1930. *The Genetical Theory of Natural Selection.* Oxford: Clarendon Press.

Fitelson, B. 2006. "Some Remarks on the 'Intelligent Design' Controversy." *Harvard Review of Philosophy*, forthcoming.

Fitelson, B. and Sober, E. 1998. "Plantinga's Probability Arguments against Evolutionary Naturalism." *Pacific Philosophical Quarterly* 79: 115–29.

Fitelson, B., Stephens, C., and Sober, E. 1999. "How Not to Detect Design – Critical Notice: William A. Dembski, *The Design Inference.*" *Philosophy of Science* 66: 472–88.

Floridi, L. 2004a. "Open Problems in the Philosophy of Information." *Metaphilosophy* 4: 554–82.

Floridi, L. 2004b. "Outline of a Theory of Strongly Semantic Information." *Mind and Machines* 14: 197–221.

Forrest, B. 2001. "The Wedge at Work: How Intelligent Design Creationism is Wedging Its Way into the Cultural and Academic Mainstream." In Pennock, R. T. Ed. *Intelligent Design Creationism and Its Critics: Philosophical, Theological, and Scientific Perspectives.* Cambridge, MA: MIT Press, pp. 5–53.

Forrest, B. and Gross, P. R. 2004. *Creationism's Trojan Horse: The Wedge of Intelligent Design*. New York: Oxford University Press.

Forst, C.V., and Schulten K. 1999. Evolution of Metabolisms: A New Method for the Comparison of Metabolic Pathways Using Genomics Information. *Journal of Computational. Biology* **64**: 343–60.

Forster, M. R. 1999. "Notice: No Free Lunches for Anyone, Bayesians Included." <http://www.no-free-lunch.org/Fors99.pdf>. Accessed: February 14, 2005.

Foster, P. L. 1993. "Adaptive Mutation: The Uses of Adversity." *Annual Review of Microbiology* **47**: 467–504.

Fox, R. 1971. *The Caloric Theory of Gases: From Lavoisier to Regnault*. Oxford: Oxford University Press.

Funch, P. and Kristensen, R. M. 1995. "*Cycliophora* is a New Phylum with Affinities to *Entoprocta* and *Ectoiprocta*." *Nature* **378**: 711–14.

Futuyma, D. 1983. *Science on Trial: The Case for Evolution*. New York: Pantheon.

Garson, J. 2007, forthcoming. "Function and Teleology." In Sarkar, S. and Plutynski, A. Eds. *The Blackwell Companion to the Philosophy of Biology*. Malden, MA: Blackwell.

Gee, H. 2001. *In Search of Deep Time: Beyond the Fossil Record to a New History of Life*. Ithaca, NY: Comstock Publishing.

Gerhart, J. and Kirschner, M. 1997. *Cells, Embryos, and Evolution*. Oxford: Blackwell Science.

Ghirardi, G. 2002. "Collapse Theories." In Zalta, E. N. Ed. *The Stanford Encyclopedia of Philosophy (Spring 2002 Edition)*. URL = <http://plato.stanford.edu/archives/spr2002/entries/qm-collapse/>; accessed December 18, 2005.

Ghirardi, G. C., Rimini, A., and Weber, T. 1986. "Unified Dynamics for Microscopic and Macroscopic Systems." *Physical Review D* **34**: 470–91.

Gillespie, J. H. 1991. *The Causes of Molecular Evolution*. New York: Oxford University Press.

Gingerich, P. D. 1983. "Rates of Evolution: Effects of Time and Temporal Scaling." *Science* **222**: 159–61.

Gisin, N. 1989. "Stochastic Quantum Dynamics and Relativity." *Helvetica Physica Acta* **62**: 363–71.

Gish, D. T. 1992. *Dinosaurs by Design*. Green Forest, AZ: Master Books.

Gishlick, A. 2004. "Evolutionary Paths to Irreducible Systems: The Avian Flight Apparatus." In Young, M. and Edis, T. Eds. *Why Intelligent Design Fails: A Scientific Critique of the New Creationism*. Piscataway, NJ: Rutgers University Press, pp. 58–71.

Gishlick, A., Matzke, N., and Elsberry, W. R. 2004. "Review of *Meyer, Stephen C. 2004. The origin of biological information and the higher taxonomic categories. Proceedings of the Biological Society of Washington 117(2):213–239*." See http://www.pandasthumb.org/pt-archives/000430.html; accessed December 19, 2005.

Godfrey-Smith, P. 2004. "Genes Do not Encode Information for Phenotypic Traits." In Hitchcock, C. Ed. *Contemporary Debates in the Philosophy of Science*. Malden, MA: Blackwell, pp. 275–289.

Goffart, M. 1971. *Function and Form in the Sloth*. Oxford: Pergamon Press.

Goles, E., Schulz, O., and Markus, M. 2000. "A Biological Generator of Prime Numbers." *Nonlinear Phenomena in Complex Systems* **3**: 208–13.

Goles, E., Schulz, O., and Markus, M. 2001. "Prime Number Selection of Cycles in a Predator–Prey Model." *Complexity* **6**: 33–8.

Gould, S. J. 1989. *Wonderful Life: The Burgess Shale and the Nature of History*. New York: W. W. Norton & Co.

Gould, S. J. and Lewontin, R. C. 1979. "The Spandrels of San Marco and the Panglossian paradigm." *Proceedings of the Royal Society of London B* **205**: 581–98.

Gould, S. J. and Vrba, E. S. 1982. "Exaptation – A Missing Term in the Science of Form." *Paleobiology* **8**: 4–15.

Grant, B. R. and Grant, P. R. 1989. *Evolutionary Dynamics of a Natural Population: The Large Cactus Finch of the Galápagos*. Princeton, NJ: Princeton University Press.

Gray, A. 1876. *Darwiniana*. New York: D. Appleton.

Griffiths, P. 2001. "Genetic Information: A Metaphor in Search of a Theory." *Philosophy of Science* **67**: 26–44.

Gross, P. R., Goodenough, U., Haack, S., Lerner, L. S., Schwartz, M., and Schwarts, R. 2005. *The State of State Science Standards*. Washington, DC: Thomas B. Fordham Institute.

Haldane, J. B. S. 1924. "A Mathematical Theory of Natural and Artificial Selection. Part I." *Transactions of the Cambridge Philosophical Society* **23**: 19–41.

Haldane, J. B. S. 1928. *Possible Worlds and Other Papers*. New York: Harper.

Haldane, J. B. S. 1932. *The Causes of Evolution*. London: Harper and Brothers.

Haldane, J. B. S. 1938. "Forty Years of Genetics." In Needham, J. and Pagel, W. Eds. *Background to Modern Science*. Cambridge: Cambridge University Press, pp. 223–43.

Haldane, J. B. S. 1956. Can a Species Concept Be Justified? *Systematic Association Publication* **2**: 956.

Haldane, J. B. S. 1957a. "Aunt Jobisca, the Bellman, and the Hermit." *Rationalist Annual* **1957**: 15–21.

Haldane, J. B. S. 1957b. "The Cost of Natural Selection." *Journal of Genetics* **55**: 511–24.

Harris, H. 1966. "Enzyme Polymorphism in Man." *Proceedings of the Royal Society Series B* **164**: 298–310.

Hermodson, M. 2005. "Editoral and Position Papers." *Protein Science* **14**: 2215–16.

Heuck, C. J. 1998. "Type III Protein Secretion Systems in Bacterial Pathogens of Animals and Plants." *Microbiology and Molecular Biology Reviews* **62**: 379–433.

Holden, C. 2006a. "Ohio School Board Boots Out ID." *Science* **311**: 1083.

Holden, C. 2006b. "New Dover Board to Pay $ 1 Million." *Science* **311**: 1227.

Holland, J. 1975. *Adaptation in Natural and Artificial Systems: An Introductory Analysis with Applications to Biology, Control, and Artificial Intelligence*. Ann Arbor, MI: University of Michigan Press.

Honig, B. 1999. "Protein Folding: From the Levinthal Paradox to Structure Prediction." *Journal of Molecular Biology* **293**: 283–93.

Hume, D. 1779. *Dialogues Concerning Natural Religion*. Edinburgh.

Huxley, J. S. 1942. *Evolution: The Modern Synthesis*. London: George Allen & Unwin.

Huxley, T. H. 1893. *Darwiniana*. London: Macmillan.

Huynen, M. A., Dandekar, T., and Bork, P. 1999. "Variation and Evolution of the Citric-Acid Cycle: A Genomic Perspective." *Trends in Microbiology* **7**: 281–91.

Jacob, F. 1977. "Evolution and Tinkering." *Science* **196**: 1161–6.

Jacob, F. and Monod, J. 1961. "Genetic Regulatory Mechanisms in the Synthesis of Proteins." *Journal of Molecular Biology* **3**: 318–56.

Jenkin, F. 1867. "The Origin of Species." *North British Review* **46**: 277–318.

REFERENCES

Jiang, Y. and Doolittle, R. F. 2003. "The Evolution of Vertebrate Blood Coagulation as Viewed from a Comparison of Puffer Fish and Sea Squirt Genomes." *Proceedings of the National Academy of Sciences (USA)* **100**: 7527–32.

Johannsen, W. 1909. *Elemente der exacten Erblichkeitslehre.* Jena, Germany: Gustav Fischer.

Johnson, P. E. 1990. "Evolution as Dogma: The Establishment of Naturalism." *First Things* **6**: 15–22.

Johnson, P. E. 1991. *Darwin on Trial.* Washington, DC: Regnery.

Johnson, P. E. 1995. *Reason in the Balance: The Case against Naturalism in Science, Law and Education.* Downers Grove, IL: InterVarsity Press.

Johnson, P. E. 1996. "Response to Pennock." *Biology and Philosophy* **11**: 561–3.

Judson, H. F. 1979. *The Eighth Day of Creation.* New York: Simon and Schuster.

Juhl, C. 2006. "Fine-Tuning is Not Surprising." Analysis **66**(4): 269–275.

Kane, G. L., Perry, M. J., and Zytkow, A. N. 2002. "The Beginning of the End of the Anthropic Principle." *New Astronomy* **7**: 45–53.

Kay, L. E. 2000. *Who Wrote the Book of Life? A History of the Genetic Code.* Stanford, CA: Stanford University Press.

Keller, E. F. 1992. "Between Language and Science: The Question of Directed Mutation in Molecular Genetics." *Perspectives in Biology and Medicine* **35**: 292–306.

Kimura, M. 1961. "Natural Selection as a Process of Accumulating Genetic Information in Adaptive Evolution." *Genetical Research* **2**: 127–40.

Kimura, M. 1968. "Evolutionary Rate at the Molecular Level." *Nature* **217**: 624–6.

Kimura, M. 1983. *The Neutral Theory of Molecular Evolution.* Cambridge: Cambridge University Press.

King, J. L. and Jukes, T. H. 1969. "Non-Darwinian Evolution: Most Evolutionary Change in Proteins May Be Due to Neutral Mutations and Genetic Drift." *Science* **164**: 788–98.

Kingman, J. F. C. 1982. "The Coalescent." *Stochastic Processes and their Applications* **13**: 235–48.

Kirschner, M. W. and Gerhart, J. C. 2005. *The Plausibility of Life: Resolving Darwin's Dilemma.* New Haven, CT: Yale University Press.

Kitcher, P. 1982. *Abusing Science: The Case Against Creationism.* Cambridge, MA: MIT Press.

Kitcher, P. 1985. *Vaulting Ambition: Sociobiology and the Quest for Human Nature.* Cambridge, MA: MIT Press.

Kitcher, P. 1992. "The Naturalists Return." *Philosophical Review* **101**: 53–114.

Kitcher, P. 1995. *The Advancement of Science: Science without Legend, Objectivity without Illusions.* New York: Oxford University Press.

Kitcher, P. 2001. "Born-Again Creationism." In Pennock, R. T. Ed. *Intelligent Design Creationism and Its Critics: Philosophical, Theological, and Scientific Perspectives.* Cambridge, MA: MIT Press, pp. 257–87.

Kuhn, T. 1962. *The Structure of Scientific Revolutions.* Chicago: University of Chicago Press.

Kundrát, M. 2004. "When did Theropods Become Feathered? – Evidence for Pre-Archaeopteryx Feathery Appendages." *Journal of Experimental Zoology B: Molecular and Developmental Evolution* **302**: 355–64.

Lakatos, I. 1970. "Falsification and the Methodology of Scientific Research Programmes." In Lakatos, I. and Musgrave, A. Eds. *Criticism and the Growth of Knowledge*, Cambridge: Cambridge University Press, pp. 91–195.

Lanczos, C. 1959. *The Variational Principles of Mechanics*. Toronto: University of Toronto Press.

Land, M. F. and Nilsson, D. E. 2002. *Animal Eyes*. Oxford: Oxford University Press.

Landman, O. E. 1991. "The Inheritance of Acquired Characteristics." *Annual Review of Genetics* **25**: 1–20.

Laudan, L. 1983. "The Demise of the Demarcation Problem." In Ruse, M. Ed. *But Is It Science?* Amherst, NY: Prometheus, pp. 337–350.

Leggett, A. J. 1987. *The Problems of Physics*. Oxford: Oxford University Press.

Lenski, R. E., Ofria, C., Pennock, R. T., and Adami, C. 2003. "The Evolutionary Origins of Complex Features." *Nature* **423**: 139–44.

Leslie, J. 1989. *Universes*. New York: Routledge.

Leslie, J. 1997. "The Anthropic Principle Today." In Hassing, R. F. Ed. *Final Causality in Nature and Human Affairs*. Washington, DC: Catholic University of America Press, pp. 163–87.

Leslie, J. 1998. "Cosmology and Theology." In Zalta, E. N. Ed. *Stanford Encyclopedia of Philosophy (Fall 1998 Edition)*. URL = <http://plato.stanford.edu/archives/fall1998/entries/cosmology-theology/>

Lewontin, R. C. 1970. "The Units of Selection." *Annual Review of Ecology and Systematics* **1**: 1–18.

Lewontin, R. C. 1974. *The Genetic Basis of Evolutionary Change*. New York: Columbia University Press.

Lewontin, R. C. 1978. "Adaptation." *Scientific American* **239**: 212–30.

Lewontin, R. C. 1991. "Facts and the Factitious in Natural Sciences." *Critical Inquiry* **18**: 140–53.

Lewontin, R. C. 1998. "The Evolution of Cognition: Questions We Will Never Answer." In Scarborough, D. and Sternberg, S. Ed. *An Invitation to Cognitive Science. Vol. 4. Methods, Models, and Conceptual Issues*. Cambridge, MA: MIT Press, pp. 107–32.

Lewontin, R. C. and Hubby, J. L. 1966. "A Molecular Approach to Genic Heterozygosity in Natural Populations. II. Amount of Variation and Degree of Heterozygosity in Natural Populations of *Drosophila pseudoobscura*." *Genetics* **54**: 595–609.

Lingham-Soliar, T. 2003. "Evolution of Birds: Ichthyosaur Integumental Fibers Conform to Dromaeosaur Protofeathers." *Naturwissenschaften* **90**: 428–32.

Lynch, M. 2005. "Simple Evolutionary Pathways to Complex Proteins." *Protein Science* **14**: 2217–25.

Mattick, J. S. 2004. "The Hidden Genetic Program of Complex Organisms." *Scientific American* **291**: 60–7.

May, R. M. 1973. *Stability and Complexity in Model Ecosystems*. Princeton, NJ: Princeton University Press.

Maynard Smith, J. 1978. "Optimization Theory in Evolution." *Annual Review of Ecology and Systematics* **9**: 31–56.

Maynard Smith, J. 1982. *Evolution and the Theory of Games*. Cambridge: Cambridge University Press.

Maynard Smith, J. 1983. "The Genetics of Stasis and Punctuation." *Annual Review of Genetics* **17**: 11–25.

Maynard Smith, J. 2000. "The Concept of Information in Biology." *Philosophy of Science* **67**: 177–94.

REFERENCES

Maynard Smith, J. and Szathmáry, E. 1995. *The Major Transitions in Evolution*. Oxford: Oxford University Press.

Mayr, E. 1942. *Systematics and the Origin of Species*. New York: Columbia University Press.

Mayr, E. 1961. "Cause and Effect in Biology." *Science* **134**: 1501–6.

Mayr, E. 1963. *Animal Species and Evolution*. Cambridge, MA: Harvard University Press.

Mayr, E. 1982. *The Growth of Biological Thought*. Cambridge, MA: Harvard University Press.

Mayr, E. 1983. "How to Carry Out the Adaptationist Program." *American Naturalist* **121**: 324–34.

Mayr, E. 2001. *What Evolution Is*. New York: Basic Books.

McCausland, I. 1999. "Anomalies in the History of Relativity." *Journal of Scientific Exploration* **13**: 271–90.

McMullin, E. [1991] 2001. "Plantinga's Defense of Special Creation." In Pennock, R. T. Ed. *Intelligent Design Creationism and Its Critics: Philosophical, Theological, and Scientific Perspectives*. Cambridge, MA: MIT Press, pp. 165–96.

McOuat, G. and Winsor, M. P. 1995. "J. B. S. Haldane's Darwinism in its Religious Context." *British Journal for the History of Science* **28**: 227–31.

Meléndez-Hevia, E., Waddell, T. G., and Cascante, M. 1996. "The Puzzle of the Krebs Citric Acid Cycle: Assembling the Pieces of Chemically Feasible Reactions, and Opportunism in the Design of Metabolic Pathways during Evolution." *Journal of Molecular Evolution* **43**: 293–303.

Mendel, G. 1866. "Versuche über Pflanzenhybriden." *Verhandlungen des naturforschenden Vereines in Brunn* **4**: 3–44.

Menuge, A. 2004. "Who's Afraid of ID?" In Dembski, W. A. and Ruse, R. Eds. *Debating Design: From Darwin to DNA*. New York: Cambridge University Press, pp. 32–51.

Mervis, J. 2006. "Judge Jones Defines Science – And Why Intelligent Design Isn't." *Science* **33**: 34.

Meyer, S. C. 2004. "The Origin of Biological Information and the Higher Taxonomic Categories." *Proceedings of the Biological Society of Washington* **117**: 213–39.

Miller, K. R. 1999a. *Finding Darwin's God*. New York: Harper Collins.

Miller, K. R. 1999b. "The Evolution of Vertebrate Blood Clotting." http://www.millerandlevine.com/km/evol/DI/clot/Clotting.html (accessed December 10, 2005).

Miller, K. R. 2004. "The Flagellum Unspun: The Collapse of 'Irreducible Complexity'." In Dembski, W. A. and Ruse, M. Eds. *Debating Design: From Darwin to DNA*. New York: Cambridge University Press, pp. 81–97.

Mills, D. R., Peterson, R. L., and Spiegelman, S. 1967. "An Extracellular Darwinian Experiment with a Self-Duplicating Nucleic Acid Molecule." *Proceedings of the National Academy of Sciences (USA)* **58**: 217–24.

Mills, G. C. 2002. "In Defense of Intelligent Design." *Perspectives on Science and Christian Faith* **54**: 260–63.

Mishler, B. D. and Donoghue, M. J. 1982. "Species Concepts: A Case for Pluralism." *Systematic Zoology* **31**: 491–503.

Montagu, A. Ed. 1983. *Science and Creationism*. New York: Oxford University Press.

Mooney, C. 2005. *The Republican War on Science*. New York: Basic Books.

Moorhead, P. S. and Kaplan, M. M. Eds. 1967. *Mathematical Challenges to the Neo-Darwinian Interpretation of Evolution*. Philadelphia: Wistar Institute.

Moran, P. A. P. 1964. "On the Nonexistence of Adaptive Topographies." *Annals of Human Genetics* **27**: 383–93.

Morgan, T. H. 1926. *The Theory of the Gene*. New Haven, CT: Yale University Press.

Muller, H. J. 1962. *Studies in Genetics*. Bloomington, IN: Indiana University Press.

Mulley, J. and Holland, P. 2004. "Small Genome, Big Insights." *Nature* **431**: 916–17.

Musgrave, I. 2004. "Evolution of the Bacterial Flagellum." In Young, M. and Edis, T. Eds. *Why Intelligent Design Fails: A Scientific Critique of the New Creationism*. New Brunswick, NJ: Rutgers University Press, pp. 72–84.

Nagel, E. 1956. *Logic without Metaphysics and Other Studies in the Philosophy of Science*. New York: Free Press.

Nelson, G. 1989. "Species and Taxa: Systematics and Evolution." In Otte, D. and Endler, J. A. Eds. *Speciation and Its Consequences*. Sunderland, MA: Sinauer, pp. 60–81.

Newell, N. D. 1982. *Creation and Evolution: Myth or Reality*. New York: Columbia University Press.

Newman, C. M., Cohen, J. E., and Kipnis, C. 1985. "Neo-Darwinian Evolution ImpliesPunctuated Equilibria." *Nature* **315**: 400–1.

Newman, M. E. J. and Palmer, R. G. 2003. *Modeling Extinction*. New York: Oxford University Press.

Newman, J. H. 1973. *The Letters and Diaries of John Henry Newman*. Vol. 25. Oxford: Clarendon Press.

Nilsson, D.-E. and Pelger, S. 1994. A pessimistic estimate of the time required for an eye to evolve. *Proceedings of the Royal Society (London), Biological Sciences* **256**: 53–8.

Numbers, R. L. 1992. *The Creationists: The Evolution of Scientific Creationism*. New York: Knopf.

Oakley, T. H. and Cunningham, C. W. 2002. "Molecular Phylogenetic Evidence for the Independent Evolutionary Origin of an Arthropod Compound Eye." *Proceedings of the National Academy of Sciences (USA)* **99**: 1426–30.

Ohta, T. 1973. "Slightly deleterious mutant substitutions in evolution." *Nature* **246**: 96–8.

Ohta, T. 1996. "Development of Neutral and Nearly Neutral Theories." *Theoretical Population Biology* **49**: 128–42.

Ohta, T. 2000. "Molecular Evolution: Nearly Neutral Theory." *Nature Encyclopedia of Life Sciences*. London: Nature Publishing Group. <http://www.els.net/>. [doi:10.1038/npg.els.0001801]. Accessed March 2, 2005.

Oltean, M. 2004. "Searching for a Practical Evidence of the No Free Lunch Theorems." *Lecture Notes in Computer Science*: 472–483.

Orgel, L. E. 1973. *The Origins of Life*. New York: John Wiley & Sons.

Orr, H. A. 1996-7. "Darwin v. Intelligent Design (Again)." *Boston Review* December/January, 28–31.

Orr, H. A. 2002. "Book Review: No Free Lunch." *Boston Review* <http://www.bostonreview.net/BR27.3/orr.html>. Accessed: Feburary 14, 2005.

Oster, G. F. and Wilson, E. O. 1978. *Caste and Ecology in the Social Insects*. Princeton, NJ: Princeton University Press.

Paley, W. 1802. *Natural Theology, or, Evidences of the Existence and Attributes of the Deity, Collected from the Appearances of Nature*. London: Rivington.

REFERENCES

Peacocke, A. R. 1979. *Creation and the World of Science*. Oxford: Clarendon Press.

Pearle, P. 1986. "Models for Reduction." In Penrose, R. and Isham, C. J. Eds. *Quantum Concepts in Space and Time*. Oxford: Oxford University Press, pp. 84–108.

Pennock, R. T. 1996. "Naturalism, Evidence, and Creationism: The Case of Philip Johnson." *Biology and Philosophy* **11**: 543–9.

Pennock, R. T. 1999. *Tower of Babel: The Evidence against the New Creationism*. Cambridge, MA: MIT Press.

Pennock, R. T. Ed. 2001. *Intelligent Design Creationism and Its Critics: Philosophical, Theological, and Scientific Perspectives*. Cambridge, MA: MIT Press.

Perakh, M. 2003. "The No Free Lunch Theorems and Their Applications to Evolutionary Algorithms." <http://www.nctimes.net/~mark/bibl_science/orr_demb_NFL.htm>. Accessed: February 13, 2005.

Perakh, M. 2004a. "Why There is a Free Lunch After All: William Dembski's Wrong Answer to Irrelevant Questions." In Young, M. and Edis, T. Eds. *Why Intelligent Design Fails: A Scientific Critique of the New Creationism*. New Brunswick, NJ: Rutgers University Press, pp. 153–71.

Perakh, M. 2004b. *Unintelligent Design*. Amherst, NY: Prometheus Books.

Pincock, S. 2005. "Creationism: From the US with Love." *The Scientist* **19**(4): 12–13 (28 February).

Plantinga, A. 1996. "Methodological Naturalism?" In van der Meer, J. M. Ed. *Facets of Faith Science. Vol. 1. Historiography and Modes of Interaction*. Lanham, MD: University Press of America, pp. 177–221.

Plantinga, A. 1993. *Warrant and Proper Function*. New York: Oxford University Press.

Pourciau, B. 2001. "A New Translation of and Guide to Newton's *Principia*." *Annals of Science* **58**: 85–91.

Provine, W. B. 1971. *The Origins of Theoretical Population Genetics*. Chicago: University of Chicago Press.

Prum, R. O. and Brush, A. H. 2002. "The Evolutionary Origin and Diversification Of Feathers." *Quarterly Review of Biology* **77**: 261–95.

Prum, R. O. and Brush, A. H. 2003. "Which Came First, the Feather or the Bird?" *Scientific American* **288**: 84–93.

Ratzsch, D. L. 2001. *Nature, Design, and Science: The Status of Design in Natural Science*. Albany, NY: State University of New York Press.

Raup, D. M. 1991. *Extinction: Bad Genes or Bad Luck?* New York: W. W. Norton.

Raven, P. H. 1976. "Systematics and Plant Population Biology." *Systematic Botany* **1**: 284–316.

Rees, M. J. 1999. *Just Six Numbers: The Deep Forces that Shape the Universe*. New York: Basic Books.

Reza, F. 1961. *An Introduction to Information Theory*. New York: McGraw-Hill.

Reznick, D. N., Shaw, F. H., Rodd, F. H., and Shaw, R. G. 1997. "Evaluation of Evolution in Natural Populations of Guppies (*Poecilla reticulata*)." *Science* **275**: 1934–7.

Richards, R. J. 1987. *Darwin and the Emergence of Evolutionary Theories of Mind and Behavior*. Chicago: University of Chicago Press.

Romanes, G. J. 1896. *Life and Letters*. London: Longmans, Green.

Ronshaugen, M., McGinnis, N., and McGinnis, W. 2002. "Hox Protein Mutation and Macroevolution of the Insect Body Plan." *Nature* **415**: 914–17.

Rosenberg, A. 1996. "A Field Guide to Recent Species of Naturalism." *British Journal of Philosophy of Science* 47: 1–29.

Rosenhouse, J. 2001. "How Anti-Evolutionists Abuse Mathematics." *Mathematical Intelligencer* 23: 3–8.

Rosenhouse, J. 2002. "Probability, Optimization Theory, and Evolution." *Evolution* 56: 1721–2.

Roseveare, N. T. 1982. *Mercury's Perihelion from Le Verrier to Einstein*. Oxford: Clarendon Press.

Ruse, M. 1982. *Darwinism Defended*. Reading, MA: Addison-Wesley.

Ruse, M. 2001. "Methodological Naturalism under Attack." In Pennock, R. T. Ed. *Intelligent Design Creationism and Its Critics: Philosophical, Theological, and Scientific Perspectives*. Cambridge, MA: MIT Press, pp. 363–85.

Ruse, M. 2003. *Darwin and Design: Does Evolution Have a Purpose?* Cambridge, MA: Harvard University Press.

Samuel, A., Petersen, J., and Reese, T. 2001. "Envelope Structure of Synechococcus sp. WH8113, a Nonflagellated Swimming Cyanobacterium." *BMC Microbiology* 1(1): 4.

Sarkar, S. 1991. "Lamarck *contre* Darwin, Reduction *versus* Statistics: Conceptual Issues in the Controversy over Directed Mutagenesis in Bacteria." In Tauber, A. I. Ed. *Organism and the Origins of Self*. Dordrecht: Kluwer, pp. 235–71.

Sarkar, S. 1996. "Biological Information: A Skeptical Look at Some Central Dogmas of Molecular Biology." In Sarkar, S. Ed. *The Philosophy and History of Molecular Biology: New Perspectives*. Dordrecht, Germany: Kluwer, pp. 187–231.

Sarkar, S. 1997. "The Itô Formalism and Stochastic Modifications of Quantum Dynamics." In Cohen, R. S., Horne, M. and Stachel, J. Eds. *Experimental Metaphysics: Quantum Mechanical Studies in Honor of Abner Shimony*. Dordrecht, Germany: Kluwer, pp. 157–69.

Sarkar, S. 1998a. *Genetics and Reductionism*. New York: Cambridge University Press.

Sarkar, S. 1998b. "Wallace's Belated Revival." *Journal of Biosciences* 23: 3–7.

Sarkar, S. 2000. "Information in Genetics and Developmental Biology: Comments on Maynard-Smith." *Philosophy of Science* 67: 208–13.

Sarkar, S. 2004. "Evolutionary Theory in the 1920s: The Nature of the 'Synthesis'." *Philosophy of Science* 71: 1215–26.

Sarkar, S. 2005. *Molecular Models of Life: Philosophical Papers on Molecular Biology*. Cambridge, MA: MIT Press.

Sarkar, S. 2006. "Maynard Smith, Optimization, and Evolution." *Biology and Philosophy* 20(5): 951–66.

Scheuer, P. A. G. and Mandel, S. P. H. 1959. "An Inequality in Population Genetics." *Heredity* 31: 519–24.

Schneider, T. D. 2000. "Evolution of Biological Information." *Nucleic Acids Research* 28: 2794–9.

Schrödinger, E. 1944. *What is Life? The Physical Aspect of the Living Cell*. Cambridge: Cambridge University Press.

Scott, E. C. 2004. *Evolution vs. Creationism : An Introduction*. Westport, CT: Greenwood Press.

Shahshahani, S. 1979. "A New Mathematical Framework for the Study of Linkage and Selection." *Memoirs of the American Mathematical Society* 17(211): 1.

REFERENCES

Shallit, J. 2002. "William Dembski, No Free Lunch." *Biosystems* **66**: 93–9.

Shallit, J. and Elsberry, W. R. 2004. "Playing Games with Probablity: Dembski's Complex Specified Information." In Young, M. and Edis, T. Eds. *Why Intelligent Design Fails: A Scientific Critique of the New Creationism*. New Brunswick, NJ: Rutgers University Press, pp. 121–138.

Shanks, N. 2004. *God, the Devil, and Darwin*. New York: Oxford University Press.

Shannon, C. E. 1948. "A Mathematical Theory of Communcation." *Bell System Technical Journal* **27**: 379–423, 623–56.

Shermer, M. 2002. *In Darwin's Shadow: The Life and Science of Alfred Russel Wallace*. New York: Oxford University Press.

Shimony, A. 1971. "Perception from an Evolutionary Point of View." *Journal of Philosophy* **68**: 571–83.

Shimony, A. 1981. "Integral epistemology." In Brewer, M. B. and Collins, B. E. Eds. *Scientific Inquiry and the Social Sciences: A Volume in Honor of Donald T. Campbell*. San Francisco: Jossey-Bass, 98–123.

Sniegowski, P. D. and Lenski, R. E. 1995. "Mutation and Adaptation: The Directed Mutation Controversy in Evolutionary Perspective." *Annual Review of Ecology and Systematics* **26**: 553–78.

Sober, E. 1988. Reconstructing the Past: Parsimony, Evolution, and Interference. Cambridge, MA: MIT Press.

Sober, E. 1999. "Testability." *Proceedings and Addresses of the American Philosophical Association* **73**: 47–76.

Sober, E. 2002. "Intelligent Design and Probability Reasoning." *International Journal for the Philosophy of Religion* **52**: 65–80.

Sober, E. 2004. "The Design Argument." In Mann, W. Ed. *Blackwell Guide to the Philosophy of Religion*. Malden, MA: Blackwell, pp. 27–54.

Stachel, J. 1995. "History of Relativity." In Brown, L. M., Pais, A., and Pippard, B. Eds. *Twentieth Century Physics*. New York: American Institute of Physics, pp. 249–356.

Stein, H. 1972. "On the Conceptual Structure of Quantum Mechanics." In Colodny, R. G. Ed. *Paradigms and Paradoxes: Philosophical Challenges of the Quantum Domain*. Pittsburgh, PA: University of Pittsburgh Press, pp. 367–438.

Stenger, V. J. 1998. "Anthropic Design and the Laws of Physics." *Reports of the National Center for Science Education* **18**(3): 8–12.

Stenger, V. J. 2000. "Natural Explanations for the Anthropic Coincidences." *Philo* **3**(2): 50–67.

Sterelny, K. 2000. "The 'Genetic Program' Program: A Commentary on Maynard Smith on Information in Biology." *Philosophy of Science* **67**: 195–202.

Stockwell, D. R. B. and Peters, D. 1999. "The GARP Modelling System: Problems and Solutions to Automated Spatial Prediction." *International Journal of Geographical Information Science* **13**: 143–58.

Strahler, A. N. 1987. *Science and Earth History: The Evolution/Creation Controversy*. Buffalo, NY: Prometheus Books.

Strickberger, M. W. 2000. *Evolution*. 3rd ed. Sudbury, MA: Jones and Bartlett.

Sulloway, F. J. 1979. "Geographical Isolation in Darwin's Thinking: The Vicissitudes of a Crucial Idea." *Studies in the History of Biology* **3**: 23–65.

Suppes, P. 1993. "The Transcendental Character of Determinism," *Midwest Studies in Philosophy* **18**: 242–57.

Svirizhev, Y. M. 1972. "Optimum Principles in Population Genetics." In Ratner, V. A. Ed. *Studies on Theoretical Genetics*. Novosibirsk: USSR Academy of Science, pp. 86–102.

Swinburne, R. 1990. "Argument from the Fine-Tuning of the Universe," In Leslie, J. Ed. *Physical Cosmology and Philosophy*. New York: Macmillan, pp. 154–73.

Swinburne, R. 1991. *The Existence of God*. Oxford: Clarendon Press.

Takahata, N. 2000. "Molecular Evolution: Neutral Theory." *Nature Encyclopedia of Life Sciences*. London: Nature Publishing Group. <http://www.els.net/>. [doi:10.1038/npg.els.0001800]. (Accessed March 2, 2005.)

Tauber, A. I. and Sarkar, S. 1992. "The Human Genome Project: Has Blind Reductionism Gone Too Far?" *Perspectives on Biology and Medicine* **35**(2): 220–35.

Taylor, J. S. and Raes, J. 2004. "Duplication and Divergence: The Evolution of New Genes and Old Ideas." *Annual Review of Genetics* **38**: 615–43.

Thomas, A. L. R. 1998. "Cambrian Explosion Blown out of the Water." *Trends in Ecology and Evolution* **13**: 129.

Thomas, A. L. R. and Garner, J. P. 1998. "Are Birds Dinosaurs?" *Trends in Ecology and Evolution* **13**: 129–30.

Thomas, N. A., Bardy, S. L., and Jarrell, K. F. 2001. "The Archaeal Flagellum: A Different Kind of Prokaryotic Motility Structure." *FEMS Microbiology Reviews* **25**: 147–74.

Thornhill, R. H. and Palmer, C. T. 2000. *A Natural History of Rape: Biological Bases of Sexual Coercion*. Cambridge, MA: MIT Press.

Thornhill, R. H. and Ussery, D. W. 2000. "A Classification of Possible Routes of Darwinian Evolution." *Journal of Theoretical Biology* **203**: 111–16.

Tipler, F. J. 1995. *The Physics of Immortality: Modern Cosmology, God and the Resurrection of the Dead*. New York: Anchor.

Trachtenberg, S., Gilad, R., and Geffen, N. 2003. "The Bacterial Linear Motor of *Spiroplasma melliferum* BC3: From Single Molecules to Swimming Cells." *Molecular Microbiology* **47**: 671–97.

Tribus, M. 1961. *Thermostatistics and Thermodynamics*. Princeton, NJ: D. van Nostrand Company, Inc.

Unwin, D. M. 1998. "Feathers, Filaments and Theropod Dinosaurs." *Nature* **391**: 119–20.

Ussery, D. W. 1999. "A Biochemist's Response to 'The Biochemical Challenge to Evolution'." *Bios* **70**: 40–5.

Ussery, D. W. 2004. "Darwin's Transparent Box: The Biochemical Evidence for Evolution." In Young, M. and Edis, T. Eds. *Why Intelligent Design Fails: A Scientific Critique of the New Creationism*. New Brunswick, NJ: Rutgers University Press, pp. 48–71.

Valentine, J. W., Jablonski, D., and Erwin, D. H. 1999. "Fossils, Molecules and Embryos: New Perspectives on the Cambrian Explosion." *Development* **126**: 851–59.

Van Valen L. 1973. "A New Evolutionary Law." *Evolutionary Theory* **1**: 1–30.

Vorzimmer, P. 1963. "Charles Darwin and Blending Inheritance." *Isis* **54**: 371–90.

Wallace, A. R. 1855. "On the Law Which Has Regulated the Introduction of New Species." *Annals and Magazine of Natural History* **16**: 184–96.

Wallace, A. R. 1858. "On the Tendency of Varieties to Depart Indefinitely from the Original Type." *Journal of the Proceedings of the Linnaean Society. Zoology* **3**: 53–62.

REFERENCES

Wallace, A. R. 1864. "The Origin of Human Races and the Antiquity of Man Deduced From the Theory of 'Natural Selection'." *Journal of the Anthropological Society of London* **2**: 158–70.

Wallace, A. R. 1869. *The Malay Archipelago, the Land of the Orang-Utan and the Bird of Paradise.* London: Macmillan.

Wallace, A. R. 1876. *The Geographical Distribution of Animals.* 2 Vols. London: Macmillan.

Wallace, A. R. 1889. *Darwinism: An Exposition of the Theory of Natural Selection with Some of Its Applications.* London: Macmillan.

Watson, J. D. and Crick, F. H. C. 1953a. "Molecular Structure of Nucleic Acids – A Structure for Deoxyribose Nucleic Acid." *Nature* **171**: 737–8.

Watson, J. D. and Crick, F. H. C. 1953b. "Genetical Implications of the Structure of Deoxyribonucleic Acid." *Nature* **171**: 964–7.

Waterton, C. 1973. *Wanderings in South America, the North-west of the United States, and the Antilles, in the Years 1812, 1816, 1820 and 1824.* Oxford: Oxford University Press.

Weatherford, J. 2005. *Genghis Khan and the Making of the Modern World.* New York: Three Rivers Press.

Weldon, W. F. R. 1893. "On Certain Correlated Variations in Carcinus moenas." *Proceedings of the Royal Society (London)* **54**: 318–29.

Weinberg, S. 1993. *Dreams of a Final Theory: The Search for the Fundamental Laws of Nature.* London: Vintage.

Weismann, A. 1889. *Essays upon Heredity and Kindred Subjects.* Oxford: Clarendon Press.

Wells, J. 2000. *Icons of Evolution: Science or Myth? Why Much of What We Teach about Evolution is Wrong.* Washington, DC: Regnery.

Wells, J. 2005. "Do Centrioles Generate a Polar Ejection Force?" *Rivista di Biologia/ Biology Forum* **98**: 71–96.

Wilkins, J. S. 2004. "The Origin of Species Concepts, History, Characters, Modes and Synapomorphies." PhD Dissertation. Department of History and Philosophy of Science, University of Melbourne.

Wilkins, J. S. and Elsberry, W. R. 2001. "The Advantages of Theft over Toil: The Design Inference and Arguing from Ignorance." *Biology and Philosophy* **16**: 711–24.

Williams, S. M. and Sarkar, S. 1994. "Assortative mating and the adaptive landscape." *Evolution* **48**: 868–75.

Wilson, C. and Wilson, B. 2001. *Crash Goes Darwin . . . and His Origin of Species.* Victoria, Australia: Pacific Christian Ministries.

Wilson, E. O. 1978. *On Human Nature.* Cambridge, MA: Harvard University Press.

Wilson, E. O. 1984. *Biophilia: The Human Bond with Other Species.* Cambridge, MA: Harvard University Press.

Wimsatt, W. C. 1972. "Teleology and the Logical Structure of Function Statements." *Studies in the History and Philosophy of Science* **3**: 1–80.

Wolpert, D. H. 2003. "William Dembski's Treatment of the No Free Lunch Theorems is Written in Jello." <http://www.talkreason.org/articles/jello.cfm>. Accessed: Feburary 13, 2005.

Wolpert, D. H. and Macready, W. G. 1995. "No Free Lunch Theorems for Search." Technical Report SFI-TR-95-02-010. Sante Fe: Santa Fe Institute. Available at: <www.no-free-lunch.org/WoMa95.pdf>. Accessed: February 18, 2005.

Wolpert, D. H. and Macready, W. G. 1997. "No Free Lunch Theorems for Optimization." *IEEE Transactions on Evolutionary Computation* **1**: 67–82.

Wolpert, D. H. and Macready, W. G. 2005. "Coevolutionary Free Lunches." *IEEE Transactions on Evolutionary Computation* **9**: 721–35.

Woodmorappe, J. 1996. *Noah's Ark: A Feasibility Study*. Santee, CA: Institute for Creation Research.

Wright, S. 1931. "Evolution in Mendelian Populations." *Genetics* **16**: 97–159.

Wright, S. 1967. "'Surfaces' of Selective Value." *Proceedings of the National Academy of Sciences (USA)* **58**: 165–72.

Xiao, S., Zhang, Y., and Knoll, A. H. 1998. Three-dimensional preservation of algae and animal embryos in a Neoproterozoic phosphorite. *Nature* **391**: 553–8.

Xu, X. and Doolittle, R. F. 1990. "Presence of a Vertebrate Fibrinogen-Like Sequence in an Echinoderm." *Proceedings of the National Academy of Sciences (USA)* **87**: 2097–101.

Yonekura, K., Maki-Yonekura, S., and Namba, K. 2002. "Growth Mechanism of the Bacterial Flagellar Filament." *Research in Microbiology* **153**: 191–97.

Young, W. 1985. *Fallacies of Creationism*. Calgary: Detrelig Enterprises.

Zhang, J. 2003. "Evolution by Gene Duplication: An Update." *Trends in Ecology and Evolution* **18**: 292–7.

Index

INDEX

INDEX